Carbonnier

Gladys Horiuchi

Edwin C. Warner

Robin Kelley O'Connor

Alistair Robertson

(Louis) LATOUR

Marion R. Shanken

L F Bouchard

Rodney D. Strong

Rio Roffen

Stéfan M

James Trezise

R. Benter

Richard L. Arrowood

David S. Stare

Louis P. Martini

Eric P. Wente

Alan Lewis

Mike Stephens

Sio dei Medici

Ed Sbragia

John L. Meir

WINDOWS ON THE WORLD

Complete
Wine Course

Kevin Zraly

STERLING PUBLISHING CO., INC.
NEW YORK

Acknowledgments

I would like to express my appreciation to M. Shanken Communications, Inc., New York City, publishers of *Impact* wine and spirits newsletter; *Market Watch* magazine; and *Wine Spectator,* for supplying information used in this book. I am indebted to the winemakers and grape growers throughout the world who contributed their expertise and enthusiasm for this project. The signatures on the endpapers represent some of the people whose help was invaluable to me.

Original edition and this revision edited by Felicia Sherbert
Production editor: Hannah Reich
Earlier versions edited by Stephen Topping, Robert Hernandez, and Keith L. Schiffman
Maps: Jeffrey L. Ward
Design: Richard Oriolo

LIBRARY OF CONGRESS CATALOGING-IN-PUBLICATION DATA AVAILABLE

1   3   5   7   9   10   8   6   4   2

Published by Sterling Publishing Company, Inc.
387 Park Avenue South, New York, N.Y. 10016
© 2001 by Kevin Zraly
Distributed in Canada by Sterling Publishing
c/o Canadian Manda Group, One Atlantic Avenue, Suite 105
Toronto, Ontario, Canada M6K 3E7
Distributed in Great Britain and Europe by Cassell PLC
Wellington House, 125 Strand, London WC2R 0BB, England
Distributed in Australia by Capricorn Link (Australia) Pty Ltd
P.O. Box 6651, Baulkham Hills, Business Centre, NSW 2153, Australia
PRINTED IN CHINA

Sterling ISBN 0-8069-6699-8

Contents

Dedication

First and foremost, to my parents, Charles and Kathleen, and to my sisters, Sharon and Kathy, who have been a constant source of encouragement and understanding throughout my life.

To John Novi, for allowing me to learn about wines at the Depuy Canal House in High Falls, New York.

To Craig Claiborne, *New York Times* restaurant critic, for giving the Depuy Canal House a four-star rating in 1970, which helped the restaurant's wine list grow to include 125 selections.

To Father Sam Matarazzo, who inspired me to take my study of wine to Europe.

To Peter Bienstock, who shared his older vintages with me.

To Herb Schutte, who gave me my first job in the wine business.

To Ron Koster and to Ulster County Community College, where I taught my first wine course.

To Joe Baum, creator of Windows on the World, who had the original concept of hiring a young American as cellarmaster.

To Alan Lewis, first director of Windows on the World, who hired me and was instrumental in the wine program.

To Mohonk Mountain House in New Paltz, New York, where ideas come easy.

To Kathleen Talbert, whose concepts helped greatly in the writing of this book.

To Burton Hobson, chairman of Sterling Publishing Co., Inc., who had the faith to put "another wine book" on the market.

To Lincoln Boehm, president of Sterling Publishing Co., Inc., whose passion for wine and food is the big reason for the annual update of this book.

To Felicia Sherbert, my editor, without whom this book could not have been written.

To Andrea Immer, a wizard at everything, whose research and editorial contributions were essential.

To David Emil, president of Windows on the World, who together with Joe Baum resurrected the "new" Windows on the World Restaurant and the Windows on the World Wine School in 1996.

To Gina D'Angelo, my assistant, for her excellent work and research on this 2001 edition.

And most of all to my wife, Ana, and our best vintages, Anthony (1991), Nicolas (1993), Harrison (1997), and Adriana (1999).

Foreword

Whenever I think of the year 2001, I remember the movie *2001: A Space Odyssey*, which was released around the time I began my study of wine. My teacher/student wine odyssey began in 1971, when I took my first and only wine course at the famed Waldorf Astoria.

I still have great memories today of my Monday night classes, which turned into the format I used to teach class on the following Tuesdays! One of the most gratifying things to me is that today, some of my former students are now the teachers. I can honestly say that after all these years, I am still having a tremendous amount of fun learning new things every day, and I feel lucky that I chose to make wine my profession.

It all began in 1970 when, as a college student, I started working as a waiter in the Depuy Canal House Tavern in High Falls, New York, two hours north of New York City. At that time, Craig Claiborne, the *New York Times* restaurant critic, came to review the Canal House with two other great chefs, Jacques Pepin and Pierre Franey. Although we had just opened and I was the oldest waiter at 19, Mr. Claiborne bestowed the ultimate four-star rating on our restaurant. All of a sudden, we were besieged by customers, especially from New York City.

I quickly became the bartender (we were only 32 seats and never had need of a bartender before) and had to order all the beverages, including wine. I thought our wine list was pretty good. We had the top three: red, white, and rosé! Our customers wanted more. And I had to do it.

It's still hard for me to believe that over thirty years ago I was so afraid of opening a bottle of wine, I used to pay one of the chefs $1 for every bottle he opened.

By the time I left the Canal House to go to Windows on the World in 1976, I had assembled a wine list of 125 selections. During that time,

I had to try a lot of wines. I remember vividly my first glass of fine wine and recall that from that point on, all I wanted to do was learn all I could about wine.

Back in those days, you started with French wines, then moved on to Italian, Spanish, or German wines; there was little talk of California wines. I went to bookstores and libraries in search of books that could increase my knowledge. The books I found were often encyclopedic in nature—500-page volumes that made the topic of wine seem overwhelming.

Before I knew it, my interest in wine had developed into a passion, until finally it became my profession. Working in a restaurant, I came to realize that diners didn't need to know everything there is to know about wine, but I also discovered that most of them did want to learn more than they already knew.

Although I had only been studying wine for a year, I started teaching my first wine course in 1971. As any teacher will tell you, all you need to be is one step ahead of your students! And teachers also tell you that you learn by teaching. The more I taught, the more I wanted to learn. By this time, I had already explored all the vineyards in New York, but had to wait until I was 21 to visit California, which I did in my twenty-first summer, hitchhiking back and forth.

I finally finished college (my parents thought it was a good idea to have something to fall back on in case the "wino" thing didn't pan out) and I immediately left for Europe. I spent the next year visiting all the major wineries and châteaus I had ever read about. It was an experience of a lifetime! But that trip taught me something else about wine—wine is history, geography, language, culture, economics, food, merchandising, marketing, religion...and the list goes on. But at the end of the day, to sit back and open a great bottle of wine with family and friends makes my profession even more enjoyable.

Back from Europe, I decided it was time to challenge myself in the wine capital of the world—New York. I got a job as a salesman and within four months was calling on the yet-to-be-opened Windows on the World. Lucky me again! They were looking for a young American to oversee their wine program. They offered me the job; I liked the 107-story view and accepted.

I was fortunate to work with restaurant guru Joseph Baum, who not only created Windows on the World, but created The Four Seasons Restaurant and re-created the legendary Rainbow Room. Joe was also a teacher and thought it would be a great idea to continue my wine teaching at Windows at the World. The Windows on the World Wine School began a year after the restaurant opened, in 1977. Since then, we've had over 10,000 graduates and it's been a great 24 years.

The big question back in 1977 was, which wine book should I give my students? I tried several different books, but my students kept asking for something easier to read. The solution seemed simple to me: Someone had to write an introductory guide. As time went on, I was fortunate to meet some of the authors of the great wine books I had read. I asked some of these authors if they'd consider writing a simpler guide to wine, but they usually responded that there was no need for such a book.

I had never intended to write a book, but I became convinced that someone had to fill the need, and so it began. The *Windows on the World Complete Wine Course* is one of my greatest accomplishments. I would have been happy just to sell one book—to help demystify wine for just one person. Instead, to date we have sold more than 1,000,000 copies of this book.

This is the fifteenth update of the book since it was first published in 1985. But in the ever-changing world of wine, fifteen years is an eternity. I suppose many authors faced with the opportunity to revise would try to add more information to their book, but I have learned that less is more. So I have tried to make the book even simpler and, I hope, clearer.

I would like to thank all my colleagues in this business—the restaurant owners, hoteliers, retailers, wholesalers, importers, educators, and hospitality management schools—who have recommended this book to the new and "old" students of wine.

I wish I had had a book this easy to read when I began my journey. Enjoying wine should be easy, and I hope you enjoy my simple guide to wine!

I welcome all comments, suggestions, and even corrections, and would be happy to answer any wine questions you might have.

Write to:

Kevin Zraly
Windows on the World
One World Trade Center, 106th Floor
New York, NY 10048

Introduction

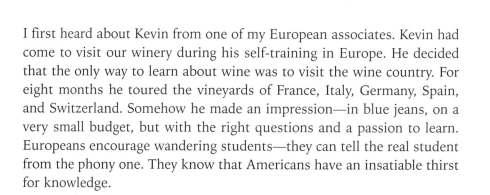

I first heard about Kevin from one of my European associates. Kevin had come to visit our winery during his self-training in Europe. He decided that the only way to learn about wine was to visit the wine country. For eight months he toured the vineyards of France, Italy, Germany, Spain, and Switzerland. Somehow he made an impression—in blue jeans, on a very small budget, but with the right questions and a passion to learn. Europeans encourage wandering students—they can tell the real student from the phony one. They know that Americans have an insatiable thirst for knowledge.

Kevin's interest in wine started during his student days in New Paltz, New York. He took a job as a part-time waiter at the Depuy Canal House Tavern in nearby High Falls, and ended up as the manager of the only four-star restaurant in the Catskills. Since his job included the ordering of wine, he decided to learn more on the subject.

He returned to New York City knowing a lot about wine, and was hired by a wine-and-liquor wholesaler to sell accounts that were more interested in Wild Irish Rose than in Meursault and Château Lafite. Before you knew it, he was the wine buyer and sommelier at Windows on the World, which ultimately turned out to be the largest wine account in America, possibly in the whole world. The job title was cellarmaster, and he continued to expand the responsibilities of the position. He created what is probably the most innovative and most frequently revised wine list in the world. After all, with knowledge and a word processor and computer there is no longer any need to carve a wine list in stone. He trained a staff second-to-none to suggest and serve the wine, and, inevitably, he started a wine school. That wine school, being in the financial center of New York, has taught more top executives than any other how to select and enjoy wine.

The reward for success in America is promotion. Kevin was named Wine Director in 1980. Besides teaching the wine classes, he started entirely new ventures along with *Wine Spectator*: The California Wine Experience and the New York Wine Experience, each a three-day spectacular, where 1,000 people from across the country listened to lectures, attended tastings, seminars, and happenings, and met the people who made wine.

It was inevitable that Kevin would write a wine book sooner or later—and that it would be different from any other wine book. It is not written to impress the world with Kevin's knowledge or insight, both of which he has enough of and to spare. It was written to be less rather than more. It is reminiscent of that old saying: "If I had more time, I would have written a shorter book." Well, Kevin has written a shorter book. He has written the essential wine book, a succinct guide to the essentials—a basic guide that does not weigh you down with unnecessary information or erudition, which would only hamper you in your journey through the labyrinth of wine. And yet this no-nonsense guide is not lacking in the necessary trivia to make the material entertaining as well as informative—those little hooks of extraneous facts which are so essential for the mind to remember facts. The information is presented in a well-designed format, it is easy to use as a guide or reference book, and yet it is interesting enough to read at one sitting. Small wonder, then, that his publisher tells me that, since its initial publication in 1985, Kevin's book has been the best-selling book on wine.

In addition, the section on how to create a wine list and stock a wine cellar in a restaurant is the best account I have ever read on the subject. It is both diverse and economical, and it will no doubt serve as a blueprint for many a wine list across the land. The section titled "Wine Service in Restaurants and at Home" is a delightfully informative look at the ritual of ordering wine.

This book represented one of the first of a number of innovative, education ventures by Kevin in the world of wines. He gains new ideas for "spreading the wine faith" in his extensive contacts with the neophyte and the connoisseur. There exists an enormous amount of information about wine, which most other writers seem to complicate. This early venture has gained Kevin an enthusiastic new following among wine lovers and new wine drinkers.

—PETER M. F. SICHEL

Prelude to Wine

You're in a wine shop looking for that "special" wine to serve at a dinner party. Before you walked in, you had at least an idea of what you wanted, but now, as you scan the shelves, you're overwhelmed. "There are so many wines," you think to yourself, "...and so many prices." You take a deep breath, boldly pick up a bottle that looks impressive, and buy it. Then you hope your guests will like your selection.

Does this sound a little farfetched? For some of you, yes. The truth is, this is a very common occurrence for the wine beginner, and even the intermediate, but it doesn't have to be that way. Wine should be an enjoyable experience. By the time you finish this book, you'll be able to buy with confidence from a retailer, or even look in the eyes of a wine steward and ask with no hesitation for the selection of your choice. But first let's start with the basics—the foundation of your wine knowledge. Read carefully, because you'll find this section invaluable as you relate it to the chapters that follow. You may even want to refer back to this section occasionally to reinforce what you learn.

For the purpose of this book, wine is the fermented juice of grapes.

What's fermentation?

Fermentation is the process by which the grape juice turns into wine. The simple formula for fermentation is:

$$\textbf{Sugar + Yeast = Alcohol + Carbon Dioxide (CO}_2\textbf{)}$$

The fermentation process begins when the grapes are crushed and ends when all of the sugar has been converted to alcohol or when the alcohol level has reached around fifteen percent, which kills off the yeast.

Sugar is naturally present in the ripe grape. Yeast also occurs naturally, as the white bloom on the grape skin. However, this natural yeast is not always used in today's winemaking. In many cases, laboratory strains of pure yeast have been isolated, each strain contributing something unique to the style of wine. The carbon dioxide dissipates into the air, except in the case of Champagne and other sparkling wines, where this gas is retained through a special process.

What are the three major types of wine?

Table wine: approximately 8–15 percent alcohol

Sparkling wine: approximately 8–12 percent alcohol + CO_2

Fortified wine: 17–22 percent alcohol

All wine fits into at least one of these categories.

Why do the world's fine wines come only from certain areas?

A combination of factors are at work. The areas with a reputation for fine wines have the right soil and favorable weather conditions, of course. But, in addition, these areas look at winemaking as an important part of their history and culture.

Is all wine made from the same kind of grape?

No. The major wine grapes come from the species *Vitis vinifera*. In fact, both European and American winemakers use the *Vitis vinifera*, which includes many different varieties of grapes—both red and white. However, there are other grapes used for winemaking. The native grape variety in America is the species *Vitis labrusca*, which is grown widely in New York State. *Hybrids*, crosses between *Vitis vinifera* and *Vitis labrusca*, are planted primarily on the East Coast of the United States.

Where are the best locations to plant grapes?

Grapes are agricultural products that require specific growing conditions. Just as you wouldn't try to grow oranges in New York, you wouldn't try to grow grapes at the North Pole. There are limitations on where vines can be grown. Some of these limitations are: the growing season, the number of days of sunlight, the angle of the sun, average temperature, and rainfall. Soil is of primary concern, and proper drainage is a requisite. The right

86% of a bottle of wine is water.

God's Gift to Wine Lovers
My favorite winemaking regions on earth are:
Napa
Sonoma
Bordeaux
Burgundy
Champagne
Rhône Valley
Tuscany
Piedmont
Mosel
Rhine
Rioja
Douro (Port)

Top five countries in wine grape acreage worldwide
1. Spain
2. Italy
3. France
4. Turkey
5. U.S.

A Sampling of the Major Grapes:

VITIS VINIFERA
Chardonnay
Cabernet Sauvignon

VITIS LABRUSCA
Concord
Catawba

HYBRIDS
Seyval Blanc
Baco Noir

Winemakers say that winemaking begins in the vineyard with the growing of the grapes. This is crucial to the whole process.

amount of sun ripens the grapes properly to give them the sugar/acid balance that makes the difference between fair, good, and great wine.

Does it matter which types of grapes are planted?

Yes, it does. Traditionally, many grape varieties produce better wines when planted in certain locations. For example, most red grapes need a longer growing season than do white grapes, and red grapes are usually planted in warmer (more southerly) locations. In colder northern regions—in Germany and northern France, for instance—most vineyards are planted with white grapes. In the warmer regions of Italy, Spain, and Portugal, the red grape thrives.

When's the harvest?

Grapes are picked when they reach the proper sugar/acid ratio for the style of wine the vintner wants to produce. Go to a vineyard in June and taste one of the small green grapes. Your mouth will pucker because the grape is so tart and acidic. Return to the same vineyard—even to that same vine—in September or October, and the grapes will taste sweet. All those months of sun have given sugar to the grape as a result of photosynthesis.

June
3% acid
0 Brix

July
2.3% acid
10 Brix

August
1.7% acid
15 Brix

Harvest
September
0.9% acid
22 Brix

What effect does weather have on the grapes?

Weather can interfere with the quality of the harvest, as well as with its quantity. In the spring, as vines emerge from dormancy, a sudden frost may stop the flowering, thereby reducing the yields. Even a strong windstorm can affect the grapes adversely at this crucial time. Not enough rain, too much rain, or rain at the wrong time can also wreak havoc.

Rain just before the harvest will swell the grapes with water, diluting the juice and making thin, watery wines. Lack of rain, as in the drought period in California's North Coast counties in the late 1980s, will affect the balance of wines for those years. A severe drop in temperature may affect the vines even outside the growing season. Case in point: The wine regions of New York State experienced an unusually bitter cold winter in 1993–94. The result was a severe loss of production for the following year, particularly in those vineyards planted with the less-than-hardy European grape varieties.

What can the vineyard owner do in the case of adverse weather?

A number of countermeasures are available to the grower. Some of these measures are used while the grapes are on the vine; others are part of the winemaking process.

PROBLEM	RESULTS IN	SOLUTION
Frost	Reduced yield	Various frost protection methods: giant flame-throwers to warm vines
Not enough sun	Unripe grapes	Chaptalization (the addition of sugar to the must—fresh grape juice—during fermentation)
Too much rain	Thin, watery wines	Move vineyard to a drier climate
Mildew	Rot	Spray with copper sulfate
Drought	Scorched grapes	Irrigate or pray for rain
Phylloxera	Dead vines	Graft vines onto resistant rootstock

What's Phylloxera?

Phylloxera, a grape louse, is one of the grapevine's worst enemies, since it eventually kills the entire plant. An epidemic infestation in the 1870s came close to destroying all the vineyards of Europe. Luckily, the roots of native American vines were immune to this louse. After this was discovered, all the European vines were pulled up and grafted onto phylloxera-resistant American rootstocks.

Can white wine be made from red grapes?

Yes. The color of wine comes entirely from the grape skins. By removing the skins immediately after picking, no color is imparted to the wine, and it will be white. In the Champagne region of France, a large percentage of the grapes grown are red, yet most of the resulting wine is white. California's White Zinfandel is made from red Zinfandel grapes.

One of the few countries to escape phylloxera is Chile. Luckily, Chilean wine producers imported their vines from France in the 1860s, before phylloxera attacked the French vineyards.

In the early 1980s, phylloxera was found in the vineyards of California. Winemakers have been replanting the vineyards at a cost of $15,000 to $25,000 per acre. The total replanting bill is estimated to run up to $2 billion.

Of the 37,000 acres of vineyards planted in the Napa Valley, over 22,000 had to be replanted as a result of phyloxera.

Walnuts and tea also
contain tannin.

Certain grapes, like
Cabernet Sauvignon,
have more tannin than
others, for example Pinot
Noir.

The first known refer-
ence to a specific vintage
was made by Roman his-
torian Piny the Elder,
who rated the wines of
121 B.C. "of the highest
excellence."

Three major wine
collectibles that will age
more than ten years:
  1. Great châteaus of
     Bordeaux
  2. Best producers of
     California Cabernet
     Sauvignon
  3. Finest producers of
     Vintage Port

The earliest evidence of
wine dates back at least
7,000 years!

What's tannin, and is it desirable in wine?

Tannin is a natural substance that comes from the skins, stems, and pips of the grapes, and even from the wooden barrels in which certain wines are aged. It acts as a preservative; without it, certain wines wouldn't con-tinue to improve in the bottle. In young wines, tannin can be very astrin-gent and make the wine taste bitter. Generally, red wines have a higher level of tannin than do whites, because red grapes are usually left to fer-ment on their skins.

Is acidity desirable in wine?

All wine will have a certain amount of acidity. Generally, white wines have more acidity than do reds, though winemakers try to have a balance of fruit and acid. An overly acidic wine is also described as tart or sour.

What's meant by "vintage"? Why is one year con-sidered better than another?

A vintage indicates the year the grapes were harvested, so every year is a vintage year. A vintage chart reflects the weather conditions for various years. Better weather results in a better rating for the vintage.

Are all wines meant to be aged?

No. It's a common misconception that all wines improve with age. In fact, more than 90 percent of all the wines made in the world are meant to be consumed within one year, and less than 1 percent of the world's wines are meant to be aged for more than 5 years.

How is wine production regulated worldwide?

Each major wine-producing country has government-sponsored control agencies and laws that regulate all aspects of wine production and set cer-tain minimum standards that must be observed. Here are some examples:

France: Appellation d'Origine Contrôlée (A.O.C.)

Italy: Denominazione di Origine Controllata (D.O.C.)

United States: Bureau of Alcohol, Tobacco, and Firearms (B.A.T.F.)

Germany: Ministry of Agriculture

Spain: Denominación de Origen (D.O.)

On Tasting Wine

You can read all the books (and there are plenty) written on wine to become more knowledgeable on the subject, but you should taste wines to truly enhance your understanding. Reading covers the more academic side of wine, while tasting is more enjoyable and practical. A little of each will do you the most good.

The following are the necessary steps for tasting wine. You may wish to follow them with a glass of wine in hand.

Wine tasting can be broken down into five basic steps: Color, Swirl, Smell, Taste, and Savor.

Color

The best way to get an idea of the color of the wine is to get a white background—a napkin or linen tablecloth—and hold the glass of wine in front of it. The range of colors that you may see depends, of course, on whether you're tasting a white or red wine. Here are the colors for both, beginning with the youngest wine and moving to an older wine:

WHITE WINE	RED WINE
pale yellow-green	purple
straw yellow	ruby
yellow-gold	red
gold	brick red
old gold	red-brown
yellow-brown	brown
maderized	
brown	

Color tells you a lot about the wine. Since we start with the white wines, I'll tell you three reasons why a white wine may have more color:

1. It's older.

2. Different grape varieties give different color. (For example, Chardonnay usually gives off a deeper color than does Riesling.)

3. The wine was aged in wood.

In class, I always begin by asking my students what color the wine is. It's not unusual to hear that some believe that the wine is pale yellow-green, while others say it's gold. Everyone begins with the same wine,

"There are no standards of taste in wine, cigars, poetry, prose, etc. Each man's own taste is the standard, and a majority vote cannot decide for him or in any slightest degree affect the supremacy of his own standard."

—Mark Twain, 1895

If you can see through a red wine, generally it's ready to drink!!

As white wines age, they gain color. Red wines, on the other hand, lose color as they age.

but color perceptions vary. There are no right or wrong answers, because perception is subjective. So you can imagine what happens when we actually taste the wine!

Swirl

Why do we swirl wine? To allow oxygen to get into the wine: Swirling releases the esters, ethers, and aldehydes that combine with oxygen to yield the bouquet of the wine. In other words, swirling aerates the wine and gives you a better smell.

Everyone does a great job swirling wine. You can do it any way you want—with your left hand, your right hand, with two fingers, behind your back....But I must warn you right now: You will start swirling everything—your milk, soft drinks, your morning coffee!

Some wine experts say that if you put your hand over the glass while you swirl, you will get a better bouquet and aroma.

Smell

This is the most important part of wine tasting. You can only perceive four tastes—sweet, sour, bitter, and salt—but the average person can smell over 2,000 different scents, and wine has over 200 of its own. Now that you've swirled the wine and released the bouquet, I want you to smell the wine at least three times. You will find that the third smell will give you more information than the first smell did. What does the wine smell like? What type of nose does it have? Smell is the most important step in the tasting process and most people simply don't spend enough time on it.

Pinpointing the nose of the wine helps you to identify certain characteristics. The problem here is that many people in class want me to tell them what the wine smells like. Since I prefer not to use pretentious words, I may say that the wine smells like a French white Burgundy. Still, I find that this doesn't satisfy the majority of the class. They want to know more. I ask these people to describe what steak and onions smell like. They answer, "Like steak and onions." See what I mean?

The best way to learn what your own preferences are for styles of wine is to "memorize" the smell of the individual grape varieties. For white, just try to memorize the three major grape varieties: Chardonnay, Sauvignon Blanc, and Riesling. Keep smelling them, and smelling them, and smelling them until you can identify the differences, one from the other. For the reds it's a little more difficult, but you still can take three major grape varieties: Pinot Noir, Merlot, and Cabernet Sauvignon. Try to memorize those smells without using flowery words, and you'll understand what I'm talking about.

Bouquet is the total smell of the wine.

Aroma is the smell of the grapes.

The "nose" is a word that wine tasters use to describe the bouquet and aroma of the wine.

This just in: It is now known that each nostril can detect different smells.

For those in the wine school who remain unconvinced, I hand out a list of 500 different words commonly used to describe wine. Here is a small excerpt:

acetic	character	legs	seductive
aftertaste	corky	light	short
aroma	delicate	maderized	soft
astringent	developed	mature	stalky
austere	earthy	metallic	sulfury
baked-burnt	finish	moldy	tart
balanced	flat	nose	thin
big-full-heavy	fresh	nutty	tired
bitter	grapey	off	vanilla
body	green	oxidized	woody
bouquet	hard	pétillant	yeasty
bright	hot	rich	young

What kind of wine do I like? I like my wine bright, rich, mature, developed, seductive, and with nice legs!!

Another interesting point is that you're more likely to recognize some of the defects of a wine through your sense of smell.

Following is a list of some of the negative smells in wine:

SMELL	WHY
Vinegar	Too much acetic acid in wine
Sherry	Oxidation
Dank, wet-mold, cellar smell (referred to as "corked wine")	Wine absorbs the taste of a defective cork
Sulfur (burnt matches)	Too much sulfur dioxide

Sulfur dioxide is used in many ways in winemaking. It kills bacteria in wine, prevents unwanted fermentation, and acts as a preservative. It sometimes causes a burning and itching sensation in your nose.

Every wine contains a certain amount of sulfites. It is a natural by-product of fermentation.

Taste

To many people, tasting wine means taking a sip and swallowing immediately. To me, this isn't tasting. Tasting is something you do with your taste buds. You have taste buds all over your mouth—on both sides of the tongue, underneath, on the tip, and extending to the back of your throat. If you do what many people do, you take a gulp of wine and bypass all of those important taste buds.

The average person has 5,000 taste buds.

What should you think about when tasting wine?

There is now new evidence that people may have five tastes: sweet, sour, bitter, salt, and possibly umami, a.k.a. MSG.

Be aware of the most important sensations of taste and where they occur on your tongue and in your mouth. As I mentioned earlier, you can only perceive four tastes: sweet, sour, bitter, and salt (but there's no salt in wine, so we're down to three). Bitterness in wine is usually created by high alcohol and high tannin. Sweetness only occurs in wines that have some residual sugar left over after fermentation. Sour (sometimes called "tart") indicates the acidity in wine.

Sweetness—Found on the tip of the tongue. If there's any sweetness in a wine whatsoever, you'll get it right away.

Fruit and Varietal Characteristics—Found in the middle of the tongue.

Acidity—Found at the sides of the tongue, the cheek area, and the back of the throat. White wines and some lighter-style red wines usually contain a higher degree of acidity.

Tannin—The sensation of tannin begins in the middle of the tongue. Tannin frequently exists in red wines or white wines aged in wood. When the wines are too young, tannin dries the palate to excess. If there's a lot of tannin in the wine, the tannin can actually coat your whole mouth, blocking the fruit. Remember, tannin is not a taste. It is a tactile sensation.

Aftertaste—The overall taste and balance of the components of the wine that lingers in your mouth. How long does the balance last? Usually a sign of a high-quality wine is a long, pleasing aftertaste. The taste of many of the great wines lasts anywhere from one minute to three minutes, with all their components in harmony.

Savor

After you've had a chance to taste the wine, sit back for a few moments and savor it. Think about what you just experienced, and ask yourself the following questions to help focus your impressions. Was the wine:

Light, medium, or full-bodied?

For a white wine: How was the acidity? Very little, just right, or too much?

For a red wine: Is the tannin in the wine too strong or astringent? Is it pleasing? Or is it missing?

What is the strongest component (residual sugar, fruit, acid, tannin)?

Wine Textures
Light—skim milk
Medium—whole milk
Full—heavy cream

How long did the balance of the components last? (10 seconds, 60 seconds, etc.)

To your taste, is the wine worth the price?

Is the wine ready to drink?

What kind of food would you enjoy with the wine?

This brings us to the most important point. The first thing you should consider after you've tasted a wine is whether or not you like it. Is it your style?

You can compare tasting wine to browsing in an art gallery. You wander from room to room looking at the paintings. Your first impression tells whether you like one or not. Once you decide you like a piece of art, you want to know more: Who was the artist? What is the history behind the work? How was it done? And so it is with wine. Usually, once oenophiles discover a new wine that they like, they have to know all about it—the winemaker, the grapes, exactly where the crop was planted, the blend, if any, and the history behind the wine.

"One not only drinks wine, one smells it, observes it, tastes it, sips it, and--one talks about it."

–King Edward VII

How do you know if a wine is good or not?

The definition of a good wine is one that you enjoy. Do not let others dictate taste to you!

When's a wine ready to drink?

This is one of the most frequently asked questions at the Windows on the World Wine School. The answer is very simple: when all components of the wine are in balance to your particular taste.

The 60-Second Wine Expert

Over the last few years I have insisted that my students spend at least one minute of silence after they swallow the wine. I use a "one-minute wine expert" tasting sheet in my classes for students to record their impressions. The minute is divided into four sections: 0–15 seconds, 15–30 seconds, 30–45 seconds, and the final 45–60 seconds. Try this with your next glass of wine.

0-15 seconds: If there is any residual sugar/sweetness in the wine, I will experience it now. If there is no sweetness in the wine, the acidity is usually at its strongest sensation in the first 15 seconds. I am also looking for the fruit level of the wine and its balance with the acidity.

I never rate the wine in the first 15 seconds because the first taste is a

Step One: Look at the color of the wine.
Step Two: Smell the wine three times
Step Three: Put the wine in your mouth and leave it there for three to five seconds.
Step Four: Swallow the wine.
Step Five: Wait and concentrate on the wine for sixty seconds before discussing it.

shock to the taste buds. I will begin to formulate my opinion of the wine from 30 seconds to 60 seconds.

15–30 seconds: After the sweetness or acidity I am looking for great fruit sensation. After all, that is what I am paying for! By the time I reach 30 seconds, I am hoping for balance of all the components. By this time, I can identify the weight of the wine. Is it light, medium, or full-bodied? I am now starting to think about what kind of food I can pair with this wine. (See pages 165-166.)

30–45 seconds: Not all wines need 60 seconds of thought. Lighter-style wines such as Riesling will usually show their best at this point. The fruit, acid, and sweetness of a great German Riesling should be in perfect harmony from this point on. For quality red and white wines, acidity— which is a very strong component (especially in the first 30 seconds)— should now be in balance with the fruit of the wine.

45–60 seconds: Very often wine writers use the term "length" to describe how long the components, balance, and flavor continue in the mouth. I am concentrating on the length of the wine in this last 15 seconds. In big, full-bodied red wines from Bordeaux, the Rhône Valley, and Cabernets from California, as well as Barolos and Barbarescos from Italy, and even some full-bodied Chardonnays, I am concentrating on the level of tannin in the wine. As the acidity and fruit balance are my major concerns in the first 30 seconds, it is now the tannin and fruit balance that I am looking for in the last 30 seconds. If the fruit, tannin, and acid are all in balance at 60 seconds, then I feel that the wine is probably ready to drink. Does the tannin overpower the fruit? If it does at the 60-second mark, I will then begin to question whether I should drink the wine now or put it away for more aging.

In 45–60 seconds, I will make my decision about whether or not I like the style of the wine.

It is extremely important to me that if you want to learn the true taste of the wine, you take at least one minute to concentrate on all of its components. In my classes it is amazing to see over 100 students silently taking one minute to analyze a wine. Some close their eyes, some bow their heads in deep thought, while others write notes.

One last note: 60 seconds to me is a minimum time to wait before making a decision about the wine. Many great wines continue to show balance well past 120 seconds. The best wine I ever tasted lasted over three minutes. That's three minutes of perfect balance of all components!

For further reading: Michael Broadbent's *Pocket Guide to Wine Tasting*, Jancis Robinson's *Vintage Timecharts*, and Alan Young's *Making Sense of Wine*.

White Grapes of the World

Now that you know the basics of how wine is made and how to taste it, you're almost ready to begin the first three classes on white wines.

Before you do, simplify your journey by letting me answer the question most frequently asked by my wine students on what will help them most in learning about wine. The most important thing is to understand the major grape varieties and where they are grown in the world.

The purpose of this book is not to overwhelm you with information about every grape under the sun. My job as a wine educator is to try to narrow down this overabundance of grape data. So let's start off with the three major grapes you need to know to understand white wine. They are listed here in order from the lightest style to the fullest:

Riesling   Sauvignon Blanc   Chardonnay

This is not to say that world-class wine is not made from any other white grapes, but we have to start somewhere.

One of the first things I show my students in Class One is a list of these three grape varieties, indicating where they grow best in the world. The grapes are ranked from the lightest to the fullest-bodied, and the major countries and regions are listed that produce the highest quality wine from the corresponding grape varieties. It looks something like this:

GRAPES	WHERE THEY GROW BEST
Riesling	Germany; Alsace, France; New York State
Sauvignon Blanc	Loire Valley, France; Bordeaux, France; New Zealand; California (Fumé Blanc)
Chardonnay	Burgundy, France; California; Australia; Champagne, France

There are world-class Rieslings, Sauvignon Blancs, and Chardonnays made in other countries, but in general these regions are known best for wine made from these grapes.

Fifty major white wine grape varieties are grown throughout the world. In California alone, over 24 white grape varieties are planted.

Other white grapes and regions you may wish to explore:

GRAPES	WHERE THEY GROW BEST
Albariño	Spain
Chenin Blanc	Loire Valley, France; California
Gewürz-traminer	Alsace, France
Pinot Grigio /Pinot Gris	Italy Alsace, France
Sémillon	Bordeaux (Sauternes); Australia
Viognier	Rhône, France; California

California, Australia, and Chile usually list the grape variety on the label. French, Italian, and Spanish wines usually list the region, village, or vineyard where the wine is made, but not the grape.

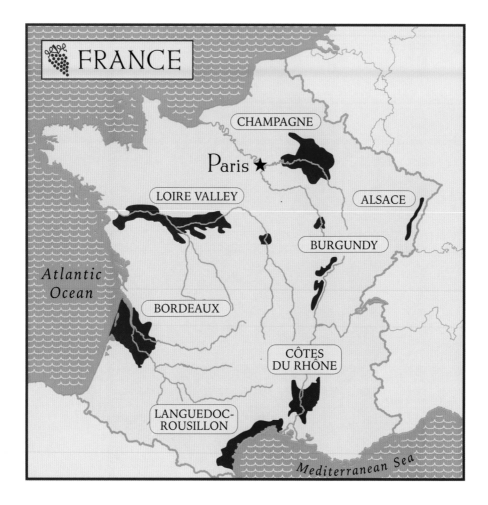

FRANCE

CHAMPAGNE

Paris ★

LOIRE VALLEY

ALSACE

BURGUNDY

Atlantic
Ocean

BORDEAUX

CÔTES
DU RHÔNE

LANGUEDOC-
ROUSILLON

Mediterranean Sea

The White Wines of France

Understanding French Wine

Before we begin our first "class," "The White Wines of France," I think you should know a few important points about all French wines. Take a look at a map of France to get familiar with the main wine-producing areas. As we progress, you'll understand why geography is so important.

Here's a quick rundown of which areas produce which kinds of wine:

WINE REGIONS	MAJOR GRAPES
Champagne—sparkling wine	Pinot Noir, Chardonnay
Loire Valley—mostly white	Sauvignon Blanc, Chenin Blanc
Alsace—mostly white	Riesling, Gewürtztraminer
Burgundy—red and white	Pinot Noir, Chardonnay
Bordeaux—red and white	Sauvignon Blanc, Semillon, Merlot, Cabernet Sauvignon, Cabernet Franc
Côtes du Rhône—mostly red	Syrah, Grenache
Languedoc-Roussillon—red and white	Merlot, Cabernet Sauvignon, Savignon Blanc, Chardonnay

I'm sure that you've had a French wine at one time or another. Why? Because French wines have the reputation of being among the best. There's a reason for this, and it goes back to quality control.

French winemaking is regulated by strict government laws that are set up by the *Appellation d'Origine Contrôlée*. If you don't want to say "Appellation d'Origine Contrôlée" all the time, you can simply say the "A.O.C." This is the first of many wine lingo abbreviations you'll learn in this book.

California, Australia, and Chile usually list the grape variety on the label. French, Italian, and Spanish wines usually list the region, village, or vineyard where the wine was made, but not the grape.

Only 35% of all French wines are worthy of A.O.C. designation.

There are more than 350 A.O.C. French wines.

Hectare—metric measure; 1 hectare = 2.471 acres

Hectoliter—metric measure; 1 hectoliter = 26.42 U.S. gallons.

The region most active in the production of Vin de Pays varietal wines is the Midi, also called Languedoc-Roussillon, in southwest France. Called in the past the "wine lake" because of the vast quantities of anonymous wine made there, the Languedoc has more than 700,000 acres of vineyards, almost twice as many as California, and produces more than 200 million cases a year, about a third of the total French crop.

Why would Georges Duboeuf, Louis Latour and many other famous winemakers start wineries in the Midi? For one thing, Midi vineyard land is much cheaper than land in places such as Burgundy or Bordeaux, so the winemakers can produce moderately priced wines and still get a good return on their investment.

A.O.C.

Established in the 1930s, the Appellation d'Origine Contrôlée laws set minimum requirements for each wine-producing area in France. The A.O.C. laws also can help you decipher French wine labels, since the A.O.C. controls the following:

	EXAMPLE	EXAMPLE
1. Geographic origin	Chablis	Pommard
2. Grape variety: Which grapes can be planted where.	Chardonnay	Pinot Noir
3. Minimum alcohol content: This varies depending upon the particular area where the grapes are grown.	10%	10.5%
4. Vinegrowing practices: For example, a vintner can produce only so much wine per acre.	40 hectoliters/acre	35 hecto-liters/acre

Appellation d'Origine Vins Délimités de Qualité Supérieure—Known as A.O.V.D.Q.S., this is a step below A.O.C. wines and represents 1 percent of production.

Vins de Pays—This is a category that's growing in importance. A 1979 French legal decision liberalized the rules for this category, permitting the use of non-traditional grapes in certain regions, and even allowing vintners to label wines with the varietal name rather than with the regional name. For exporters to the American market, where consumers are becoming accustomed to buying wines by grape variety—Merlot or Chardonnay, for example—this change makes their wines much easier to sell.

Vins de Table—These are ordinary, simple table wines and represent almost 35 percent of all wines produced in France.

Most French wine is meant to be consumed as a simple beverage. Many of the vins de table are marketed under proprietary names and are the French equivalent of California jug wines. Don't be surprised if you go into a grocery store in France to buy wine and find it in a plastic wine container with no label on it! You can see the color through the plastic—either red, white, or rosé—but the only marking on the container is the alcohol content, ranging from 9 to 14 percent. You choose your wine depending on what you have to do during the rest of the day!!

When you buy wines, keep these distinctions in mind, because there's not only a difference in quality, but also in price.

What are the four major white-wine-producing regions of France?

Alsace   Loire Valley   Bordeaux   Burgundy

Let's start with Alsace and the Loire Valley, because these are the two French regions truly known for white wines. As you can see from the map at the beginning of this chapter, Alsace, the Loire Valley, and Chablis (a white-wine-producing region of Burgundy) have one thing in common: They're all located in the northern region of France. These areas produce white wines predominantly, because of the shorter growing season and the cooler climate, both of which are best suited for growing white grapes.

Alsace

I often find that people are confused about the difference between wines from Alsace and those from Germany. Why do you suppose this is?

First of all, Alsace and Germany grow the same grape varieties. When you think of Riesling, what are your associations? You'll probably answer "Germany" and "sweetness." That's a very typical response. However, after the winemaker from Alsace harvests his Riesling, he makes his wine much differently from the wine of his German counterpart. The winemaker from Alsace ferments every bit of the sugar in the grape, while in Germany the winemaker adds a small amount of the naturally sweet unfermented grape juice back into the wine, which creates the typical German style. Ninety-nine percent of all Alsace wines are totally dry.

Another fundamental difference between wine from Alsace and wine from Germany is the alcohol content. Wine from Alsace has 11 to 12 percent alcohol, while most German wine has a mere 8 to 9 percent.

Just to confuse you a bit more, both wines are bottled in similarly shaped bottles that are tall with a tapering neck.

PRODUCT OF FRANCE

MARQUE DÉPOSÉE

MOREAU
BLANC RESERVE

VIN DE TABLE FRANCAIS

MIS EN BOUTEILLE PAR
J. MOREAU & FILS
NEGOCIANT A 89800 . FRANCE

750 ml.   Alc. 11% by vol.

Famous non-A.O.C. French wines that are available in the United States include: Valbon, Moreau, Boucheron, Chantefleur, and René Junot.

Champagne is another major white-wine producer, but that's a chapter in itself.

From 1871 to 1919, Alsace was part of Germany.

All wines produced in Alsace are A.O.C.-designated wines, and represent nearly 20% of all A.O.C. white wines in France.

Alsace produces 8% red wines from the Pinot Noir grape. These generally are consumed in the region and are rarely exported.

Wine labeling in Alsace is different from other French regions administered by the A.O.C., because Alsace is the only region that labels its wine by specific grape variety. All Alsace wines that put the name of the grape on the label must contain 100% of that grape.

Great Sweet (Late Harvest) Wines from Alsace
Vendange Tardive
Seléction de Grains Nobles

In the last ten years, there have been more Pinot Blanc and Riesling grapes planted in Alsace than any other variety.

There are 35,000 acres of grapes planted in Alsace, but the average plot of land for each grower is only five acres.

What are the white grapes grown in Alsace?

The four grapes you should know are:

> Riesling—accounts for 23 percent
>
> Gewürztraminer—accounts for 19 percent
>
> Pinot Blanc—accounts for 20 percent
>
> Tokay–Pinot Gris—accounts for 7 percent

What type of wine is produced in Alsace?

As we mentioned earlier, virtually all the Alsace wines are dry. Riesling is the major grape planted in Alsace, and it is responsible for the highest-quality wines of the region. The other wine Alsace is known for is Gewürztraminer, which is in a class by itself. Most people either love it or hate it, because Gewürztraminer has a very distinctive style. *"Gewürz"* is the German word for "spice," which aptly describes the wine.

Pinot Blanc is a "new-style" wine for the region, and it's becoming increasingly popular with the growers of Alsace.

How should I select an Alsace wine?

Two factors are important in choosing a wine from Alsace: the grape variety and the reputation and style of the shipper. Some of the most reliable shippers are:

Hugel & Fils	Domaine Zind-Humbrecht
F. E. Trimbach	Domaine Weinbach
Léon Beyer	Domaine Marcel Deiss
Dopff "Au Moulin"	

Why are the shippers so important?

Because the majority of the landholders in Alsace don't grow enough grapes for it to be economically feasible to produce and market their own wine. Instead, they sell their grapes to a shipper who produces, bottles, and markets the wine under his own name. The art of making high-quality wine lies in the selection of grapes made by each shipper.

What are the different quality levels of Alsace wine?

The vast majority of the wine is a shipper's varietal: A very small percentage is labeled with a specific vineyard's name, especially in the appellation "Alsace Grand Cru." Some wines are also labeled "Réserve" or "Réserve Personelle," which terms are not legally defined. Their importance is determined by the shipper's reputation.

Should I lay down my Alsace wines for long aging?

In general, most Alsace wines are made to be consumed young—that is, one to five years after they're bottled. As in any fine-wine area, there is a small percentage of great wines produced in Alsace that may be aged for ten years or more.

What are the recent trends in Alsace wine?

What I've learned over the last ten years is that the more I drink Alsace wines, the more I like them. They're fresh, they're "clean," they're easy to drink, they're very compatible with food.

I think Riesling is still the best grape, but Pinot Blanc, which is lighter in style, is a perfect apéritif wine at a very good price.

Most Alsace wines are very affordable, of good quality, and are available in most markets.

Best Bets for Recent Vintages of Alsace
1994 1995 1996 1997 1998

WINE AND FOOD

During a visit to Alsace, I spoke with two of the region's best-known producers to find out which types of food they enjoy with Alsace wines. Here's what they prefer:

Étienne Hugel—"Alsace wines are not only suited to classic Alsace and other French dishes. For instance, I adore Riesling with such raw fish specialties as Japanese sushi and sashimi, while our Gewürztraminer is delicious with smoked salmon and brilliant with Chinese, Thai, and Indonesian food."

Mr. Hugel describes Pinot Blanc as "round, soft, not aggressive...an all-purpose wine...can be used as an apéritif, with all kinds of *pâté* and *charcuterie*, and also with hamburgers. Perfect for brunch—not too sweet or flowery."

Hubert Trimbach—"Riesling with fish—blue trout with a light sauce." He recommends Gewürztraminer as an apéritif, or with *foie gras* or any *pâté* at the end of the meal; with Muenster cheese, or a stronger cheese such as Roquefort.

Sometimes you'll see "Grand Cru" on an Alsace label. This wine can be made only from the best grape varieties of Alsace. There are over 50 different vineyards entitled to be called "Grand Cru."

The Alsace region has little rainfall, especially during the grape harvest, and the town of Colmar, the Alsace wine center, is the second driest city in France. That's why they say a "one-shirt harvest" will be a good vintage.

FOR THE TOURISTS
Visit the beautiful wine village of Riquewihr, whose buildings date from the fifteenth-sixteenth century.

FOR THE FOODIES
Alsace has three three-star Michelin restaurants in a 30-mile radius.

Alsace is also known for its fruit brandies—"eaux-de-vie":
Framboise—raspberries
Kirsch—cherries
Mirabelle—yellow plums
Fraise—strawberries
Poire—pears

FOR FURTHER READING:
Alsace, by S. F. Hallgarten;
Alsace, by Pamela Van Dyke Price.

Loire Valley

Starting at the city of Nantes, a bit upriver from the Atlantic Ocean, this valley stretches inland for 600 miles along the Loire River.

There are two grape varieties you should be familiar with:

Sauvignon Blanc   Chenin Blanc

In the Loire Valley, 56% of the A.O.C. wines produced are white, and 96% of those are dry.

The Loire Valley is famous not only for its wines, but also as a summer retreat for royalty. Elegant and sometimes enormous châteaus embellish the countryside.

The distinct nose (bouquet) of Pouilly-Fumé comes from a combination of the Sauvignon Blanc grape and the soil of the Loire Valley.

My students are often confused about Pouilly-Fumé and Pouilly-Fuissé, expecting similarly named wines to be related. But Pouilly-Fumé is made from 100% Sauvignon Blanc and comes from the Loire Valley, while Pouilly-Fuissé is made from 100% Chardonnay and comes from the Mâconnais region of Burgundy.

The Loire Valley also produces the world-famous Anjou Rosé.

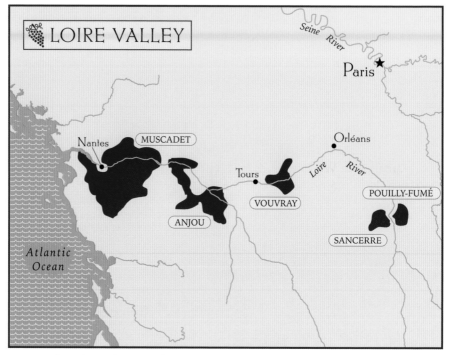

Rather than choosing by grape variety and shipper, as you would in Alsace, choose Loire Valley wines by style and vintage. Here are the main styles:

Pouilly-Fumé—A dry wine that has the most body and concentration of all the Loire Valley wines. It's made with 100 percent Sauvignon Blanc.

Muscadet—A light, dry wine, made from 100 percent Melon grape.

Sancerre—Striking a balance between full-bodied Pouilly-Fumé and light-bodied Muscadet, it's made with 100 percent Sauvignon Blanc.

Vouvray—The "chameleon"; it can be dry, semisweet, or sweet. It's made from 100 percent Chenin Blanc.

How did Pouilly-Fumé get its name, and what does "Fumé" mean?

Many people ask me if Pouilly-Fumé is smoked, because they automatically associate the word "fumé" with smoke. One of the many theories about the origin of the word comes from the white morning mist that blankets the area. As the sun burns off the mist, it looks as if smoke is rising.

When are the wines ready to drink?

Generally, Loire Valley wines are meant to be consumed young. The exception is a sweet Vouvray, which can be laid down for a longer time.

Here are more specific guidelines:

Pouilly-Fumé—three to five years

Sancerre—two to three years

Muscadet—one to two years

What are the most recent trends in Loire Valley wines?

Ten years ago, at Windows on the World, we started promoting Sancerre over Pouilly-Fumé. Both are made with the same grape variety, but the Sancerre was less expensive. Today, with a demand for both wines, they have become much more expensive, with Sancerre sometimes even more expensive than Pouilly-Fumé.

Muscadet, on the other hand, remains a good value. In fact, I think these wines are being made even better than they were ten years ago.

Best Bets for Recent Vintages of Loire Valley
1996 1997 1999

WINE AND FOOD

Baron Patrick Ladoucette—owner of Ladoucette Pouilly-Fumé (and incidentally the largest producer of Pouilly-Fumé)—recommends the following wine and food combinations:

Pouilly-Fumé— "Smoked salmon; turbot with hollandaise; white meat chicken; veal with cream sauce."

Sancerre— "Shellfish, simple food of the sea, because Sancerre is drier than Pouilly-Fumé."

Muscadet— "All you have to do is look at the map to see where Muscadet is made: by the sea where the main fare is shellfish, clams, and oysters."

Vouvray— "A nice semi-dry wine to have with fruit and cheese."

Most Pouilly-Fumé and Sancerre wines are not aged in wood.

BEST PRODUCERS
Sancerre: Archambault, Roblin, Lucien Crochet, Jean Vacheron, Château de Sancerre, Domaine Fournier
Pouilly-Fumé: Guyot, Michel Redde, Ch. de Tracy, Dagueneau, Ladoucette, Colin
Vouvray: Huet
Muscadet: Marquis de Goulaine, Sauvignon, Metareau

If you see the words *sur-lie* on a Muscadet wine label, it means that the wine was aged on its lees (sediment).

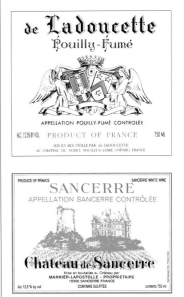

For further reading: *A Wine and Food Guide to the Loire,* by Jacqueline Friedrich.

Two-thirds of Bordeaux wines are red and one-third are white.

Marquis Robert de Goulaine—owner of Marquis de Goulaine—recommends the following wine and food combinations:

"My favorite wine and food combination for Pouilly-Fumé is to have it with a turbot sauce hollandaise. Pouilly-Fumé, because of its long-lasting bouquet and taste in the mouth, needs a rich sauce of that type.

"Sancerre, being floral, with a slightly grassy bouquet, is ideal with the local Loire Valley goat cheese.

"Muscadet is good with a huge variety of excellent and fresh 'everyday' foods, including all the seafood from the Atlantic Ocean, the fish from the river—pike, for instance—game, poultry, and cheese (mainly goat cheese). Of course, there is a must in the region of Nantes: freshwater fish with the world-famous butter sauce, the *beurre blanc*, invented at the turn of the century by Clémence, who happened to be the chef at Goulaine. If you prefer, try Muscadet with a dash of crème de cassis (black currant); it is a wonderful way to welcome friends!

"Vouvray, sipped on its own as an apéritif on a warm, long summer afternoon, will always be a treat. During a meal, it would be a wonderful, unusual alternative to complement foie gras or an apricot tart."

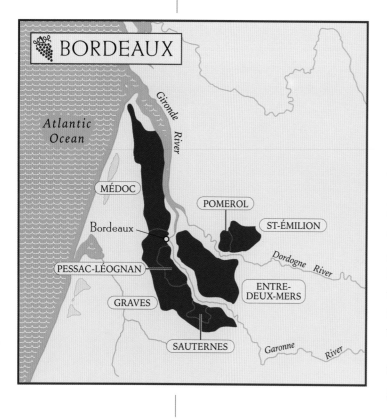

The White Wines of Bordeaux

Doesn't Bordeaux always mean red wine?

That's a misconception. Actually, two of the five major areas of Bordeaux are known for their excellent white wines—Graves and Sauternes. Sauternes is world-famous for its sweet white wine.

The major white grape varieties used in both areas are:

Sémillon   **Sauvignon Blanc**

Graves

How are the white Graves wines classified?

There are two levels of quality distinction:

Graves   **Pessac-Léognan**

The most basic Graves is simply called "Graves." The best wines are produced in Pessac-Léognan. Those labeled "Graves" are from the southern portion of the region closest to Sauternes, while Pessac-Léognan is in the northern half of the region, next to the city of Bordeaux. The best wines are known by the name of a particular château, a special vineyard that produces the best-quality grapes. The grapes grown for these wines enjoy better soil and better growing conditions overall. The classified château wines and the regional wines of Graves are always dry.

How should I select a Graves wine?

My best recommendation would be to purchase a classified château wine. Here they are:

Château Bouscaut*
Château Carbonnieux*
Domaine de Chevalier
Château Couhins-Lurton
Château La Louvière*
Château La Tour-Martillac
Château Laville-Haut-Brion
Château Malartic-Lagravière
Château Olivier*

*The largest producers and the easiest to find.

What are the most recent trends in the white wines of Bordeaux?

Some of the major changes in French white wines have occurred in the Bordeaux region. The winemakers have changed the style through more modern winemaking techniques, as well as by being more careful with their selection in the vineyard, thus resulting in a much higher quality of white Bordeaux wines.

The word "Graves" means gravel—the type of soil found in the region.

When people think of dry white Bordeaux wines, they normally think of the major areas of Graves or Pessac-Léognan, but some of the best value/quality white wines produced in Bordeaux come from the area called Entre-Deux-Mers.

The wine production of Graves is divided evenly between red and white.

Classified white château wines are hard to find, since they make up only 3% of the total production of white Graves.

The style of classified white château wines varies with the ratio of Sauvignon Blanc and Sémillon used. Château Olivier, for example, is made with 65% Sémillon, and Château Carbonnieux with 65% Sauvignon Blanc.

WINE AND FOOD

Denise Lurton-Moulle (Château La Louvière, Château Bonnet)—With Château La Louvière Blanc, grilled sea bass with a *beurre blanc*, shad roe, goat cheese soufflé. With Château Bonnet Blanc, oysters on the half-shell, fresh crab salad, mussels, and clams.

Antony Perrin (Château Carbonnieux)—With a young Château Carbonnieux Blanc, chilled lobster consommé, or shellfish, such as oysters, scallops, or grilled shrimps. With an older Carbonnieux, a traditional sauced fish course or with a goat cheese.

Jean-Jacques de Bethmann (Château Olivier)—Oysters, lobster, Rouget du Bassin d'Arachon.

Sauternes/Barsac

All French Sauternes are sweet, meaning that not all the grape sugar has turned into alcohol during fermentation. A dry French Sauternes doesn't exist. The Barsac district, adjacent to Sauternes, has the option of choosing between Barsac or Sauternes as its appellation.

What are the two different quality levels in style?

1. Regional ($)
2. Classified château ($$$)/($$$$)

Sauternes is still producing one of the greatest sweet wines in the world. With the great vintages of 1988, 1989, 1990, 1996, and 1997, you'll be able to find excellent regional Sauternes, if you buy from the best shippers. These wines represent good value for your money, considering the labor involved in production, but they won't have the same intensity of flavor as a classified château.

What are the main grape varieties in Sauternes?

Sémillon   Sauvignon Blanc

When buying regional Sauternes look for these reputable shippers: Baron Philippe de Rothschild and B&G.

There's more Sémillon planted in Bordeaux than there is Sauvignon Blanc.

If the same grapes are used for both the dry Graves and the sweet Sauternes, how do you explain the extreme difference in styles?

First and most important, the best Sauternes is made primarily with the Sémillon grape. Second, to make Sauternes, the winemaker leaves the grapes on the vine longer. He waits for a mold called *Botrytis cinerea* (noble rot) to form. When this "noble rot" forms on the grapes, the water within them evaporates and they shrivel. Sugar becomes concentrated as the grapes "raisinate." Then, during the winemaking process, not all the sugar is allowed to ferment into alcohol: hence, the high-residual sugar.

How are Sauternes classified?

FIRST GREAT GROWTH—GRAND PREMIER CRU

Château d'Yquem*

FIRST GROWTH—PREMIERS CRUS

Château La Tour Blanche*   Château Climens* (Barsac)

Château Lafaurie-Peyraguey*   Château Guiraud*

Clos Haut-Peyraguey*   Château Rieussec*

Château de Rayne-Vigneau*   Château Rabaud-Promis

Château Suduiraut*   Château Sigalas-Rabaud*

Château Coutet* (Barsac)

SECOND GROWTHS—DEUXIÈMES CRUS

Château Myrat (Barsac)   Château Nairac* (Barsac)

Château Doisy-Daëne (Barsac)   Château Caillou (Barsac)

Château Doisy-Védrines* (Barsac) Château Suau (Barsac)

Château Doisy-Dubroca (Barsac)   Château de Malle*

Château d'Arche   Château Romer du Hayot*

Château Filhot*   Château Lamothe

Château Broustet (Barsac)   Château Lamothe-Guignard

*These are the Châteaus most readily available in the U.S.

Other sweet-wine producing in Bordeaux: Ste-Croix-du-Mont, Loupiac

Sauternes is expensive to produce because several pickings must be completed before the crop is entirely harvested. The harvest can last into November.

Doesn't Château d'Yquem make a dry white wine? Yes, it does, and it's called Chateau "Y".
A dry wine made in Sauternes cannot be called Appellation Sauternes by law. It can only be called Appellation Bordeaux.

Château Rieussec is owned by the same owners as Château Lafite-Rothschild.

Not classified, but outstanding quality: Château Fargues, Château Gilette, Château Raymond Lafon.

Sauternes is a wine you can age. In fact, most classified château wines in good vintages can easily age for ten to thirty years.

Best Bets for Vintages of Sauternes
1967 1975 1976 1983 1986 1988
1989 1990 1995 1996 1997

Just Desserts

My students always ask me, "What do you serve with Sauternes?" Here's a little lesson I learned when I first encountered the wines of Sauternes.

Many years ago, when I was visiting the Sauternes region, I was invited to one of the châteaus for dinner. Upon arrival, my group was offered appetizers of foie gras, and, to my surprise, Sauternes was served with it. All the books I had ever read said you should serve drier wines first and sweeter wines later. But since I was a guest, I thought it best not to question my host's selection.

When we sat down for the first dinner course, we were once again served a Sauternes. This continued through the main course—which happened to be rack of lamb—when another Sauternes was served.

I thought for sure our host would serve a great old red Bordeaux with the cheese course, but I was wrong again. With the Roquefort cheese was served a very old Sauternes.

With dessert soon on its way, I got used to the idea of having a dinner with Sauternes, and waited with anticipation for the final choice. You can imagine my surprise when a red Bordeaux—Château Lafite-Rothschild—was served with dessert!

My point is that Sauternes doesn't have to be served only with dessert. Actually, all the Sauternes went well with the courses, because all the sauces complemented the wine and food.

By the way, the only wine that *didn't* go well with dinner was the Château Lafite-Rothschild with dessert, but we drank it anyway!!

Perhaps this anecdote will inspire you to serve Sauternes with everything. Personally, I prefer to enjoy Sauternes by itself; I'm not a believer in the dessert wine category. This dessert wine is dessert in itself.

The White Wines of Burgundy

Where's Burgundy?

Burgundy is a region located in central eastern France. Its true fame is as a wine-producing area.

What's Burgundy?

This may sound like a silly question, but many people are confused about what a Burgundy really is, because the name is often misused on the market.

For our purposes, Burgundy is one of the major wine-producing regions that holds an A.O.C. designation in France. *Burgundy is not a synonym for red wine, although many red wines are simply labeled "Burgundy."* Many of these Burgundy wines are ordinary table wines. They may come from California, South Africa, Australia, or Chile, and bear little resemblance to the styles of authentic French Burgundy wines.

The largest city in Burgundy is known not for its wines, but for another world-famous product. The city is Dijon, and the product is mustard.

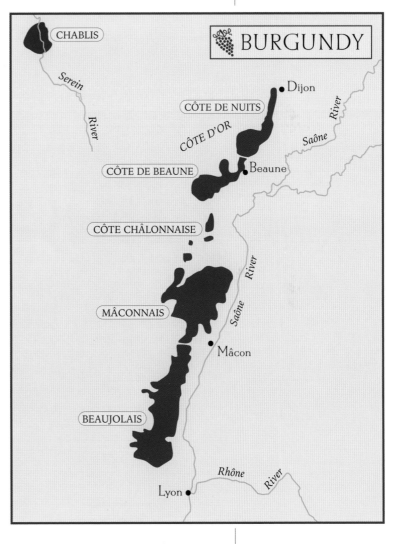

Although Chablis is part of the Burgundy region, it is a three-hour drive south from there to the Mâconnais area.

Côte d'Or Production
78% Red
22% White

What are the main areas of Burgundy?

Chablis

Côte d'Or } Côte de Nuits

Côte de Beaune

Côte Châlonnaise

Mâconnais

Beaujolais

Before we explore Burgundy, region by region, it's important to know the types of wine that are produced there. Take a look at the chart below: It breaks down the types of wine and tells you the percentage of reds to whites.

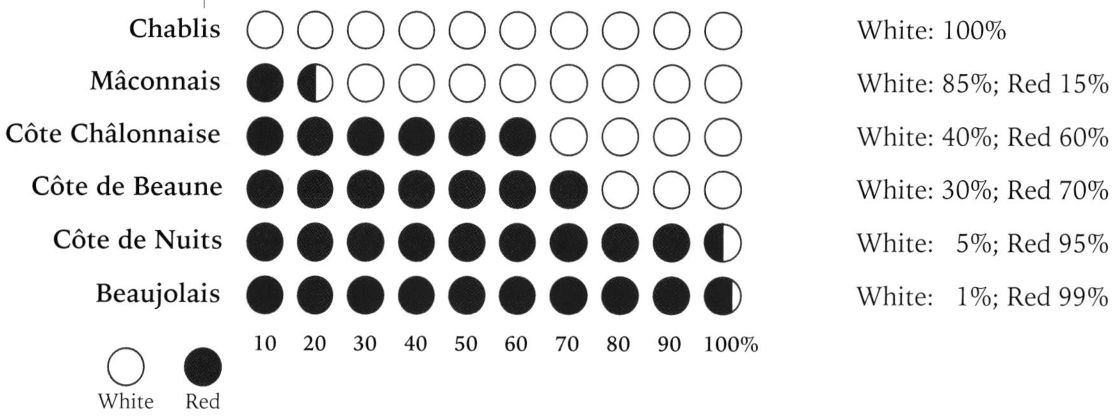

Region	Chart	Percentage
Chablis	○○○○○○○○○○	White: 100%
Mâconnais	●◐○○○○○○○○	White: 85%; Red 15%
Côte Châlonnaise	●●●●●●○○○○	White: 40%; Red 60%
Côte de Beaune	●●●●●●●○○○	White: 30%; Red 70%
Côte de Nuits	●●●●●●●●●◐	White: 5%; Red 95%
Beaujolais	●●●●●●●●●◐	White: 1%; Red 99%

10 20 30 40 50 60 70 80 90 100%

○ White   ● Red

Burgundy is another one of those regions so famous for its red wines that people sometimes forget that some of the finest white wines of France are also produced there. The three areas in Burgundy that produce world-famous white wines are:

Chablis   Côte de Beaune   Mâconnais

If it's any comfort to you, you need to know only one white grape variety—Chardonnay. All the great white Burgundies are made from 100 percent Chardonnay.

Is there only one type of white Burgundy?

Although Chardonnay is used to make all the best French white Burgundy wines, the different areas produce many different styles. Much of this has to do with where the grapes are grown and the vinification procedures. For example, in Chablis, because of its northerly climate, its wines will have more acidity than those of the southern region of Mâconnais.

With regard to vinification procedures, after the grapes are harvested in the Chablis and Mâconnais areas, 95 percent are fermented and aged in stainless-steel tanks. In the Côte de Beaune, after the grapes are harvested, a good percentage of the wines are fermented in small oak barrels and also aged in oak barrels. The wood adds complexity, depth, body, flavor, and longevity to the wines.

White Burgundies have one trait in common: They are dry.

There are more than 250 grape growers in Chablis, but only a handful age their wine in wood.

The Story of Kir

The apéritif "Kir" has become very popular. It is a mixture of white wine and crème de cassis (made from black currants). It was the favorite drink of the former mayor of Dijon, Canon Kir, who originally mixed the sweet cassis to balance the acidity of the white Burgundy wine made from the Aligoté grape.

Another white grape found in the Burgundy region is the Aligoté. It is a lesser grape variety and usually the grape name appears on the label.

A Note on the Use of Wood

Each wine region in the world has its own way of producing wines. Wine was always fermented and aged in wood—until the introduction of cement tanks, glass-lined tanks, and most recently, stainless-steel tanks. Despite these technological improvements, many winemakers prefer to use the more traditional methods. For example, many of the wines from the firm of Louis Jadot are fermented in wood as follows:

One-third of the wine is fermented in new wood.

One-third of the wine is fermented in year-old wood.

One-third of the wine is fermented in older wood.

Jadot's philosophy is that the better the vintage, the more the wood aging; the lesser the vintage, the less the wood aging. A lesser-vintage wine will usually not be aged in new wood for fear the wine would be overpowered by it. The younger the wood, the more flavor and tannin it gives to the wine.

How are the white wines of Burgundy classified?

The type of soil and the angle and direction of the slope are the primary factors determining quality. Here are the levels of quality:

Village Wine—
Bears the name of a specific village. ($ = good)

Premier Cru—
From a specific vineyard with special characteristics, within one of the named villages. Usually a Premier Cru wine will list the village first and the vineyard second. ($$ = better)

Grand Cru—
From a specific vineyard that possesses the best soil and slope in the area and meets or exceeds all other requirements. In most areas of Burgundy, the village won't appear on the label—only the vineyard name is used. ($$$$ = best)

Chablis

Chablis is the northernmost area in Burgundy, and it produces only white wine.

Isn't Chablis just a general term for white wine?

The name "Chablis" suffers from the same misinterpretation and overuse as does the name "Burgundy." Because the French didn't take the necessary precautions to protect the use of the name "Chablis," it's now randomly applied to many ordinary bulk wines from other countries. Chablis has come to be associated with some very undistinguished wine, *but this is not the case with French Chablis*. In fact, the French take their Chablis very seriously. There is a special classification of Chablis.

What are the quality levels of Chablis?

Petit Chablis—The most ordinary Chablis; rarely seen in the United States.

Chablis—A wine that comes from grapes grown anywhere in the Chablis district.

Chablis Premier Cru—A very good quality of Chablis that comes from specific high-quality vineyards.

Chablis Grand Cru—The highest classification of Chablis, and the most expensive because of its limited production. There are only seven vineyards in Chablis entitled to be called Grand Cru.

Also look for regional Burgundy wine, such as Bourgogne Blanc or Bourgogne Rouge.

Most Premier Cru wines give you the name of the vineyard on the label, but others are simply called "Premier Cru," which is a blend of different "cru" vineyards.

The average yield for a village wine in Burgundy is 360 gallons per acre. For the Grand Cru wines it is 290 gallons per acre, a noticeably larger concentration, which produces a more flavorful wine.

All French Chablis is made of 100% Chardonnay.

Of these quality levels, the best price/value wine is a Chablis Premier Cru.

There are only 245 acres planted in Grand Cru vineyards.

Village	Premier Cru	Grand Cru

If you're interested in buying only the best Chablis, here are the seven Grands Crus and the most important Premiers Crus vineyards:

THE GRAND CRU VINEYARDS OF CHABLIS

Les Clos   Blanchots

Vaudésir   Preuses

Valmur   Grenouilles

Bougros

THE TOP PREMIER CRU VINEYARDS OF CHABLIS

Vaillons   Fourchaume

Montée de Tonnerre   Montmains

Monts de Milieu   Côte de Vaulorent

Lechet

What has been the most important recent change in Chablis?

The cold, northerly climate of Chablis poses a threat to the vines. Back in the late 1950s, Chablis almost went out of business because the crops were ruined by frost. Through modern technology, and with improved methods of frost protection, vintners have learned to control this problem, so more and better wine is being produced.

The winter temperatures in some parts of Chablis can match those of Norway.

How should I buy Chablis?

The two major aspects to look for in Chablis are the shipper and the vintage. Here is a list of the most important shippers of Chablis to the United States:

Albert Pic & Fils
A. Regnard & Fils
Domaine Laroche
Joseph Drouhin
J. Moreau & Fils
Guy Robin
Robert Vocoret
Louis Jadot
Jean Dauvissat
René Dauvissat
François Raveneau
William Fèvre
Louis Michel

Best Bets for Recent Vintages of Chablis
1995 1996❖ 1997 1998

Note: ❖ signifies exceptional vintage

When should I drink my Chablis?

Chablis—within two years of the vintage
Premier Cru—between two and four years
Grand Cru—between three and eight years

Côte de Beaune

This is one of the two major areas of the Côte d'Or. Very few of the wines from this area are white, but they are some of the finest examples of dry white wine produced in the world and are considered a benchmark for winemakers everywhere.

The largest Grand Cru, in terms of production, is Corton-Charlemagne, which represents more than 50% of all white Grand Cru wines.

Côte de Beaune

Here is a list of my favorite villages and vineyards in the Côte de Beaune that produce white wines.

VILLAGE	PREMIER CRU VINEYARDS	GRAND CRU VINEYARDS
Aloxe-Corton		Corton-Charlemagne
		Charlemagne
Beaune	Clos des Mouches	None
Meursault	Les Perrières	None
	Les Genevrières	
	La Goutte d'Or	
	Les Charmes	
	Blagny	
	Poruzots	
Puligny-Montrachet	Les Combettes	Montrachet*
	Les Caillerets	Bâtard-Montrachet*
	Les Pucelles	Chevalier-Montrachet
	Les Folatières	Bienvenue-Bâtard-Montrachet
	Clavoillons	
	Les Referts	
Chassagne-Montrachet	Les Ruchottes	Montrachet*
	Morgeot	Bâtard-Montrachet*
		Criots-Bâtard-Montrachet

*The vineyards of Bâtard-Montrachet and Montrachet overlap between the villages of Puligny-Montrachet and Chassagne-Montrachet.

The three most important white wine villages of the Côte de Beaune are Meursault, Puligny-Montrachet, and Chassagne-Montrachet. All three villages produce their white wine from the same grape—100 percent Chardonnay.

Village $	Premier Cru $$	Grand Cru $$$$

As Robert Drouhin, a leading winemaker in Burgundy, says: "The difference between the Village wine, Puligny-Montrachet, and the Grand Cru Montrachet, is not in the type of wood used in aging or how long the wine is aged in wood. The primary difference is in the location of the vineyards, *i.e.*, the soil and the slope of the land."

What makes each Burgundy wine different?

In Burgundy, one of the most important factors in making a good wine is *soil*. Soil makes the difference between a Village, a Premier Cru, and a Grand Cru wine. Another major factor that makes the wines different in style is the vinification procedure the winemaker uses—the recipe. It's the same as if you were to compare the chefs at three gourmet restaurants. They may start out with the same ingredients, but it's what they do with those ingredients that matters.

Best Bets of Côte de Beaune White
1995❖ 1996❖ 1997 1999

Note: ❖signifies exceptional vintage

Côte Châlonnaise

The Côte Châlonnaise is the least known of the major wine districts of Burgundy. Although the Châlonnaise is best known for such red wines as Givry and Mercurey (see the chapter on the red wines of Burgundy), it *does* produce some very good white wines that not many people know about, which means value for you. I'm referring to the wines of **Montagny** and **Rully**. These wines are of the highest quality produced in the area, similar to the white wines of the Côte d'Or.

Look for the wines of Antonin Rodet, Louis Latour, Moillard, and Olivier Leflaive.

Mâconnais

The southernmost white-wine-producing area in Burgundy, the Mâconnais has a climate warmer than that of the Côte d'Or and Chablis. Mâcon wines, in general, are pleasant, light, uncomplicated, reliable table wines, and are a great value.

What are the quality levels of Mâconnais wines?

From basic to best:

Mâcon Blanc
Mâcon Supérieur
Mâcon-Villages
St-Véran
Pouilly-Vinzelles
Pouilly-Fuissé

Of all Mâcon wines, Pouilly-Fuissé is unquestionably one of the most popular. It is among the highest-quality Mâconnais wines, fashionable to drink in the United States long before most Americans discovered the splendors of wine. As wine consumption increased in America, Pouilly-Fuissé and other famous areas such as Pommard, Nuits-St-Georges, and Chablis became synonymous with the best wines of France, and could always be found on any restaurant's wine list.

In my opinion, Mâcon-Villages is the best value. Why pay more for Pouilly-Fuissé—sometimes three times as much—when a simple Mâcon will do just as nicely?

Best Bets of Recent Vintages of Mâcon White
1996 1997 1998

Overview

Now that you're familiar with the many different white wines of Burgundy:

How do you choose the right one for you?

First look for the vintage year. With Burgundy, it's especially important to buy a good year. After that, your choice becomes a matter of taste and cost. If price is no object, aren't you lucky?

More than four-fifths of the wines from the Mâconnais are white.

There is a village named Chardonnay in the Mâconnais area, where it is said the grape's name originated.

In an average year, around 450,000 cases of Pouilly-Fuissé are produced—not nearly enough to supply all the restaurants and retail shops for worldwide consumption.

Pouilly-Fuissé prices in many years have ended up higher than some of the great wines of Puligny-Montrachet and Meursault!

Since Mâcon wines are usually not aged in oak, they are ready to drink after one to three years.

Also, after some trial and error, you may find that you prefer the wines of one shipper over another. Here are some of the shippers to look for when buying white Burgundy:

1997
MEURSAULT
APPELLATION MEURSAULT CONTROLÉE
CE VIN A ÉTÉ ÉLEVÉ ET MIS EN BOUTEILLE PAR
BOUCHARD PÈRE & FILS
CHÂTEAU DE BEAUNE, CÔTE D'OR, FRANCE
PRODUIT DE FRANCE · PRODUCT OF FRANCE

If you're taking a client out on a limited expense account, a safe wine to order is a Mâcon. If the sky's the limit, go for the Meursault!

Estate-bottled wine: The wine is made, produced, and bottled by the owner of the vineyard.

Puligny-Montrachet
« LES REFERTS »
APPELLATION PULIGNY-MONTRACHET 1ᵉʳ CRU CONTROLÉE
WHITE BURGUNDY TABLE WINE
Mis en bouteilles par
Etienne Sauzet
PULIGNY-MONTRACHET · CÔTE-D'OR · FRANCE
SHIPPED BY ROBERT HAAS SELECTIONS*, BORDEAUX, BEAUNE

Domaine Leflaive's wines are named for characters and places in a local medieval tale. The Chevalier of Puligny-Montrachet, lonely for his son who was off fighting in the Crusades, amused himself in the ravinelike vineyards (Les Combettes) with a local maiden (Pucelle), only to welcome the arrival of another son (Bâtard-Montrachet) nine months later.

Bouchard Père & Fils
Joseph Drouhin
Louis Jadot
Louis Latour
Ropiteau Frères
Mommessin
Prosper Maufoux
Labouré-Roi
Chartron et Trébuchet
Olivier Leflaive Frères

1996
PULIGNY-MONTRACHET
APPELLATION PULIGNY-MONTRACHET CONTROLÉE
PRODUCED AND BOTTLED BY
BOUCHARD PÈRE & FILS
CHÂTEAU DE BEAUNE, CÔTE D'OR, FRANCE
PRODUIT DE FRANCE · PRODUCT OF FRANCE
WHITE BURGUNDY WINE

Although 80 percent of Burgundy wines are sold through shippers, some fine estate-bottled wines are available in limited quantities in the United States. Some of the better ones are:

Domaine Leflaive (Meursault, Puligny-Montrachet)
Domaine Bachelet-Ramonet (Chassagne-Montrachet)
Domaine Bonneau du Martray (Corton-Charlemagne)
Domaine Matrot (Meursault)
Domaine Étienne Sauzet (Chassagne-Montrachet, Puligny-Montrachet)
Domaine Boillot (Meursault)
Domaine des Comtes Lafon (Meursault)
Domaine Coche-Dury (Meursault, Puligny Montrachet)

What are the recent trends in white Burgundy?

If anything, white Burgundy wines have gotten better over the last ten years. With the great vintages of 1995, 1996, and 1997, they continue to be high-priced but, for great Chardonnays, they're still worth it. Mâcon wines remain one of today's great values in the world of wine, being made from 100 percent Chardonnay grapes, yet usually priced under $10 a bottle.

One of the most interesting things I have seen on the labels of French wines in the U.S. market, particularly from the Mâconnais, is the inclusion of the grape variety. French winemakers have finally realized that Americans buy wines by grape varieties.

I have also found that the major shippers have continued to make high-quality wines.

WINE AND FOOD

When you choose a white Burgundy wine, you have a whole gamut of wonderful food possibilities. Let's say that you decide upon a wine from the Mâconnais area. Very reasonably priced, Mâconnais wines are suitable for picnics, as well as for more formal dinners. Or, you might select one of the fuller-bodied Côte de Beaune wines that can even stand up to a hearty steak, or if you prefer, an all-purpose wine, Chablis. Here are some tempting combinations offered by the winemakers.

Christian Moreau—A basic village Chablis is good as an apéritif and with hors d'oeuvres and salads. A great Premier Cru or Grand Cru Chablis needs something more special, such as lobster. It's an especially beautiful match if the wine has a few years' age on it.

Pierre Henry Gagey (Louis Jadot)— "My favorite food combination with white Burgundy wine is, without doubt, Homard Grillé Breton (blue lobster). Only harmonious, powerful, and delicate wines are able to go with the subtle, thin flesh and very fine taste of the Breton lobster."

Mr. Gagey says that Chablis is a great match for oysters, snails, and shellfish, but a "Grand Cru Chablis should be had with trout."

On white wines of the Côte de Beaune, Mr. Gagey gets a bit more specific. "With Village wines, which should be had at the beginning of the meal, try a light fish or quenelles (light dumplings)."

"Premier Cru and Grand Cru wines can stand up to heavier fish and shellfish such as lobster—but with a wine such as Corton-Charlemagne, smoked Scottish salmon is a tasty choice."

Mr. Gagey's parting words on the subject: "Never with meat."

Louis Latour—"With Corton-Charlemagne, fillet of sole in a light Florentine sauce. Otherwise, the Chardonnays of Burgundy complement roast chicken, seafood, and light-flavored goat cheese particularly well." Mr. Latour believes that one should have Chablis with oysters and fish.

Robert Drouhin—With a young Chablis or St-Véran, Mr. Drouhin enjoys shellfish. "Fine Côte d'Or wines match well with any fish or light white meat such as veal or sweetbreads. But please, no red meat."

For further reading on Burgundy wines, I recommend *Burgundy,* by Anthony Hanson, *Burgundy,* by Robert M. Parker, Jr., *Making Sense of Burgundy,* by Matt Kramer, and *The Great Domaines of Burgundy,* by Remington Norman.

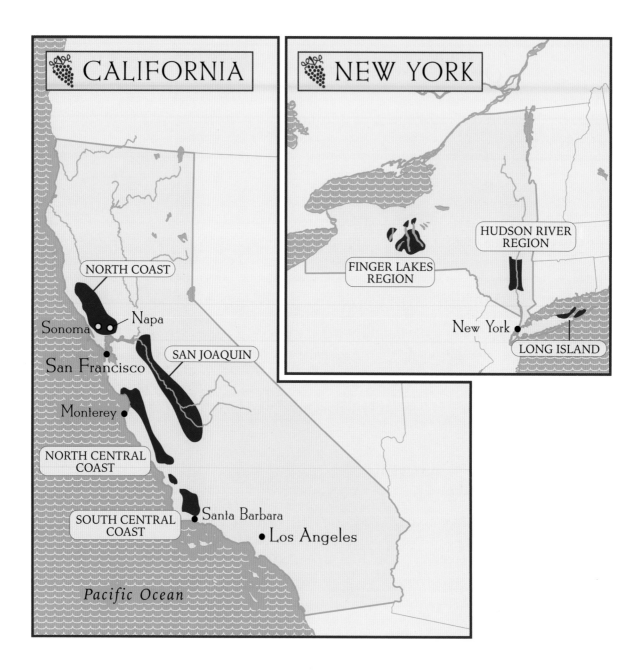

CALIFORNIA

NORTH COAST

Sonoma • Napa

San Francisco

SAN JOAQUIN

Monterey

NORTH CENTRAL
COAST

SOUTH CENTRAL
COAST

Santa Barbara

• Los Angeles

Pacific Ocean

NEW YORK

HUDSON RIVER
REGION

FINGER LAKES
REGION

New York

LONG ISLAND

The White Wines of California, New York & the Pacific-Northwest

Before discussing the wines of California and New York, let's take a look at American drinking habits. Wine has never been America's favorite beverage. In fact, forty percent of all Americans don't drink alcohol at all, and another thirty percent don't drink wine. (They prefer beer or distilled spirits.) This leaves only thirty percent of Americans who drink one glass of wine each week, the definition for a "wine drinker" in the U.S. In the final analysis, 75 percent of all wine is consumed by five percent of the population.

The leading beverage in the United States is soda, the typical American consuming an average of fifty gallons per year. Beer is in second place with 31 gallons per person. According to Gallup, wine drinking jumped by over a third in the U.S. from 1990 to 1998, leading an overall increase in alcohol consumption. Still, wine consumption has only increased to a modest two gallons per person.

Of the thirty percent of consumers who enjoy wine, the preference is decidedly American. Over eighty percent of all wines consumed by Americans are produced in the United States. Less than twenty percent are imported. Within the U.S., California accounts for ninety percent of wine production and New York ranks number two, producing six percent.

American Viticultural Areas

In the previous chapter, we discussed the white wines of France and the *appellation contrôlée* system. In the United States, we are beginning to develop a more systematic understanding of viticultural regions. So what you could describe as a U.S. appellation system is something called A.V.A., which stands for "American Viticultural Area." The first A.V.A. was established in 1980.

The top five wine-consuming countries
1. France
2. Italy
3. United States
4. Germany
5. Spain

The world's top per capita wine-consuming countries

Rank	Country	Gallons/person
1.	Luxembourg	17
2.	France	16
3.	Italy	15.5
4.	Portugal	14
5.	Slovenia	14
35.	United States	2

The top wine-producing states are:

Rank	State	# of Wineries
1.	California	1,056
2.	New York	136
3.	Washington	125
4.	Oregon	116

Thomas Jefferson, America's first wine connoisseur, had 200 acres of vineyards planted in Virginia.

Leading Wine
Producers of the
World
1. France
2. Italy
3. Spain
4. United States
5. Argentina

Grapes are grown and
wine is produced in more
than 40 of the 50 states.

In 1999 there were over
2,000 wineries in the
United States, up from
580 in 1975.

There are 210 growing
days on Long Island,
compared to 150 in the
Finger Lakes.

New York's Hudson
Valley boasts the oldest
active winery in the
United States—
Brotherhood, which
recorded its first vintage
in 1839.

Examples of *Vitis vinifera*
grapes are Riesling,
Sauvignon Blanc,
Chardonnay, Pinot Noir,
Merlot, and Cabernet
Sauvignon.

There are 125 wineries in
New York State. There
are 60 in the Finger
Lakes, 28 in the Hudson
Valley and 24 in Long
Island.

Vintners are discovering, as their European counterparts did years ago, which grapes grow best in which particular soils and climatic conditions. There are over 125 viticultural areas in the United States. I believe the A.V.A. concept is important to wine buying, and will continue to be so as individual A.V.A.'s become known for certain grape varieties or wine styles.

For example, let's look at Napa Valley, which is probably the best known A.V.A. in the United States. Within the Napa Valley region, there is a smaller inner district called Carneros, which has the coolest climate in the Napa Valley. Since Chardonnay and Pinot Noir need a cooler growing season to mature properly, these grape varieties are especially suited to that A.V.A.

Before turning to the exciting world of California wines, I'd like to talk about two other major winemaking regions in the United States: New York State and the Pacific Northwest.

New York State

New York is the second-largest wine-producing state in the United States. The three premium wine regions in New York are:

Finger Lakes—with the largest wine production east of California

Hudson River Region—with a great concentration of premium farm wineries

Long Island—New York's fastest-growing wine region

Which grapes grow in New York State?

There are three main categories:

Native American (*Vitis labrusca)*

European (*Vitis vinifera*)

French-American (hybrids)

Native American Varieties

The *Vitis labrusca*, or Native American varieties, are very popular among grape growers in New York because they are hardy grapes that can withstand cold winters. Among the most familiar grapes of the *Vitis labrusca* family are Concord, Catawba, and Delaware. Until the last decade, these

The Beginning of Winemaking in the United States

When colonists came to America in the 1600s, many of them settled in New England. They were very pleased to find native American vines already growing wild (*Vitis labrusca*), so they didn't have to worry about importing their own.

The first thing they did was to prune the existing vines and plant more of the same. Three years later—the time it takes before a mature grape crop can produce wine—they harvested the grapes and made the wine. After they tasted the first vintage, they were disappointed that it didn't taste the same as the wine they had drunk in their homeland.

So they decided to bring in their own European *Vitis vinifera* vines—actually, cuttings of the vines, to America. Once again, ships from Europe landed on the East Coast and the colonists planted the *Vitis vinifera* vines.

What happened? Nothing. The vines didn't grow. The cold was blamed, but actually the European vines lacked immunity to local plant diseases and pests. If the colonists had had access to today's methods to control these problems, the *Vitis vinifera* grapes would have thrived on the East Coast, just as they do today.

---

were the grapes that were used to make most New York wines. In describing these wines, words such as "foxy," "grapey," "Welch's," and "Manischewitz" are often used. These words are a sure sign of *Vitis labrusca*.

European Varieties

Forty years ago, some New York wineries began to experiment with the traditional European (*Vitis vinifera*) grapes. Dr. Konstantin Frank, a Russian viticulturist skilled in cold-climate grape-growing, came to the United States and catalyzed efforts to grow *Vitis vinifera* in New York. This was unheard of—and laughed at—years ago. Other vintners predicted that he'd fail, that it was impossible to grow *vinifera* in New York's cold and capricious climate.

"What do you mean?" Dr. Frank replied. "I'm from Russia—it's even colder there."

Most people still laughed, but Charles Fournier of Gold Seal Vineyards was intrigued enough to give Konstantin Frank a chance to prove his theory.

Sure enough, Dr. Frank was successful with the *vinifera* and has produced some world-class wines, especially his Riesling and Chardonnay. So have many other New York wineries, thanks to the vision and courage of Dr. Frank and Charles Fournier.

"It's Not Your Father's Kosher Wine"
Kosher wines around the world have vastly improved in quality. For years, kosher wines were thought of only as sweet wines. Today you can buy great examples of kosher Chardonnay and Cabernet Sauvignon.

Dr. Konstantin Frank

NEW YORK
Johannisberg Riesling
1997

DRY

ALC 11.5% VOL

French-American Varieties

Some New York winemakers have planted French-American hybrid varieties, which combine European taste characteristics with American vine hardiness to withstand New York's cold winters. These varieties were originally developed by French viticulturists in the 19th century. Seyval Blanc and Vidal are the most promising white wine varieties; Baco Noir and Chancellor are the best reds.

What have been the trends in New York wines over the last twenty years?

The most significant developments have been in the wines of Long Island, which has experienced the fastest growth of new vineyards. In the last 20 years, its grape-growing acreage has increased from 100 acres to more than 2,800 acres, with more expansion expected in the future.

The predominant use of *Vitis vinifera* varieties allows Long Island wineries to compete more effectively in the world market, and Long Island's longer growing season offers more potential for red grapes.

The Hudson Valley has seen the addition of a major winery, called Millbrook, which has shown that this region can produce world-class wines—not only white, but red, from such grapes as Merlot, Pinot Noir, and Cabernet Franc.

The wines of the Finger Lakes region continue to get better as the winemakers work with grapes that thrive in the cooler climate, including European varieties such as Riesling, Chardonnay, and Pinot Noir.

There are 24 wineries on Long Island, and the two A.V.A.'s are North Fork and The Hamptons.

Today, more than eighty New York State wineries produce *vinifera* wines. Wineries to look for in New York State are:

THE FINGER LAKES
Dr. Konstantin Frank
Glenora
Herman Weimer
Wagner
Fox Run

THE HUDSON VALLEY
Millbrook

LONG ISLAND
Lenz
Hargrave
Pindar
Palmer
Christina
Pelligrini
Bedel

The first winery on Long Island was started in 1972 by Alex and Louisa Hargrave.

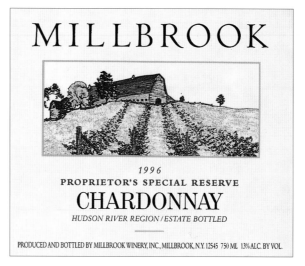

The Pacific Northwest

Washington State

In Washington, the climatic conditions are a little cooler than in California, and the winegrowing regions are protected from Washington's famous rains by the Cascade Mountains. The two major white grapes are Chardonnay and Riesling. Sémillon, Sauvignon Blanc, and Pinot Noir are grown there as well.

There are three major A.V.A.'s: Columbia Valley, Yakima, and Walla Walla. Some of the wineries to look for include Columbia Crest, Columbia Winery, Hogue Cellars, L'Ecole #41, Leonetti Cellars, Woodward Canyon Winery, and the largest winery, Chateau Ste. Michelle.

Oregon

Oregon, because of its climate, is becoming well known for Burgundian-style wines. By Burgundian style I'm referring to Chardonnay and Pinot Noir, which are the major grapes planted in Oregon. The major A.V.A. in Oregon is the Willamette Valley, near Portland. Other A.V.A.'s include Rogue Valley and Umpqua.

Wineries to look for include Adelsheim, Eyrie Vineyards, Erath, Ponzi Vineyards, Rex Hill, Cristom, Sokol Blosser, and Tualatin. Also, the famous Burgundy producer Joseph Drouhin owns a winery in Oregon called Domain Drouhin, producing, not surprisingly, Burgundy-style wines.

Of course, very good wines are produced throughout the United States, in such places as Idaho, Michigan, and Texas, but a discussion of each is beyond the scope of this book. For further reading, I recommend *The Wines of America*, by Leon D. Adams, and *American Wine*, by Anthony Dias Blue.

Cabernet Sauvignon and Merlot grow well in Washington State's Columbia Valley, which is on the same latitude as Bordeaux, France.

The 1998 vintage in Washington State is considered by many winemakers to be the highest quality harvest ever!

Vital Statistics
OREGON:
7,500 acres, 120 wineries
WASHINGTON:
over 20,000 acres, 100 wineries
NAPA VALLEY
36,115 acres, over 240 wineries

North American Wine Grape Production, 1999
(in tons)

California	2,900,000
New York	170,000
Washington	80,000
Oregon	16,500

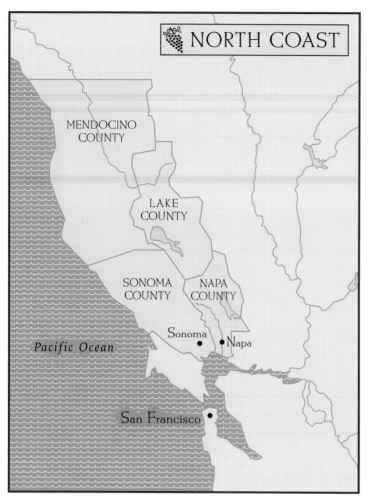

California

No winegrowing area in the world has come so far so quickly as California. It seems ironic, because Americans historically have not been interested in wine. But from the moment Americans first became "wine conscious," winemakers rose to the challenge in the typical American way. They made it their mission to create a product and to go as far as possible with it: "We'll beat out the competition; we'll show that we're the best and can compete with the best." Fifteen years ago we were asking if California wines were entitled to be compared to European wines. Now, California wines are available worldwide—shipments for export have increased dramatically over recent years to countries such as Japan, Germany, and England. California wines are now accepted worldwide.

The 20 Top-Selling California Wines
1. Carlo Rossi
2. Franzia
3. Gallo Label
4. Gallo Reserve Cellars
5. Almaden
6. Inglenook
7. Sutter Home
8. Robert Mondavi
9. Beringer
10. Paul Masson
11. Glen Ellen
12. Vendange
13. Peter Vella
14. Fetzer
15. Sebastiani
16. Kendall-Jackson
17. William Wycliff
18. Taylor California Cellars
19. Blossom Hill
20. Turning Leaf

Source: *U.S. Wine Stats*

How did California come so far so fast in the wine industry?

California has many elements for winemaking success, including:

Location—Napa and Sonoma, the two major quality-wine regions, are one and a half hours from San Francisco by car. The proximity of these regions to the city encourages people to visit often and taste the wines.

Weather—Plenty of sunshine, warm temperatures, and a long growing season all add up to good conditions for growing many grape varieties. California is certainly subject to sudden changes in weather—as is any other wine-growing region in the world—but a fickle climate is not a major worry to Californians.

The University of California at Davis, and Fresno State University—These schools have been the training grounds for many young California winemakers. They teach new techniques and a truly scientific study of wine: the soil, the different strains of yeast, temperature-controlled fermentation, and other winemaking and viticultural techniques.

Money and Marketing Strategy—This factor simply cannot be overemphasized. Perhaps marketing does not make the wine, but it certainly helps sell it. Going back to 1967, when the now defunct National Distillers bought Almaden, large corporations with tremendous resources and expertise in advertising and promotion entered the wine business and brought California wines to the attention of buyers around the world. Other corporate participants included Pillsbury, Coca-Cola, and even Otsuka Pharmaceutical Company of Japan.

From the Corporate Ladder to the Vine

The pioneers of the back-to-the-land movement:

"FARMER"	WINERY	PROFESSION
Robert Travers	Mayacamas	Investment banker
David Stare	Dry Creek	Civil engineer
Tom Jordan	Jordan	Geologist
Rodney Strong	Rodney Strong	Dancer/Choreographer
James Barrett	Chateau Montelena	Attorney
Tom Burgess	Burgess	Air Force pilot
Brooks Firestone	Firestone	Take a guess!

Early California winemakers sent their children to study oenology at Geisenheim (Germany) or Montpellier (France). Today, many European winemakers send their children to the University of California at Davis and to Fresno State University.

The University of California at Davis graduated only five students from its oenology department in 1966. Today, over thirty years later, it has a waiting list of students from all over the world.

So you want to buy a vineyard in California? Today, one acre in the Napa Valley costs $50,000 to $60,000 unplanted, and it takes an additional $6,000 per acre to plant. This per-acre investment sees no return for three to five years. To this, add the cost of building the winery, buying the equipment, and hiring the winemaker.

Creative Financing
Overheard at "The Diner" in Yountville, Napa: "How do you make a small fortune in the wine business?" "Start with a large fortune and buy a winery."

What are the advantages of being a California winery owner?
1. You can wear all the latest styles from the L.L. Bean catalog.
2. You can bone up a lot on ecology and organic farming.
3. You can grow a beard, drive a pickup truck, and wear suspenders.

What do the Smothers Brothers, Christina Crawford, Fess Parker, Wayne Rogers, and Francis Ford Coppola have in common? They all own vineyards in California.

As one California winemaker said: "We release no wine before the bank tells us that it's ready."

Why is California wine so confusing?

The renaissance of the California wine industry only began about 30 years ago. Within that short period of time, over 700 new wineries have been established in California. Today, there are more than 900 wineries in California, most of them making more than one wine, and the price differences are reflected in the styles (you can get a Chardonnay wine in any price range from $5 to $75—so how do you choose?). The constant changes in the wine industry through experimentation keep California winemaking in a state of flux.

What are the latest trends in the wines of California?

There has been a trend toward wineries specializing in particular grape varieties. Fifteen years ago, I would have talked about which wineries in California were the best. Today, I'm more likely to talk about which winery makes the best Chardonnay; which winery makes the best Sauvignon Blanc; and the same would hold true for the reds, narrowing it down to who makes the best Cabernet, Pinot Noir, or Merlot.

The era of great experimentation with winemaking techniques is slowly coming to an end, and now the winemakers are just making the finest possible wines they can from what they've learned in the '80s and '90s. I do expect to see some further experimentation to determine which grape varieties grow best in the various A.V.A.'s and microclimates. One of the biggest changes in the last fifteen years is that wineries have also become more food-conscious in winemaking, adjusting their wine styles to go better with various kinds of food by lowering alcohol levels and increasing the acidity.

Chardonnay and Cabernet Sauvignon remain the two major grape varieties, but much more Merlot is being planted in California. Sauvignon Blanc (also called Fumé Blanc) wines have improved. They're easier to consume young, although they still don't have the cachet of a Chardonnay. However, other white-grape varieties, such as Riesling and Chenin Blanc, aren't meeting with the same success, and they're harder to sell today. Still, just to keep it interesting, some winemakers are introducing some additional European varietals to the California wine scene, including Italy's Sangiovese, and Grenache and Viognier from France.

Another big change is that American wine drinkers are moving away from generic wines toward varietal wines.

Fifteen years ago, diners would come into Windows on the World and ask for a glass of Chablis. Today, they not only ask for Chardonnay, but they'll also ask, "Which Chardonnays do you have?" California has been very successful in creating affordable varietal wines. At the same time, even Gallo, which was known for its generic wines, produces a $30 bottle of Chardonnay and a $60 bottle of Cabernet Sauvignon, and critics have raved about the quality of the wine.

Also, many of the corporate players are no longer in the game. For example, Coca-Cola realized it could make more money selling soft drinks, so it abandoned the wine business.

Finally, one must not forget the impact of the plant louse phylloxera, which has been killing the vines of California for the past few years. It has required large-scale replanting of many California vineyards, which has led to the improvement in vineyard management techniques and, ultimately, in wine quality.

What's California's winemaking history?

Although California wines have come into national and international prominence only recently—within the past thirty years—the winemaking industry in the state is more than 200 years old.

The California Gold Rush of 1849 started a mass migration to the West Coast. While many were following the call "Go west, young man," not so many were getting rich panning for gold. What did they do? The same thing any businessman would do to survive—change businesses.

I'm sure you'll recognize the names of some of the early European winemakers:

FINLAND: Gustave Niebaum (Inglenook)—1879

FRANCE: Paul Masson—1852
Étienne Thée and Charles LeFranc (Almaden)—1852
Pierre Mirassou—1854
Georges de Latour (Beaulieu)—1900

GERMANY: Beringer Brothers—1876
Carl Wente—1883

IRELAND: James Concannon—1883

ITALY: Giuseppe and Pietro Simi—1876
John Foppiano—1895
Samuele Sebastiani—1904
Louis Martini—1922
Adolph Parducci—1932

Date of the first known vintage produced in California: 1782.

Quick History

1769: Padre Junípero Serra came to California from Mexico with the *Vitis vinifera* grape to plant for his missions.

1831: Jean Louis Vignes brought the first European grape cuttings of classic wine varieties to California.

1861: Count Agoston Haraszthy brought 100,000 *Vitis vinifera* vine cuttings from Europe. The story goes that it was the governor of California who selected Haraszthy to go to Europe to buy the cuttings. Even at this early date, California saw the potential for a wine industry.

1899: California wines were winning medals in international competition by the late 1800s.

In 1861, Mrs. Lincoln served American wines in the White House.

When Robert Louis Stevenson honeymooned in the Napa Valley in 1880, he described the efforts of local vintners to match soil and climate with the best possible varietals: "One corner of land after another...this is a failure; that is better; this is best. So bit by bit, they grope about for their Clos de Vougeot and Lafite...and the wine is bottled poetry."

In 1920 there were more than 700 wineries in California. By the end of Prohibition there were 160.

In 1930, there were 188,000 acres of vineyards in California. Today, there are more than 400,000 acres.

The best-known wineries of California in the 1950s:
Wente
Martini
Inglenook
Beaulieu
Korbel
Concannon
Beringer
Krug
Paul Masson
Almaden

Since the land was free and open, many chose farming as the most logical option, and one of the most popular crops was grapes. This led to the real beginning of the California wine industry.

Now, don't get the idea that frustrated gold miners created the whole California winemaking industry. In fact, many Europeans who settled in California brought their grapes and winemaking tradition with them.

In 1919 something terrible happened, at least for the wine industry—Prohibition! Prohibition lasted fourteen miserable years, until 1933.

What effect did Prohibition have on the California wine industry?

By the end of Prohibition, most of the wineries had gone out of business. The only wineries to survive legitimately were those that produced table grapes for home winemaking and, of course, for sacramental wine.

Beringer, Beaulieu, and the Christian Brothers are a few of the wineries that survived this dry time by supplying sacramental wine. Since these wineries didn't have to interrupt production during Prohibition, they had a jump on those that had to start all over again after the amendment was repealed in 1933.

One Way to Get Around Prohibition...

During Prohibition, people used to buy grape concentrate from California and have it shipped to the East Coast. The top of the container was stamped in big, bold letters: CAUTION: DO NOT ADD SUGAR OR YEAST OR ELSE FERMENTATION WILL TAKE PLACE!

Of course, we know the formula: Sugar+Yeast=Alcohol. Do you want to guess how many people had the sugar and yeast ready the very moment the concentrate arrived?

When did California begin to make better-quality wines?

As early as the 1940s, Frank Schoonmaker, an importer and writer, and one of the first American wine experts, convinced some California winery owners to market their best wines, using varietal labels.

Robert Mondavi may be one of the best examples of a winemaker who concentrated solely on varietal wine production. In 1966, Mondavi left the Charles Krug Winery and started the Robert Mondavi Winery. His role was important to the evolution of varietal labeling of California wines. He was among the first major winemakers to make the switch that led to higher-quality winemaking.

What are the main viticultural areas of California?

The map at the beginning of the chapter should help familiarize you with the winemaking regions. It's easier to remember them if you divide them into four groups:

North Coast
Napa County

Sonoma County

Mendocino County

Lake County

North Central Coast
Monterey County

Santa Clara County

Livermore

South Central Coast
San Luis Obispo County

Santa Barbara County

San Joaquin Valley
Central Valley

Although you may be most familiar with the names Napa and Sonoma, only twelve percent of all California wine comes from these two regions combined. In fact, the bulk of California wine is from the San Joaquin Valley, where mostly "jug" wines are produced. This region accounts for 54 percent of the wine grapes planted. Maybe that doesn't seem too exciting—that the production of jug wine dominates the California winemaking industry—but Americans are not atypical in this respect. In France, for example, the A.O.C. (Appellation d'Origine Contrôlée) wines account for only 35 percent of all French wines, while the rest are everyday table wines.

Robert Mondavi was a great promoter for the California wine industry. "He was able to prove to the public what the people within the industry already knew—that California could produce world-class wines," said Eric Wente.

The Napa Valley had more than 5.1 million visitors in 1998.

Acres of wine grapes planted in Napa: 36,115
Number of wineries: over 240

Acres of wine grapes planted in Sonoma: 40,510
Number of wineries: over 150

Acres of wine grapes planted in Mendocino: 13,522
Number of wineries: 36

There are 70 A.V.A.'s in California. Some of the best known are:
Napa Valley
Sonoma Valley
Russian River Valley
Alexander Valley
Dry Creek Valley
Los Carneros
Anderson Valley
Santa Cruz Mountain
Livermore Valley
Paso Robles
Edna Valley
Fiddletown
Stag's Leap

Gallo sells nearly one out of every four bottles of American wine. They produce more than 51 million cases per year—almost a million cases per week.

A Note on Jug Wines

The phrase "jug wine" refers to simple, uncomplicated, everyday drinking wine. You're probably familiar with these types of wine: They're usually labeled with a generic name, such as "Chablis" or "Burgundy." Inexpensive and well made, these wines were originally bottled in jugs, rather than in conventional wine bottles, hence the name "jug wine." They are very popular and account for the largest volume of California wine sold in the United States.

Ernest & Julio Gallo, who began their winery in 1933, are the major producers of jug wines in California. In fact, many people credit the Gallo brothers with converting American drinking habits from spirits to wine. Several other wineries also produce jug wines, among them Almaden, Paul Masson, and Taylor California Cellars.

In my opinion, the best-made jug wines in the world are from California. They maintain both consistency and quality from year to year.

The Gallo "University"

The Ernest & Julio Gallo Winery celebrated its 65th year in the wine industry in 1998. The two brothers were in business long before California wines became popular internationally. Not only is theirs the largest winery in the world, but it also has a reputation for maintaining the highest standards in the production of its wines. Many of the famous winemakers of today's smaller California wineries learned their trade under the guidance of Ernest & Julio Gallo.

Here's a short list of some of Gallo's "graduates," and the wineries where they've worked:

WINEMAKER	WINERY
Bill Bonetti	Sonoma Cutrer
Jerry Luper	Chateau Montelena,
	Chateau Bouchaine,
	Rutherford Hill
Dick Peterson	Monterey Vineyards
Philip Togni	Togni Vineyards
Walter Schug	Schug Winery
Ed Sbragia	Beringer

What is the major white-grape variety grown in California?

The most important white wine grape grown in California is Chardonnay. This green-skinned European (*Vitis vinifera*) grape is considered the finest white-grape variety in the world. It is responsible for all the great French white Burgundies, such as Meursault, Chablis, and Puligny-Montrachet. In California, it has been the most successful white grape, yielding a wine of tremendous character and magnificent flavor. The wines are often aged in small oak barrels, increasing their complexity. In the vineyard, yields are fairly low and the grapes command high prices. Chardonnay is always dry, and benefits from aging more than any other American white wine. Superior examples can keep and develop well in the bottle for five years or longer.

The two leading white table wines produced in the United States in 1999:
1. Chardonnay
2. Sauvignon Blanc/Fumé Blanc

More than 300 different California wineries market Chardonnay.

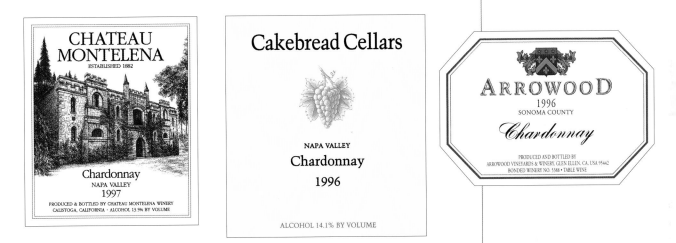

Why do some Chardonnays cost more than other varietals?

In addition to everything we've mentioned before, many wineries age these wines in wood—sometimes for more than a year. Oak barrels have doubled in price over the last five years, averaging $600 per barrel. Add to this the cost of the grapes and the length of time before the wine is actually sold, and you can see why the best of the California Chardonnays cost more than $25.

What makes one Chardonnay different from another?

Put it this way: There are many brands of ice cream on the market. They use similar ingredients, but there is only one Ben & Jerry's. The same is true for wine. Among the many things to consider: Is a wine aged in wood or stainless steel? How long does it remain in the barrel (part of the style of the winemaker)? Where do the grapes come from?

Is there any Chardonnay in a California Chablis?

Probably not, since Chardonnay is the most expensive grape used to make some of the best-quality wines in California (that's one reason to remember the varietal name "Chardonnay").

"Why," you ask, "did you say, in the last chapter, that Chablis must have 100 percent Chardonnay?"

Good question! In France the standards set by the Appellation d'Origine Contrôlée (A.O.C.) regulations require this percentage. Early California winemakers, however, "borrowed" the names of famous European wine-making regions, such as Chablis, and applied them to their own wines, regardless of the grape variety used to produce them.

Best Bets For California Chardonnay
1994   1995   1996   1997   1999

What are the other major California white-wine grapes?

Sauvignon Blanc—Sometimes labeled Fumé Blanc. This is one of the grapes used in making the dry white wines of the Graves region of Bordeaux, and the white wines of Sancerre and Pouilly-Fumé in the Loire

California has been blessed with great vintages in the 1990's.

Why is Sauvignon Blanc often labeled as Fumé Blanc? Robert Mondavi found that no one was buying Sauvignon Blanc, so he changed its name to Fumé Blanc. Strictly a marketing maneuver—it was still the same wine. Result: Sales took off. The only mistake Mondavi made was not trademarking the name, so now anyone can use it (and many producers do).

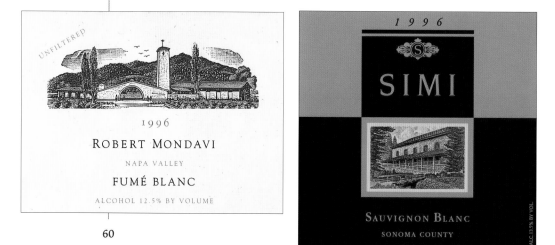

60

Valley of France. This grape is capable of producing as good a wine in California as it does in France. It is sometimes aged in small oak barrels and occasionally blended with the Sémillon grape.

Chenin Blanc—This is one of the most widely planted grapes in the Loire Valley. In California, the grape yields a very attractive, soft, light-bodied wine. It is usually made very dry or semi-sweet; it is a perfect apéritif wine, simple and fruity.

Gewürztraminer—This grape is commonly grown both in Germany and in Alsace, France. The wine is often finished in a slightly sweet to medium-sweet style to counter the grape's tendency towards bitterness, but dry versions have also shown quite well.

Johannisberg Riesling—The true Riesling responsible for the best German wines of the Rhein and Mosel—and the Alsace wines of France—is also called White Riesling, or just Riesling. This grape produces white wine of distinctive varietal character in every style from bone-dry to very sweet dessert wines, which are often much better by themselves than with dessert. The smell of Riesling at its finest is always lively, fragrant, and both fruity and flowery.

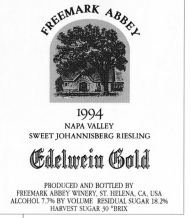

In 1981, the B.A.T.F. requested that the Wine Institute propose industry-wide standard definitions for the terms "Late Harvest" and other similar designations that link wine style to picking time. The categories proposed with their associated grape-sugar levels at harvest generally follow the terms established by the German Wine Law of 1971 (see pages 71–73):

> **Early Harvest**—Equivalent to a German Kabinett, this term refers to wine made from grapes picked at a maximum of 20° Brix.
>
> **Regular or Normal**—No specific label designation will be used to connote wines made from fruit of traditional maturity levels, 20° to 24° Brix.
>
> **Late Harvest**—This term is equivalent to a German Auslese and requires a *minimum* sugar level of 24° Brix at harvest.
>
> **Select Late Harvest**—Equivalent to a German Beerenauslese, the sugar-level *minimum* is 28° Brix.
>
> **Special Select Late Harvest**—This, the highest maturity-level designation, requires that the grapes be picked at a minimum sugar content of 35° Brix, the same level necessary for a German Trockenbeerenauslese.

Brix—A scale that measures the sugar level of the unfermented grape juice.

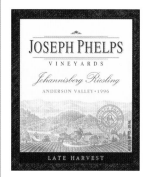

Botrytis cinerea is a mold that forms on the grapes, known also as "noble rot," which is necessary to make Sauternes and the rich German wines Beerenauslese and Trockenbeerenauslese.

California Ingenuity

Several wineries in California started to market their Late Harvest Riesling with German names such as Trockenbeerenauslese. The German government complained, and this practice was discontinued. One winemaker, though, began marketing his wine as T.B.A., the abbreviation for Trockenbeerenauslese. Again there was a complaint. This time the winemaker argued his case, saying that T.B.A. was not an abbreviation for Trockenbeerenauslese, but for *Totally Botrytis Affected.* Stay tuned for more.

How do I choose a good California wine?

One of the reasons California produces such a wide variety of wine is that it has so many different climates. Some are as cool as Burgundy, Champagne, and the Rhein, while others are as warm as the Rhône Valley, Italy, Spain, and Portugal. If that's not diverse enough, these wine-growing areas have inner districts with "microclimates," or climates-within-climates. One of the microclimates (which are among the designated A.V.A.'s) in Sonoma County, for example, is the Alexander Valley.

To better understand this concept, let's take a close look at the Clos Du Bois label.

The legal limits for the alcohol content of table wine are 7% to 13.9%, with a 1.5% allowance either way, so long as the allowance doesn't go beyond the legal limits. If the alcohol content of a table wine exceeds 14%, the label must show that. Sparkling wines may be 10% to 13.9%, with the 1.5% allowance. Appetizer wines: 17% to 20%; dessert wines: 18% to 20%. There is a 1% allowance for these last two types of wine.

If an individual vineyard is noted on the label, 95% of the grapes must have come from the named vineyard, which must be located within a federally approved A.V.A.

State:
California

County:
Sonoma

Viticultural Area:
Alexander Valley

Vineyard:
Calcaire

Winery:
Clos Du Bois

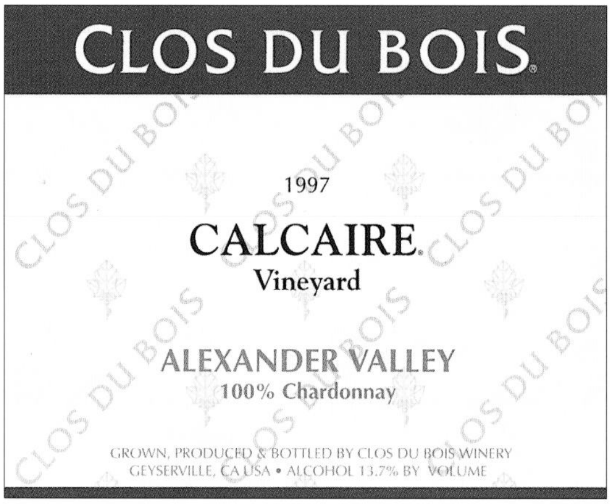

CLOS DU BOIS®
1997
CALCAIRE®
Vineyard
ALEXANDER VALLEY
100% Chardonnay
GROWN, PRODUCED & BOTTLED BY CLOS DU BOIS WINERY
GEYSERVILLE, CA USA • ALCOHOL 13.7% BY VOLUME

To better understand the concept, go back to the label. California labels tell you everything you need to know about the wine—and more. Here are some quick tips you can use when you scan the shelves at your favorite retailer. The label shown above will serve as an example.

The most important piece of information on the label is the producer's name. In this case, the producer is Clos Du Bois.

As of January 1983, if the grape variety is on the label, a minimum of 75 percent of the wine must be derived from that grape variety. If the wine was made before 1983, it must contain at least 51 percent of the labeled variety. The label shows that the wine is made from the Chardonnay grape.

If the wine bears a vintage date, 95 percent of the grapes must have been harvested that year.

If the wine is designated "California," then 100 percent of the grapes must have been grown in California.

If the label designates a certain federally recognized viticultural area (A.V.A.), such as Alexander Valley (as on our sample label), then at least 85 percent of the grapes used to make that wine must have been grown in that location.

The alcohol content is given in percentages. Usually, the higher the percentage of alcohol, the "fuller" the wine will be.

"Produced and bottled by" means that at least 75 percent of the wine was fermented by the winery named on the label.

Some wineries tell you the exact varietal content of the wine, and/or the sugar content of the grapes when they were picked, and/or the amount of residual sugar (to let you know how sweet or dry the wine is).

What's meant by "style"? How are different styles of California wine actually created?

Style refers to the characteristics of the grapes and wine. It is the trademark of the individual winemaker—an "artist" who tries different techniques to explore the fullest potential of the grapes.

Most winemakers will tell you that 95 percent of winemaking is in the quality of the grapes they begin with. The other five percent can be traced to the "personal touch" of the winemaker. Here are just a few of the hundreds of decisions a winemaker must make when developing his style of wine:

When should the grapes be harvested?

Should the juice be fermented in stainless-steel tanks or oak barrels? How long should it be fermented? At what temperature?

Should the wine be aged at all? How long? If so, should it be aged in oak? What kind of oak——American, French?

What varieties of grape should be blended, and in what proportion?

How long should the wine be aged in the bottle before it is sold?

"A winemaker's task is to bring to perfection the natural potential that is in the fruit itself."
—*Warren Winiarski, winemaker/owner, Stag's Leap Wine Cellars, Napa Valley.*

Another note on winemakers and style: In California many winemakers move around from one winery to another, just as a good chef may move from one restaurant to the next. This is not uncommon. They may choose to carry and use the same "recipe" from place to place, if it is particularly successful, and sometimes they will experiment and create new styles.

I've mentioned stainless-steel fermentation tanks so often by now that I'll give you a definition, in case you need one. These tanks are temperature controlled: They allow the winemaker to control the temperature at which the wine ferments. For example, a winemaker could ferment wines at a low temperature to retain their fruitiness and delicacy, while preventing browning and oxidation.

The list goes on. Because there are so many variables in winemaking, producers can create many styles of wine from the same grape variety—so you can choose the style that suits your taste. With the relative freedom of winemaking in the United States, the "style" of California wines continues to be "diversity."

How is California winemaking different from the European technique?

Many students ask me this, and I can only tell them I'm glad I learned all about the wines of France, Italy, Germany, Spain, and the rest of Europe before I tackled California. European winemaking has established traditions that have remained essentially unchanged for hundreds of years. These practices involve the ways grapes are grown and harvested, and in some cases include winemaking procedures.

In California, there are few traditions, and winemakers are able to take full advantage of modern technology. Furthermore, there is freedom to experiment and create new products. Some of the experimenting the California winemakers do, such as combining different grape varieties to make new styles of wine, is prohibited by some European wine-control laws. Californians thus have opportunities to try many new ideas—opportunities sometimes forbidden to European winemakers.

Another way in which California winemaking is different from European winemaking is that many Californians carry an entire line of wine. Many of the larger California wineries produce more than 20 different labels. In Bordeaux, most châteaus produce only one or two wines.

In addition to modern technology and experimentation, you can't ignore the fundamentals of wine growing: California's rainfall, weather patterns, and soils are very different from those of Europe.

What about the prices of California varietal wines?

You can't necessarily equate quality with price. Some excellent varietal wines that are produced in California are well within the budget of the average consumer. On the other hand, some varietals (primarily Chardonnay and Cabernet Sauvignon) may be quite expensive.

As in any market, it is mainly supply-and-demand that determines price. However, new wineries are affected by start-up costs, which sometimes are reflected in the price of the wine. Older, established wineries,

Eurowinemaking in California

Many well-known and highly respected European winemakers have invested in California vineyards to make their own wine. There are over 45 California wineries owned by European, Canadian, or Japanese companies. For example:

• One of the most influential joint ventures matched Baron Philippe de Rothschild, then the owner of Château Mouton-Rothschild in Bordeaux, and Robert Mondavi, of the Napa Valley, to produce a wine called Opus One.

• The owners of Château Pétrus in Bordeaux, the Moueix family, have vineyards in California. Their wine is a Bordeaux-style blend called Dominus.

• Moët & Chandon, which is part of Moët-Hennessy, owns Domaine Chandon in the Napa Valley. They also own the New York importing firm Schieffelin & Somerset Company, and Simi, a well-known winery in Sonoma.

Other European wineries with operations in California:

• Roederer has grapes planted in Mendocino County and produces Roederer Estate.

• Mumm produces a sparkling wine, called Mumm Cuvée Napa.

• Taittinger has developed its own sparkling wine called Domaine Carneros.

• The Spanish sparkling-wine house Codorniu owns a winery called Codorniu Napa; and Freixenet owns land in Sonoma County and produces a wine called Gloria Ferrer.

• The Torres family of Spain owns a winery called Marimar Torres Estate in Sonoma County.

Dominus
Napa Valley
1994
Christian Moueix
ALC. 14.1% BY VOL.-750ML
NAPA VALLEY RED WINE
CONTAINS SULFITES - PRODUCED & BOTTLED BY
DOMINUS ESTATE CORPORATION, ST. HELENA, CA., U.S.A.

U.S wine exports increased (448%) from $98 million in 1989 to $537 million in 1998.

which had long ago amortized their investments, are able to keep their prices low when the supply/demand ratio calls for it.

Remember, when you're buying California wine, price doesn't always reflect quality.

Margrit Biever and Robert Mondavi (Robert Mondavi Winery)—With Chardonnay: oysters, lobster, a more complex fish with sauce *beurre blanc,* pheasant salad with truffles. With Sauvignon Blanc: traditional white meat or fish course, sautéed or grilled fish (as long as it isn't an oily fish).

Francis Mahoney (Carneros Creek Winery)—With Chardonnay: fowl, ham, and seafood in sauces. With Sauvignon Blanc: fish, turkey, shellfish, and appetizers.

David Stare (Dry Creek)—With Chardonnay: fresh boiled Dungeness crab cooked in Zatarains crab boil, a New Orleans-style boil. Serve this with melted butter and a large loaf of sourdough French bread. With Sauvignon Blanc, "I like fresh salmon cooked in almost any manner. Personally, I like to take a whole fresh salmon or salmon steaks and cook them over the barbecue in an aluminum foil pocket. Place the salmon, onion slices, lemon slices, copious quantities of fresh dill, salt, and pepper on aluminum foil and make a pocket. Cook over the barbecue until barely done. Place the salmon in the oven to keep it warm while you take the juices from the aluminum pocket, reduce the juices, strain and whisk in some plain yogurt. Enjoy!"

Warren Winiarski (Stag's Leap Wine Cellars)—With Chardonnay: seviche, shellfish, salmon with a light hollandaise sauce.

Janet Trefethen (Trefethen Vineyards)—With Chardonnay: barbecued whole salmon in a sorrel sauce. With White Riesling: sautéed bay scallops with julienne vegetables.

Richard Arrowood (Arrowood Vineyards & Winery)—With Chardonnay: Sonoma Coast Dungeness crab right from the crab pot, with fennel butter as a dipping sauce.

Bo Barrett (Chateau Montelena Winery)—With Chardonnay: salmon, trout, or abalone, barbecued with olive oil and lemon leaf and slices.

Jack Cakebread (Cakebread Cellars)—With my 1996 Cakebread Cellars Napa Valley Chardonnay: bruschetta with wild mushrooms, leek-and-mushroom-stuffed chicken breast, and halibut with caramelized endive and chanterelles.

Ed Sbragia (Beringer Vineyards)—With Chardonnay: lobster or salmon with lots of butter.

Rodney Strong (Rodney Strong Vineyards)—With Chardonnay: Dover sole.

California wineries in the 1998 Wine Spectator Critics' Choice Selections of the Best Wineries in the World

Arrowood
Beaulieu Vineyard
Beringer
Bernardus
Bonny Doon
Buena Vista
Caymus
Chalk Hill
Chalone
Chateau St. Jean
Chateau Montelena
Clos du Bois
Codorniu Napa
Cuvaison
Dalla Valle
Diamond Creek
Domaine Carneros
Domaine Chandon
Dominus Estate
Dunn
Estancia
Far Niente
Ferrari-Carano
Fetzer

Flora Springs
Franciscan
E. & J. Gallo
Geyser Peak
Grgich Hills
Groth
Heitz
The Hess Collection
William Hill
Iron Horse
Jordan
Kendall-Jackson
Kenwood
Kistler
Laurel Glen
Markham
Matanzas Creek
Merryvale
Robert Mondavi
Mount Veeder
Mumm Cuvée Napa
Niebaum-Coppola
Opus One
Joseph Phelps

Pine Ridge
Prager
Ridge
Rochioli
Roederer Estate
Saintsbury
Sanford
Scharffenberger
Schramsberg
Shafer
Silverado Vineyards
Simi
Sonoma-Cutrer
Spottswoode
Stag's Leap Wine
  Cellars
Stag's Leap Winery
Steele
Sterling
Stonestreet
Rodney Strong
Talbott
Philip Togni

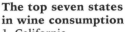

The top seven states in wine consumption
1. California
2. New York
3. Florida
4. Illinois
5. Texas
6. Washington
7. Oregon

For further reading on California wines I recommend *A Wine Atlas of California,* by Bob Thompson, *Wines of California,* by James Halliday, *California Wine,* by James Laube, and *Making Sense of California Wine,* by Matt Kramer. Lovers of gossip should have fun reading *Napa,* by James Conaway.

The White Wines of Germany

Before we begin our study of the white wines of Germany, tell me this: Have you memorized the seven Grands Crus of Chablis, the 33 Grands Crus of the Côte d'Or, and the 240 different vineyards of the Napa Valley? I hope you have, so you can begin to memorize the more than 1,400 wine villages and over 2,600 vineyards of Germany. No problem, right? What's 4,000 simple little names?

Actually, if you were to have studied German wines before 1971, you would have had 30,000 different names to remember. There used to be very small parcels of land owned by many different people; that's why so many names were involved.

In an effort to make German wines less confusing, the government stepped in and passed a law in 1971. The new ruling stated that a vineyard must encompass at least 12.5 acres of land. This law cut the list of vineyard names considerably, but increased the number of owners.

Germany produces only two or three percent of the world's wines. (Beer, remember, is the national beverage.) And what wines it does produce depends largely on the weather. Why is this? Well, look at where the wines are geographically. Germany is the northernmost country in which vines can grow. And eighty percent of the vineyards are located on hilly slopes. Germans can forget about mechanical harvesting.

The chart below should help give you a better idea of the hilly conditions vintners must contend with in order to grow grapes and produce German wines.

There has been a 10% increase in the vineyards planted over the last ten years.

France produces ten times as much wine as Germany.

In Germany, 100,000 grape-growers cultivate nearly 270,000 acres of vines, meaning the average holding per grower is 2.7 acres.

How Cold Is It?
If you were to look at a map of the world, put your finger on Germany, and then follow the 50-degree north latitude westward across into North America, you'd be pointing to the island of Newfoundland, Canada.

One mechanical harvester can do the work of sixty people.

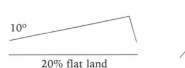

20% flat land

45°
14% hillsides

60°
66% steep hillsides

Of Mosel wines, 80% are made from the Riesling grape, while 82% of Rheingau wines are made from Riesling.

With German wines, 85 is the important number to remember.
—85% of the wines Germany produces are white.
—If a wine label gives the grape variety–Riesling, for example–85% of the wine must be made from the Riesling grape.
—If a German wine shows a vintage on the label, 85% of the grapes used must be from that year. Top German wine producers use 100% of the varietal and the vintage on the label.

With the reunification of Germany in 1989, there are now *thirteen* different regions that produce wine.

Grapes in Germany
Riesling 23%
Müller-Thurgau . . . 21%
Silvaner 7%

Germany produces red wines, too, but only 15%. Why? Red grapes simply don't grow as well as white grapes in Germany's northerly climate.

One quick way to tell the difference between a Rhein and a Mosel wine on sight is to look at the bottle. Rhein wine comes in a brown bottle, Mosel in a green bottle.

What are the most important grape varieties?

Riesling—This is by far the most widely planted and the best grape variety produced in Germany. If you don't see the name "Riesling" on the label, then there's probably very little, if any, Riesling grape in the wine. And remember, if the label gives the grape variety, then there must be at least 85 percent of that grape in the wine, according to German law. Of the grapes planted in Germany, 23 percent are Riesling.

Silvaner—This is another grape variety that accounts for seven percent of Germany's wines.

Müller-Thurgau—A cross between Riesling and Chasselas.

What are the main winemaking regions of Germany?

There are thirteen winemaking regions. Do you have to commit them all to memory like the hundreds of other names I've mentioned in the book so far? Absolutely not. Why should you worry about all thirteen when you only need to be familiar with four?

One of the reasons I emphasize these regions above the others is that in the United States you rarely see wine from the other German winegrowing regions. The other reason to look closely at these regions is that they produce the best German wines. They are:

Rheinhessen   **Pfalz** *(until 1992 known as Rheinpfalz)*
Mosel-Saar-Ruwer   **Rheingau**

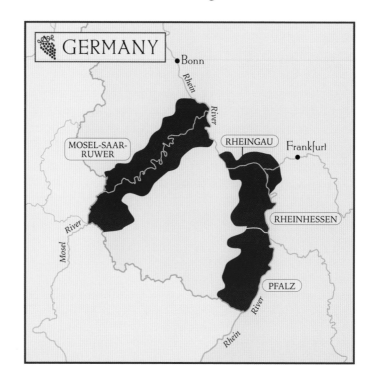

What's the style of German wines?

A balance of sweetness with acidity and low alcohol. Remember the equation:

$$\textbf{Sugar + Yeast = Alcohol + CO_2}$$

Where does the sugar come from? The sun! If you have a good year, and your vines are on a southerly slope, you'll get a lot of sun, and therefore the right sugar content to produce a good wine. In many years, however, the winemakers aren't so fortunate and they don't have enough sun to ripen the grapes. The result: higher acidity and lower alcohol. To compensate for this, some winemakers may add sugar to the must before fermentation to increase the amount of alcohol. As mentioned before, this process is called *chaptalization*. (Note: Chaptalization is not permitted for higher-quality German wines.)

The three basic styles of German wine are:

1. Trocken—Dry
2. Halbtrocken—Medium-Dry
3. Fruity—Semi-Dry to Very Sweet

A Note on Süss-Reserve

A common misconception about German wine is that fermentation stops and the remaining residual sugar gives the wine its sweetness naturally. On the contrary, some wines are fermented dry. Many German winemakers hold back a certain percentage of unfermented grape juice from the same vineyards, the same varietal, and the same sweetness level. This Süss-Reserve contains all the natural sugar and it's added back to the wine after fermentation. The finest estates do not use the Süss-Reserve method, but rely on stopping the fermentation to achieve their style.

What are the different levels of German wine?

As a result of the German law of 1971, there are two main categories. A wine is either *Tafelwein*, which means "table wine," or *Qualitätswein*, "quality wine," sometimes abbreviated QbA.

Tafelwein—The lowest designation given to a wine grown in Germany, it never carries the vineyard name. It is rarely seen in the United States.

German wines tend to be 8–10% alcohol, compared to an average 11–13% for French wine.

Given good weather, the longer the grapes remain on the vine, the sweeter they become—but the winemaker takes a risk when he does this because all could be lost in the event of bad weather.

As German winemakers say, "100 days of sun will make a good wine, but 120 days of sun will make a *great* wine."

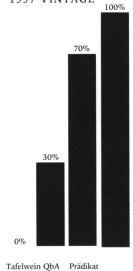

1997 VINTAGE

Tafelwein · QbA · Prädikat

Qualitätswein—literally, "quality wine."

    1. *Qualitätswein bestimmter Anbaugebiete:* QbA indicates a quality wine that comes from one of the thirteen specified regions.

    2. *Qualitätswein mit Prädikat:* This is quality wine with distinction—the good stuff. These wines may *not* be chaptalized: The winemaker is not permitted to add sugar. In ascending order of quality, price, and ripeness at harvest, here are the QmP levels:

Kabinett—Light, semi-dry wines made from normally ripened grapes. Cost: $9–$18.

Spätlese—Breaking up the word, *spät* means "late" and *lese* means "picking." Put them together and you have "late picking." That's exactly what this medium-style wine is made of—grapes that were picked after the normal harvest. The extra days of sun give the wine more body and a more intense flavor. Cost: $11–$25.

The Spätlese Rider:
The First Late-Harvest Wine

The story goes that at the vineyards of Schloss Johannisberg, the monks were not allowed to pick the grapes until the Abbot of Fulda gave his permission. During the harvest of 1775, the Abbot was away attending a synod. That year the grapes were ripening early and some of them had started to rot on the vine. The monks, becoming concerned, dispatched a rider to ask the Abbot's permission to pick the grapes. By the time the rider returned, the monks believed all was lost, but they went ahead with the harvest anyway. To their amazement, the wine was one of the best they had ever tasted. That was the beginning of Spätlese-style wines.

Auslese—Translated as "out picked," this means that the grapes are selectively picked out from particularly ripe bunches, which yields a medium to fuller-style wine. You probably do the same thing in your own garden if you grow tomatoes: You pick out the especially ripe ones, leaving the others on the vine. Cost: $15–$35.

Beerenauslese—Breaking the word down, you get *beeren*, or "berries," *aus*, or "out," and *lese*, or "picking." Quite simply (and don't let the bigger names fool you), these are berries (grapes) that are picked out individually. These luscious grapes are used to create the rich dessert wines for which Germany is known. Beerenauslese is usually made only two or three times every ten years. It's not unheard of for a good Beerenauslese to cost up to $250.

Trockenbeerenauslese—A step above the Beerenauslese, but these grapes are dried (*trocken*), so they're more like raisins. These "raisinated" grapes produce the richest, sweetest, honey-like wine—and the most expensive.

Eiswein—A very rare, sweet, concentrated wine made from frozen grapes left on the vine. They're pressed while still frozen. According to Germany's 1971 rules for winemaking, this wine must now be made from grapes that are at least ripe enough to make a Beerenauslese.

In 1921, the first Trockenbeerenauslese was made in the Mosel region.

What Is Botrytis Cinerea?

Botrytis cinerea, known as *Edelfäule* in German, is a mold that (under special conditions) attacks grapes, as was described in the section on Sauternes. I say "special" because this "noble rot" is instrumental in the production of Beerenauslese and Trockenbeerenauslese.

Noble rot occurs late in the growing season when the nights are cool and heavy with dew, the mornings have fog, and the days are warm. When noble rot attacks the grapes, they begin to shrivel and the water evaporates, leaving concentrated sugar. (Remember, 90 percent of wine is water.) Grapes affected by this mold may not look very appealing, but don't let looks deceive you: The proof is in the wine.

What's the difference between a $50 Beerenauslese and a $150 Beerenauslese (besides $100)?

The major difference is the grapes. The $50 bottle is probably made from Müller-Thurgau grapes or Silvaner, while the $150 bottle is from Riesling. In addition, the region the wine comes from will, in part, determine its quality. Traditionally, the best Beerenauslese and Trockenbeerenauslese come from the Rhein or the Mosel.

Quality is higher in wine when:

1. The wine is produced from low yields.
2. The grapes come from great vineyards.
3. The wine is produced by great winemakers.
4. The grapes were grown in a great climate or are from a great vintage.

Today, most German wines, including Beerenauslese and Trockenbeerenauslese, are bottled in spring and early summer. Many no longer receive additional cask or tank maturation, because it has been discovered that this extra barrel aging destroys the fruit.

73

When I'm ordering a German wine in a restaurant or shopping at my local retailer, what should I look for?

The first thing I would make sure of is that it comes from one of the four major regions. These regions are the Mosel-Saar-Ruwer, Rheinhessen, Rheingau, and Pfalz, which, in my opinion, are the most important quality wine-producing regions in all of Germany.

Next, look to see if the wine is a Riesling. Anyone who studies and enjoys German wines finds that Riesling shows the best-tasting characteristics. Riesling on the label is a mark of quality.

Also, be aware of the vintage. It's important, especially with German wines, to know if the wine was made in a good year.

Finally, probably the most important consideration is to buy from a reputable grower or producer. A great source for that listing is the *Gault-Millau Guide to German Wine*.

What's the difference between Rhein and Mosel wines?

Rhein wines generally have more body than do Mosels. Mosels are usually higher in acidity and lower in alcohol than are Rhein wines. Mosels show more autumn fruits like apples, pears and quince, while Rhein wines show more summer fruits like apricots, peaches, and nectarines.

Some important villages to look for:

Rheingau

Eltville

Erbach

Rüdesheim

Rauenthal

Hochheim

Johannisberg

Mosel-Saar-Ruwer

Erden

Piesport

Bernkastel

Graach

Ürzig

Brauneberg

Wehlen

Rheinhessen

Oppenheim

Nackenheim

Nierstein

Pfalz

Deidesheim

Forst

Wachenheim

Ruppertsberg

Dürkheimer

Can you take the mystery out of reading German wine labels?

German wine labels give you plenty of information. For example, see the label below.

1. **Mosel-Saar-Ruwer**—This is the region of the wine's origin. Note that the region is one of the big four we discussed earlier in this chapter.

2. **1993**—The year the grapes were harvested.

3. **Ürzig** is the town and **Würzgarten** is the vineyard from which the grapes originate. The Germans add the suffix "er" to make Ürziger, just as a person from New York is called a New Yorker.

4. **Spätlese** is the ripeness level, in this case from late-harvested grapes.

5. **Riesling** is the grape variety. Therefore, this wine is at least 85 percent Riesling.

6. **Qualitätswein mit Prädikat** is the quality level of the wine.

7. **A.P. Nr. 2 602 055 017 94** is the official testing number—proof that the wine was tasted by a panel of tasters and passed the strict quality standards required by the government.

8. **Gutsabüllung** means estate-bottled.

All Qualitätswein and Qualitätswein mit Prädikat must pass a test by an official laboratory and tasting panel to be given an official number, prior to the wine's release to the trade.

Impress your friends with this trivia:
A.P. Nr. 2 602 055 017 94
2 = the government referral office or testing station
602 = location code of bottler
055 = bottler ID number
017 = bottle lot
94= the year the wine was tasted by the board

What are the recent trends in the white wines of Germany?

As Americans' drinking tastes have shifted from generic wines to varietal wines, and so also toward drier wines, we've seen a decrease in the availability of German wines in the American

market. German wines have also been hampered in the American market by the increase in their prices. Still, I feel the lighter-style Trocken (dry), Halbtrocken (medium-dry), German Kabinetts, and even Spätleses are wines that can be easily served as an apéritif, or with very light food and also grilled food, and in particular with spicy or Pacific Rim cuisines.

Past great vintages of Beerenauslese and Trockenbeerenauslese: 1985, 1988, 1989, 1990.

Best Bets for Recent Vintages in Germany
1993   1994   1995   1996   1997   1998   1999

WINE AND FOOD

Rainer Lingenfelder (Weingut Lingenfelder Estate, Pfalz)—With Riesling Spätlese Halbtrocken: "We have a tradition of cooking freshwater fish that come from a number of small creeks in the Palatinate forest, so my personal choice would be trout, either herbed with thyme, basil, parsley, and onion, and cooked in wine, or smoked with a bit of horseradish. We find it to be a very versatile wine, a very good match with a whole range of white meat. Pork is traditional in the Palatinate region, as are chicken and goose dishes."

Johannes Selbach (Selbach-Oster, Mosel)—"What kinds of food do we have with Riesling Spätlese? Anything we like! This may sound funny but there's a wide variety of food that goes very well with a—and this is the key—fruity, only moderately sweet, well-balanced Riesling Spätlese. Start with mild curries and sesame- or ginger-flavored not-too-spicy dishes. Or try either gravlax or smoked salmon. You can even have Riesling Spätlese with a green salad in a balsamic vinaigrette, preferably with a touch of raspberry, as long as the dressing is not too vinegary. Many people avoid pairing wine with a salad, but it works beautifully.

"For *haute cuisine*, fresh duck or goose liver lightly sautéed in its own juice, or veal sweetbreads in a rich sauce. Also salads with fresh greens, fresh fruit, and fresh seafood marinated in lime or lemon juice or balsamic vinegar.

"With an old ripe Spätlese: roast venison, dishes with cream sauces, and any white-meat dish stuffed with or accompanied by fruit. It is also delicious with fresh fruit itself or as an apéritif.

With Riesling Spätlese Halbtrocken: "This is a food-friendly wine, but the first thing that comes to mind is fresh seafood and fresh fish. Also wonderful with salads with a mild vinaigrette, and with a course that's often difficult to match: cream soups. If we don't know exactly what to drink with a particular food, Spätlese Halbtrocken is usually the safe bet.

"It may be too obvious to say foie gras with Eiswein, but it is a classic."

SELBACH-OSTER

1997

ZELTINGER SCHLOSSBERG
RIESLING KABINETT

QUALITÄTSWEIN MIT PRÄDIKAT
GUTSABFÜLLUNG WEINGUT SELBACH-OSTER · D-54492 ZELTINGEN
L · A.P.NR. 2 606 319 019 98
Mosel · Saar · Ruwer
alc.8% vol · 750 ml e

Red Grapes of the World

Classes Four through Seven will now delve into the great red wines of the world. Just as you studied the major white grape varieties before the classes on white wines, as you begin this journey you should understand the major red grape varieties and where in the world they produce the best wines.

In Class Four, I start with a list of what I consider to be the major red wine grapes, ranked from lightest to fullest-bodied style, along with the region or country in which the grape grows best. By looking at this chart, not only will you get an idea of the style of the wine, but also a feeling for gradations of weight, color, tannin, and ageability.

TEXTURE	GRAPES	TANNIN LEVEL	WHERE THEY GROW BEST	COLOR LEVEL	AGEABILITY
LIGHT		LOW		LIGHTER	DRINK YOUNG
	Gamay		Beaujolais, France		
	Pinot Noir		Burgundy, France; California; Oregon; Champagne, France		
	Tempranillo		Rioja, Spain		
	Sangiovese		Tuscany, Italy		
	Merlot		Bordeaux, France; California; Washington State		
	Zinfandel		California		
	Cabernet Sauvignon		Bordeaux, France; California; Chile		
	Nebbiolo		Piedmont, Italy		
	Syrah/Shiraz		Rhône, France; Australia		
FULL-BODIED		HIGH		DEEPER	WINE TO AGE

At last count, about forty different red wine grapes were planted throughout the world. California alone grows 31 different red wine grape varieties.

In general, the lighter the color, the more perceived acidity.

Once you have become acquainted with these major red wine grapes, you may wish to explore the following:

GRAPES	WHERE THEY GROW BEST
Barbera	Italy
Dolcetto	Italy
Cabernet Franc	Bordeaux, France
Grenache	Rhone, France
Garnacha	Spain
Malbec	Bordeaux, France; Argentina

To put this chart together is extremely challenging, given all the variables that go into making wine and the many different styles that can be produced. Remember, there are always exceptions to the rule, just as there are other countries and wine regions not listed here that produce world-class wine from some of the red grapes shown. You'll begin to see this for yourself if you do your homework and taste a lot of different wines. Good luck!

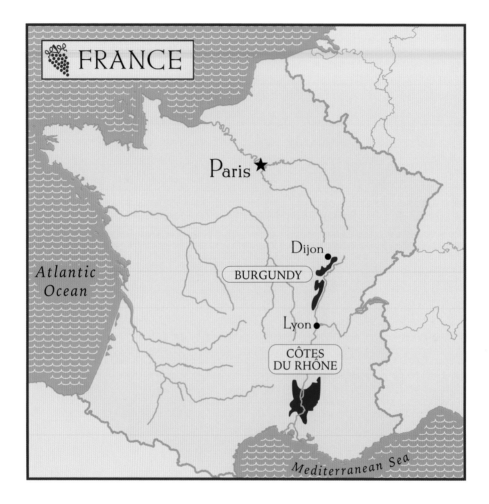

The Red Wines of Burgundy and the Rhône Valley

Now we're getting into a whole new experience in wines—the reds. Generally, my students and I become more intense and concentrate more when we taste red wines.

What's so different (beyond the obvious color)?

We're beginning to see more components in the wines—more complexities. In the white wines, we were looking mainly for the acid/fruit balance, but now, in addition, we're looking for other characteristics, such as tannin.

What's Tannin?

Tannin is what gives wine its longevity. It comes from the skins, the pits, and the stems of the grapes. Another source of tannin is wood, especially the French oak barrels in which some wines are aged or fermented.

A word used to describe the taste sensation of tannin is "astringent." Tannin is not a taste. It's a tactile sensation.

Tannin is also found in strong tea. And what can you add to the tea to make it less astringent? Milk—the fat and the proteins in milk soften the tannin. And so it is with a highly tannic wine. If you take another milk by-product, such as cheese, and have it with wine, it softens the tannin and makes the wine more appealing. Enjoy a beef entrée or one served with a cream sauce and a good bottle of red wine to experience it for yourself.

Why is Burgundy so difficult to understand?

Before we go any further, I must tell you that there are no shortcuts. Burgundy is one of the most difficult subjects in the study of wines. People get uptight about Burgundy. They say, "There's so much to know," and "It looks so hard." Yes, there are many vineyards and villages, and they're all important. But actually, there are only fifteen to 25 names you need to familiarize yourself with, if you'd like to know and speak about Burgundy wines intelligently. Not to worry. I'm going to help you decode all the mysteries of Burgundy: names, regions, and labels.

What are the main red-wine-producing areas of Burgundy?

Côte d'Or { Côte de Nuits   Beaujolais
           Côte de Beaune   Côte Châlonnaise

What major grape varieties are used in red Burgundy wines?

The two major grape varieties are Pinot Noir and Gamay. Under Appellation Contrôlée laws, all red Burgundies are made from the Pinot Noir grape. Beaujolais is produced from the Gamay grape variety.

Beaujolais

1. Made from 100 percent Gamay grapes.

2. This wine's style is typically light and fruity. It's meant to be consumed young. Beaujolais is the largest-selling Burgundy in the United States by far, probably because it's so easy to drink.

3. Beaujolais can be chilled, and it's very affordable. Most bottles cost between $7 and $12, although the price varies with the quality and the grade.

What are the quality levels of Beaujolais?

There are three different quality levels of Beaujolais:

Beaujolais—This basic Beaujolais accounts for the majority of all Beaujolais produced (Cost: $).

Beaujolais-Villages—This comes from certain villages in Beaujolais. There are 35 villages that consistently produce better wines. Most Beaujolais-Villages is a blend of wines from these villages, and usually no particular village name is included on the label (Cost: $$).

"Cru"—A "cru" is actually the name of a village that produces the highest quality of Beaujolais (Cost: $$$$).

There are ten "crus" (villages):

Brouilly
Morgon
Moulin-à-Vent
Fleurie
Côte de Brouilly
Chiroubles
Chénas
Juliénas
Saint-Amour
Régnié

Wines from the ten "crus" of Beaujolais usually do not bear the name "Beaujolais" on the label—just the name of the village. Why, you ask? Because the producers of "cru" Beaujolais don't want to have their wines confused with basic Beaujolais.

What's Beaujolais Nouveau?

Beaujolais Nouveau is even lighter and fruitier in style than your basic Beaujolais and it is best drunk young. Isn't that true of *all* Beaujolais wines? Yes, but Nouveau is different. This "new" Beaujolais is picked, fermented, bottled, and available at your local retailer in a matter of weeks. (I don't know what you call that in your business, but I call it good cash flow in mine. It gives the winemaker virtually an instant return.)

There's another purpose behind Beaujolais Nouveau: Like a preview of a movie, it offers the wine-consuming public a sample of the quality of the vintage and style that the winemaker will produce for release in the spring.

Beaujolais Nouveau is meant to be consumed within six months of bottling. So if you're holding a 1995 Beaujolais Nouveau, now is the time to give it to your "friends."

One-third of the Beaujolais grapes are used to make Beaujolais Nouveau.

There are 19 million cases of wine produced in Burgundy. Twelve million cases of that are Beaujolais!

Beaujolais Nouveau Madness

The exact date of release is the third Thursday in November, and Beaujolais Nouveau is introduced to the consumer amidst great hoopla. Restaurants and retailers all vie to be the first to offer the new Beaujolais to their customers. Some of these wine buyers go so far as to fly the wine into the United States on the Concorde.

How long should I keep a Beaujolais?

It depends on the level of quality and the vintage. Beaujolais and Beaujolais-Villages are meant to last between one and three years. "Crus" can last longer because they are more complex. I've tasted Beaujolais "crus" that were more than 10 years old and still in excellent condition. This is the exception, though, not the rule.

Which shippers/producers should I look for when buying Beaujolais?

Bouchard   Drouhin   Duboeuf   Jadot   Mommessin

"Beaujolais is one of the very few red wines that can be drunk as a white. Beaujolais is my daily drink. And sometimes I blend one-half water to the wine. It is the most refreshing drink in the world."

—Didier Mommessin

To Chill or Not to Chill?

As a young student studying wines in Burgundy, I visited the Beaujolais region, excited and naive. In one of the villages, I stopped at a bistro and ordered a glass of Beaujolais. (A good choice on my part, don't you think?) The waiter brought the glass of Beaujolais and it was *chilled*, and I thought to myself that these people had not read the right books! Every wine book I'd ever read always said you serve red wines at room temperature and white wines chilled.

Obviously, I learned from my experience that when it comes to Beaujolais Nouveau, Beaujolais, and Beaujolais-Villages, it's a good idea to give them a slight chill to bring out the fruit and liveliness (acidity) of the wines. That is why Beaujolais is my favorite red wine to have during the summer.

However, to my taste, the Beaujolais "crus" have more fruit and more tannin and are best served at room temperature.

Wine and Food

Beaujolais goes well with almost anything—especially light, simple meals and cheeses—nothing overpowering. Generally, try to match your Beaujolais with light food, such as veal, fish, or fowl. Here's what some of the experts say:

André Gagey (Louis Jadot)—"Beaujolais with simple meals, light cheeses, grilled meat—everything except sweets."

Georges Duboeuf—"A lot of dishes can be eaten with Beaujolais—what you choose depends on the appellation and vintage. With charcuteries and pâtés you can serve a young Beaujolais or Beaujolais-Villages. With grilled meat, more generous and fleshy wines, such as Juliénas and Morgon crus, can be served. With meats cooked in a sauce (for example, coq au vin), I would suggest a Moulin-à-Vent cru from a good vintage."

Didier Mommessin—"Serve with an extremely strong cheese, such as Roquefort, especially when the wine is young and strong enough for it. Also with white meat and veal."

Côte Châlonnaise

Now we're getting into classic Pinot Noir wines that offer tremendous value.

You should know three villages from this area:

Mercurey (95 percent red)

Givry (90 percent red)

Rully (50 percent red)

Mercurey is the most important, producing wines of high quality. Because they are not well known in the United States, Mercurey wines are often a very good buy.

Which shippers/producers should I look for when buying wines from the Côte Châlonnaise?

Mercurey	Faiveley
	Domaine de Suremain
	Michel Juillot
Givry	Domaine Thenard
	Domaine Jablot
	Louis Latour
Rully	Antonin Rodet

Côte d'Or

Now we're getting to the heart of Burgundy. The Côte d'Or (pronounced "coat door") means "golden slope." This region gets its name from the color of the foliage on the hillside, which in autumn is literally golden, as well as the income it brings to the winemakers. The area is very small and its best wines are among the priciest in the world. If you are looking for a $7.99 everyday bottle of wine, this is not the place.

The Côte d'Or is only 30 miles long and a half-mile wide.

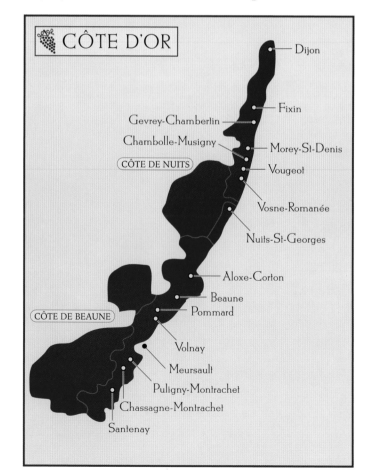

What's the best way to understand the wines of the Côte d'Or?

First, you need to know that these wines are distinguished by quality levels—generic, Village, Premier Cru vineyards, and Grand Cru vineyards. Let's look at the quality levels with the "double pyramid" shown below. As you can see, not much Grand Cru wine is produced, but it is the highest quality and extremely expensive. Generic, on the other hand, is available in abundance. Although much is produced, very few generic wines can be classified as "outstanding."

There are 33 Grand Cru vineyards:
10 white
23 red
9 from the Côte de Beaune
24 from the Côte de Nuits

There are over 400 Premier Cru vineyards in Burgundy.

Generic wines are labeled simply "Burgundy" or "Bourgogne." A higher level of generic wines will be labeled Côte de Beaune Villages or Côte de Nuits Villages, being a blend of different village wines.

DOUBLE PYRAMID

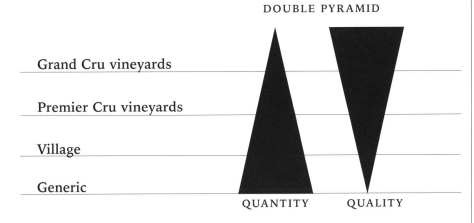

Grand Cru vineyards

Premier Cru vineyards

Village

Generic

QUANTITY   QUALITY

The Côte d'Or is divided into two regions:

Côte de Beaune—red and white wines

Côte de Nuits—the highest quality red Burgundy wines come from this region

---

The Importance of Soil to Burgundy Wines

If you talk to any producers of Burgundy wines, they'll tell you the most important element in making their quality wines is the soil in which the grapes are grown. This, together with the slope of the land and the climatic conditions, determines whether the wine is a Village wine, a Premier Cru, or a Grand Cru. This concept of soil, slope, and climatic conditions in French is known as terroir.

During one of my trips to Burgundy, it rained for five straight days. On the sixth day I saw that the workers were at the bottom of the slopes with their pails and shovels, collecting the soil that had run down the hillside and returning the soil to the vineyard. This goes to show the importance of the soil to Burgundy wines.

Another way to understand the wines of the Côte d'Or is to become familiar with the most important villages, Grand Cru vineyards, and some of the Premier Cru vineyards.

Côte de Beaune—Red

MOST IMPORTANT VILLAGES	MY FAVORITE PREMIER CRU VINEYARDS	GRAND CRU VINEYARDS
Aloxe-Corton	Fournières	Corton
	Chaillots	Corton Clos du Roi
		Corton Bressandes
		Corton Renardes
		Corton Maréchaude
Beaune	Grèves	None
	Fèves	
	Marconnets	
	Bressandes	
	Clos des Mouches	
Pommard	Épenots	None
	Rugiens	
Volnay	Caillerets	None
	Santenots	
	Clos des Chênes	
	Taillepieds	

Côte de Nuits—Red

Finally, we reach the Côte de Nuits. If you're going to spend any time studying your geography, do it now. The majority of Grand Cru vineyards are located in this area.

MOST IMPORTANT VILLAGES	MY FAVORITE PREMIER CRU VINEYARDS	GRAND CRU VINEYARDS
Gevrey-Chambertin	Clos St-Jacques	Chambertin
	Les Cazetiers	Chambertin Clos de Bèze
	Aux Combottes	Latricières-Chambertin
		Mazis-Chambertin
		Mazoyères-Chambertin
		Ruchottes-Chambertin
		Chapelle-Chambertin
		Charmes-Chambertin
		Griotte-Chambertin
Morey-St-Denis	Ruchots	Clos des Lambrays
	Les Genevrières	Clos de Tart

By far the largest red Grand Cru, in terms of production, is Corton, representing about 25% of all Grand Cru red wines.

1996

POMMARD
APPELLATION POMMARD CONTRÔLÉE

PRODUCED AND BOTTLED BY
BOUCHARD PÈRE & FILS
CHÂTEAU DE BEAUNE, CÔTE-D'OR, FRANCE
PRODUIT DE FRANCE · PRODUCT OF FRANCE
RED BURGUNDY WINE

Good Value Village Wines
Monthélie
Savigny les Beaune
Pernand-Vergelesses
Marsannay

Chambertin Clos de Bèze was the favorite wine of Napoleon, who is reported to have said: "Nothing makes the future look so rosy as to contemplate it through a glass of Chambertin." Obviously, he ran out of Chambertin at Waterloo!

MOST IMPORTANT VILLAGES	MY FAVORITE PREMIER CRU VINEYARDS	GRAND CRU VINEYARDS
Morey-St-Denis	Clos des Ormes	Clos St-Denis
		Clos de la Roche
		Bonnes Mares (partial)
Chambolle-Musigny	Les Amoureuses	Musigny
	Charmes	Bonnes Mares (partial)
Vougeot		Clos de Vougeot
Flagey-Échézeaux		Échézeaux
		Grands-Échézeaux
Vosne-Romanée	Beaux-Monts	La Grande-Rue
		Malconsorts
		Romanée-Conti
		La Romanée
		La Tâche
		Richebourg
		Romanée-St-Vivant
Nuits-St-Georges	Les St-Georges	None
	Vaucrains	
	Porets	

The Newest Grand Cru—In July 1992, La Grande-Rue, a vineyard tucked between the Grands Crus La Tâche and Romanée-Conti in Vosne-Romanée, was itself elevated to the Grand Cru level, bringing the number of Grands Crus in the Côte d'Or to 33.

Why are we bothering with all this geography? Must we learn the names of all the villages and vineyards?

I thought you'd never ask. First of all, the geography is important because it helps make you a smart buyer. If you're familiar with the most important villages and vineyards, you're more likely to make an educated purchase.

You really don't have to memorize *all* the villages and vineyards. I'll let you in on a little secret of how to choose a Burgundy wine and tell at a glance if it's a Village wine, a Premier Cru, or a Grand Cru—usually the label will tip you off in the manner illustrated here:

Has this ever happened to you? In a restaurant, you order a village wine—Gevrey Chambertin, for example—and by mistake the waiter brings you a Grand Cru Chambertin. What would you do?

$ Village Only = Village wine	$$ Village+Vineyard (Clos Saint-Jacques) = Premier Cru	$$$$ Vineyard Only (Le Chambertin) = Grand Cru

This is the method I use to teach Burgundy wine. Ask yourself the following:

Where is the wine from?
France.

What type of wine is it?
Burgundy.

Which region is it from?
Côte d'Or.

Which area?
Côte de Nuits.

Which village is the wine from?
Chambolle-Musigny.

Does the label give more details?
Yes, it tells you that the wine is from a vineyard called Musigny, which is one of the 33 Grand Cru vineyards.

It's the Law!
Beginning with the 1990 vintage, all Grand Cru Burgundies must include the words "Grand Cru" on the label.

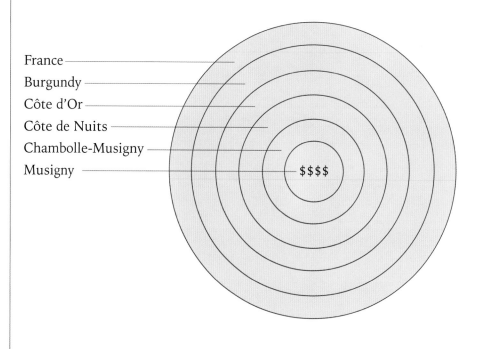

France
Burgundy
Côte d'Or
Côte de Nuits
Chambolle-Musigny
Musigny ————— $$$$

Has the style of Burgundy wines changed in the last 25 years?

There is a good deal of debate about this in the wine industry. I would have to answer that, yes, it has indeed changed. Winemakers used to make Burgundies to last longer. In fact, you couldn't drink a Burgundy for several years, if you wanted to get the fullest flavor. It simply wasn't ready. Today the winemakers of Burgundy are complying with consumer demand for Burgundy they can drink earlier. In America, it seems no one has the patience to wait. A compromise had to be made, however, and that is in the body. Many wines are lighter in style and they can be consumed just a few years after the vintage.

In Burgundy in the 1960s, wines were fermented and vatted for up to three weeks. Today's Burgundy wines are usually fermented and vatted for six to twelve days.

Why are the well-known great Burgundies so expensive?

The answer is simple—supply and demand. The Burgundy growers and shippers of the Côte d'Or have a problem all businesspeople would envy—not enough supply to meet the demand. It has been this way for years and it will continue, because Burgundy is a small region that produces a limited amount of wine. The Bordeaux wine region produces three times as much wine as Burgundy does.

If you don't want to be disappointed by the Burgundy wine you select, make sure you know your vintages. Also, due to the delicacy of the Pinot Noir grape, red Burgundies require proper storage, so make sure you buy from a merchant who handles Burgundy wines with care.

Burgundy Wine Harvest
(average number of cases over a five-year period for red and white)

Regional Appellations	2,136,674 cases
Beaujolais	11,503,617 cases
Côte Châlonnaise	357,539 cases
Côte d'Or (Côte de Nuits)	511,594 cases
Côte d'Or (Côte de Beaune)	1,391,168 cases
Chablis	755,188 cases
Mâconnais	2,136,674 cases
Other Appellations	339,710 cases
Total Burgundy Harvest	19,132,164 cases

"To Decant, or Not to Decant?" It has been my experience that in Burgundy, wine is rarely decanted, whereas in Bordeaux, it is almost always decanted. (More about decanting on pages 189–190.)

Other great Burgundy vintage years: 1969, 1978, 1985, 1988, 1989, 1990.

Best Bets for Recent Vintages of Côte d'Or
1993   1995   1996❖   1999

Note: ❖*signifies exceptional vintage*

Who are the most important shippers to look for when buying red Burgundy wine?

Bouchard Père et Fils
Joseph Drouhin
Jaffelin
Louis Jadot
Louis Latour
Labouré-Roi

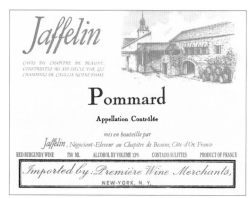

How important is the producer? Clos Vougeot is the single largest Grand Cru vineyard in Burgundy, totaling 125 acres, with seventy different owners. Each owner makes his own winemaking decisions, such as when to pick the grapes, the style of fermentation, and how much oak aging. Obviously, all Clos Vougeot is *not* created equal.

Although eighty percent of Burgundy wine is sold through shippers, some fine estate-bottled wines are available in limited quantities in the United States. Look for the following:

Maison Faiveley
Domaine Daniel Rion
Domaine Henri Gouges
Domaine Prince de Mérode
Domaine Dujac
Domaine Georges Roumier
Domaine Louis Trapet
Domaine Pierre Damoy
Domaine Henri Lamarche
Domaine de La Romanée-Conti
Domaine Jean Grivot
Domaine Mongeard-Mugneret
Domaine Leroy
Domaine Comte de Vogüé
Domaine Clerget
Domaine Parent
Domaine Groffier
Domaine Jayer
Domaine Pousse d'Or

WINE AND FOOD

To get the most flavor from both the wine and the food, some of Burgundy's famous winemakers offer these suggestions:

Jean-François Bouchard—"Lamb cooked in its own sauce—not too spicy…or veal with mushroom sauce."

Robert Drouhin—"In my opinion, white wine is never a good accompaniment to red meat, but a light red Burgundy can match a fish course (not shellfish). Otherwise, for light red Burgundies, white meat—not too many spices; partridge, pheasant, and rabbit. For heavier-style wines, lamb and steak are good choices." Personally, Mr. Drouhin does not enjoy red Burgundies with cheese—especially goat cheese.

Pierre Henry Gagey (Louis Jadot)—"With red Beaujolais wines, such as Moulin-à-Vent Château des Jacques, for example, a piece of pork like an Andouillette from Fleury is beautiful. A Gamay, more fruity and fleshy than Pinot Noir, goes perfectly with this typical meal from our *terroir*. My favorite food combination with a red Burgundy wine is Poulet de Bresse Demi d'oeil. The very thin flesh of this truffle-filled chicken and the elegance and delicacy from the great Pinot Noir, which come from the best *terroir*, go together beautifully."

Louis Latour—"With Château Corton Grancey, filet of duck in a red wine sauce. Otherwise, Pinot Noir is good with roast chicken, venison, and beef. Mature wines are a perfect combination for our local cheeses, Chambertin and Citeaux."

For further reading on Burgundy wines, I recommend *Côte d'Or,* by Clive Coates; *Burgundy,* by Anthony Hanson; *Burgundy,* by Robert M. Parker, Jr.; *Making Sense of Burgundy,* by Matt Kramer; and *The Great Domaines of Burgundy,* by Remington Norman.

The Red Wines of the Rhône Valley

Of all the wines made in the Rhône Valley, 91% are red, 6% are rose, and 3% are white.

Some of the oldest vineyards in France are in the Rhône Valley. Hermitage, for example, has been in existence for more than 2,000 years.

Many times at Windows on the World, customers ask me to recommend a big, robust red Burgundy wine to complement their rack of lamb or filet mignon. To their surprise, I don't recommend a Burgundy at all. Their best bet is a Rhône wine, which is typically a bigger and fuller wine than one from Burgundy, and which usually has a higher alcoholic content. The reason is quite simple. It all goes back to location and geography.

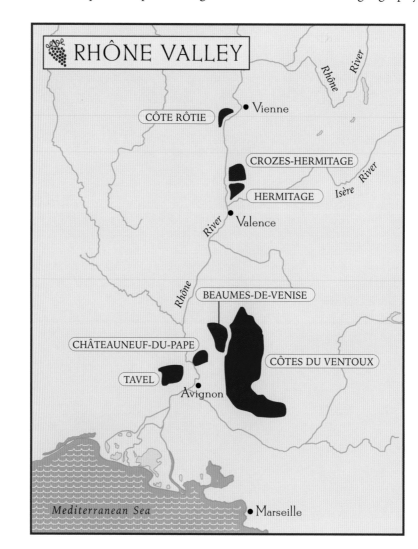

Where's the Rhône Valley?

The Rhône Valley is in southeastern France, south of the Burgundy region, where the climate is hot and the conditions are sunny. The extra sun gives the wines that added boost of alcohol, because, as you know, the sun gives the grapes the sugar that turns into alcohol. The soil is full of rocks that retain the intense summer heat during both day and night. Winemakers of the Rhône Valley are required by law to make sure their wines have a specified amount of alcohol. For example, the minimum alcoholic content required by the A.O.C. is 10.5 percent for Côtes du Rhône and 12.5 percent for Châteauneuf-du-Pape.

What are the different quality levels of the Rhône Valley?

	%of Production
1. Côtes du Rhône ($)	58%
2. Côtes du Rhône Villages ($$)	8%
3. Côtes du Rhône Crus (specific regions) ($$$$)	10%
4. Other Appelations	24%

What are the winemaking regions in the Rhône Valley?

The region is divided into two distinct areas: northern and southern Rhône. The most famous red wines that come from the northern region are:

Hermitage   Crozes-Hermitage   Côte Rôtie

The most famous red wine from the southern region is **Châteauneuf-du-Pape**, and one of the best French rosés is called **Tavel**.

Sunshine quotient (hours per year)

Burgundy	2,000
Bordeaux	2,050
Chateauneuf-du-Pape	2,750

A simple Côtes du Rhône is similar to a Beaujolais wine except the Côtes du Rhône has more body and alcohol. A Beaujolais, by A.O.C. standards, must contain a minimum of 9% alcohol—a Côtes du Rhône, 10.5%.

Over 90% of all Côtes du Rhône wines come from the southern region.

The Thirteen Crus of the Rhone Valley

North
Chateau-Grillet
Condrieu
Cornas
Côte-Rotie
Crozes-Hermitage
Hermitage
St-Joseph
St-Peray

South
Chateauneuf-du-Pape
Gigondas
Lirac
Tavel
Vacqueyras

Two distinct microclimates separate the north from the south. It is important for you to understand that these areas make distinctly different wines because of:

1. soil
2. location
3. different grape varieties used in making the wines of each area

What are the main red-grape varieties used in the Rhône Valley?

The two major grape varieties in the Rhône Valley are:

Syrah   **Grenache**

Two other important red grapes in the Rhône Valley are:
1. Cinsault
2. Mourvèdre

Which wines are made from these grapes?

The Côte Rôtie, Hermitage, and Crozes-Hermitage from the north are made primarily from the Syrah grape. These are the biggest and fullest wines from that region.

For Châteauneuf-du-Pape, as many as thirteen separate grape varieties may be included in the blend. But the best producers use a greater percentage of Grenache and Syrah in the blend.

There is no official classification for Rhône Valley wines.

What's Tavel?

It's a rosé—an unusually dry rosé, which distinguishes it from most others. It's made primarily from the Grenache grape, although nine grape varieties can be used in the blend. When you come right down to it, Tavel is just like a red wine, with all the components but less color. How do they make a rosé wine with red-wine characteristics but less color? It's all in the vatting process.

What's the difference between "short-vatted" and "long-vatted" wines?

When a wine is "short-vatted," the skins are allowed to ferment with the must (grape juice) for a short period of time—only long enough to impart that rosé color. It's just the opposite when a winemaker is producing red Rhône wines, such as Châteauneuf-du-Pape or Hermitage. The grape skins are allowed to ferment longer with the must, giving a rich, ruby color to the wine.

What's the difference between a $15 bottle of Châteauneuf-du-Pape and a $30 bottle of Châteauneuf-du-Pape?

A winemaker is permitted to use thirteen different grapes for his Châteauneuf-du-Pape recipe, as I mentioned earlier. It's only logical, then, that the winemaker who uses a lot of the best grapes (which is equivalent to cooking with the finest ingredients) will produce the best-tasting—and the most expensive—wine.

For example, a $15 bottle of Châteauneuf-du-Pape may contain only twenty percent of top-quality grapes (Grenache, Mourvèdre, Syrah, and Cinsault) and eighty percent of lesser-quality grapes; a $30 bottle may contain ninety percent of the top-quality grapes and ten percent of others.

Châteauneuf-du-Pape means "new castle of the Pope," so named for the palace in the Rhône city of Avignon in which Pope Clément V resided in the 14h century.

Here's a trivia question: What are the 13 grapes allowed in Châteauneuf-du-Pape?
Grenache
Syrah
Mourvèdre
Picpoul
Terret
Counoise
Muscardin
Vaccarèse
Picardin
Cinsault
Clairette
Roussanne
Bourboulenc

The papal coat of arms from medieval times appears on some Châteauneuf-du-Pape bottles. Only owners of vineyards are permitted to use this coat of arms on the label.

MIS EN BOUTEILLE DU CHATEAU

Château de Beaucastel

CHATEAUNEUF-DU-PAPE
APPELLATION CHATEAUNEUF-DU-PAPE CONTROLÉE

Sté FERMIÈRE DES VIGNOBLES PIERRE PERRIN
AU CHATEAU DE BEAUCASTEL COURTHEZON (V⁵ᵉ) FRANCE   750 ml
PRODUCE
OF
FRANCE   ALC. 13.5% BY VOL.
IMPORTED BY   Vineyard Brands, Inc. BIRMINGHAM, AL
SHIPPED BY ROBERT HAAS SELECTIONS, FRANCE

Older Great Vintages
North: 1983, 1985, 1988
South: 1985, 1988, 1989

Rhône Valley vintages can be tricky: A good year in the north may be a bad year in the south, and vice versa.

Hermitage is the best and the longest-lived of the Rhône wines. In a great vintage, Hermitage wines can last for fifty years.

Côtes du Rhône wine can be produced from grapes grown in either or both the northern and southern Rhône regions.

Best Bets for Red Rhône Valley Wines

North

1989❖ 1990❖ 1991❖ 1994 1995❖ 1996 1997 1998 1999

South

1990❖   1994   1995   1998❖

Note: ❖ signifies exceptional vintage

How do I buy a red Rhône wine?

You should first decide if you prefer a light Côtes du Rhône wine or a bigger, more flavorful one, such as an Hermitage. Then you must consider the vintage and the producer. Two of the oldest and best-known firms are M. Chapoutier and Paul Jaboulet Aîné. The wines of Guigal, Chave, Beaucastel, Domaine du Vieux Télégraphe, and Château Rayas are harder to find, but worth the search.

When should I drink my Rhône wine?

Tavel—within two years

Côtes du Rhône—within three years

Crozes-Hermitage—within five years

Châteauneuf-du-Pape—after five years, but higher-quality Châteauneuf-du-Pape is better at ten years.

Hermitage—seven to eight years, but best at fifteen, in a great year.

The Red Rhône Valley Roundup

Northern wines	Southern wines
Côte Rôtie	Châteauneuf-du-Pape
Hermitage	Tavel
Crozes-Hermitage	Côtes du Rhône
St. Joseph	Côtes du Rhône-Villages
Cornas	Côtes du Ventoux
	Gigondas

Grape	**Major grapes**
Syrah	Grenache
	Syrah
	Cinsault
	Mourvèdre

96

Rhône Valley Harvest
(average number of cases over a five-year period)

Côtes du Rhône regional appellation	18.8 million cases
Northern and southern Crus	2.6 million cases
Côtes du Rhône-Villages appellation	1.6 million cases
Total Rhône Valley harvest	23.0 million cases

WINE AND FOOD

Jean Pierre and François Perrin (Château de Beaucastel and La Vieille Ferme)—"The white wines of Château de Beaucastel can be drunk either very young—in the first three or four years—or should be kept for ten years or more. The combination of white meat with truffles and mushrooms is an exquisite possibility.

"Red Rhône wines achieve their perfection from ten years and beyond, and are best when combined with game and other meats with a strong flavor.

"A good dinner could be wild mushroom soup and truffles with a white Beaucastel and stew of wild hare *á la royale* (with foie gras and truffles) served with a red Château de Beaucastel."

Michel Chapoutier—With a Côtes du Rhône wine, he recommends poultry, light meats, and cheese.

Côte Rôtie goes well with white meats and small game.

Châteauneuf-du-Pape complements the ripest of cheese, the richest venison, and the most lavish civet of wild boar.

An Hermitage is suitable with beef, game, and any full-flavored cheese.

Tavel rosé is excellent with white meat and poultry.

Frédéric Jaboulet—"My grand-dad drinks a bottle of Côtes du Rhône a day and he's in his 80s. It's good for youth. It goes with everything except old fish," he jokes.

More specifically, Mr. Jaboulet says, "Hermitage is good with wild boar and mushrooms. A Crozes Hermitage, particularly our Domaine de Thalabert, complements venison or roast rabbit in a cream sauce, but you have to be very careful with the sauce and the weight of the wine.

"Beef ribs and rice go well with a Côtes du Rhône, as does a game bird like roast quail.

"Tavel, slightly chilled, is refreshing with a summer salad.

"Muscat de Beaumes-de-Venise, of course, is a beautiful match with foie gras."

A good value is Côtes du Ventoux. This relatively new appellation began in 1973. The wines that come into the American market are generally less expensive because not too many consumers know about them. One of the most widely available wines to look for in this category is La Vieille Ferme. It's inexpensive and a good value.

The two most famous white wines of the Rhône Valley are called Condrieu and Château Grillet. Both are made from the grape variety called Viognier.

For those who prefer sweet wines, try Beaumes-de-Venise, made from the Muscat grape.

There is a white Châteauneuf-du-Pape and a white Hermitage, but only a few thousand cases are produced each year.

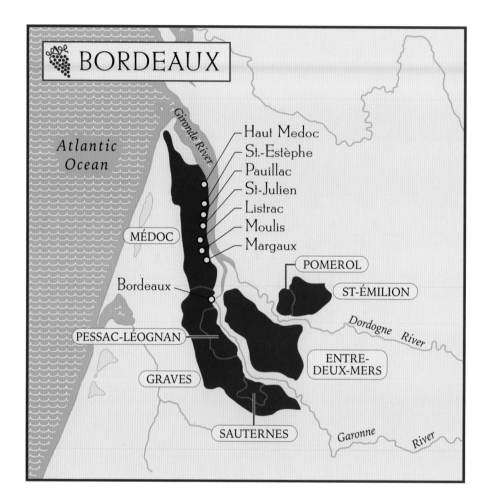

BORDEAUX

Atlantic
Ocean

Gironde River

Haut Medoc
St.-Estèphe
Pauillac
St-Julien
Listrac
Moulis
Margaux

MÉDOC

POMEROL

ST-ÉMILION

Bordeaux

PESSAC-LÉOGNAN

Dordogne River

ENTRE-
DEUX-MERS

GRAVES

SAUTERNES

Garonne River

The Red Wines of Bordeaux

This province of France is rich with excitement and history, and the best part is that the wines speak for themselves. You'll find this region much easier to learn about than Burgundy. For one thing, the plots of land are bigger, and they're owned by fewer landholders. And, as Samuel Johnson once said, "He who aspires to be a serious wine drinker must drink claret."

Some 57 wine regions in Bordeaux produce high-quality wine that enables them to carry the A.O.C. designation on the label. Of these 57 places, four stand out in my mind for red wine:

Médoc—36,783 acres (produces only red wines)

Pomerol—1,936 acres (produces only red wines)

Graves/Pessac-Léognan—10,348 acres (produces both red and dry white wines)

St-Émilion—13,436 acres (produces only red wines)

In the Médoc, there are seven important *inner* appellations you should be familiar with:

Haut Médoc—10,544 acres

St-Estèphe—3,075 acres

Pauillac—2,927 acres

St-Julien—2,223 acres

Margaux—3,364 acres

Moulis—1,353 acres

Listrac—1,595 acres

Bordeaux is much larger in acreage than Burgundy.

The English word "claret" refers to dry red wines from Bordeaux.

Of all the A.O.C. wines of France, 25% come from the Bordeaux region.

In dollar value, the United States is the fourth-largest importer of Bordeaux wines: 25% white, 75% red.

Until 1970, Bordeaux regularly produced more white wine than red. Today, red wine represents about 84% of the total crop.

Take a look at the map on page 98. As a general rule of thumb, red wines from the villages and regions on the left bank of the rivers primarily use the Cabernet Sauvignon grape and on the right bank they use Merlot.

In all of Bordeaux, there are some 86,000 acres of Cabernet Sauvignon, 124,000 acres of Merlot, and 17,000 acres of Cabernet Franc.

The major shippers of regional wines from Bordeaux are:

Barton & Guestier (B & G)
Cordier
Dourthe Kressmann
Eschenauer
Sichel
Yvon Mau
Domaines Prats
Domaines Barons de
 Rothschild
CVBG
Ets J-P Moueix
La Baronnie
Borie-Manoux
Dulong

Examples of proprietary wines you may be familiar with:

Lauretan
Maître d'Estournel
Lacour Pavillon
Mouton-Cadet
Baron Philippe
Saint Jovian
Michel Lynch

All three of these wines are owned by the same family, the Rothschilds, who also own Château Mouton-Rothschild.

Which grape varieties are grown in Bordeaux?

The three major grapes are:

Merlot   Cabernet Sauvignon   Cabernet Franc

Unlike Burgundy, where the winemaker must use 100 percent Pinot Noir to make most red wines (100 percent Gamay for Beaujolais), in Bordeaux the red wines are almost always made from a blend of grapes.

What are the different quality levels of Bordeaux wine?

Bordeaux ($) This is the lowest level of A.O.C. wine in Bordeaux—wines that are nice, inexpensive, and consistent "drinking" wines. These are sometimes known as "proprietary" wines—wines known by what you could almost call a brand name, such as Mouton-Cadet, rather than by the particular region or vineyard. These are usually the least expensive A.O.C. wines in Bordeaux.

Bordeaux + Region ($$) Regional wines come from one of the 57 different regions. Only grapes and wines made in those areas can be called by its regional name. For example, Médoc and St-Émilion. These wines are more expensive than those labeled simply Bordeaux.

Bordeaux + Region + Château ($$–$$$$) Château wines are the products of individual vineyards. There are more than 9,000 châteaus in Bordeaux. As far back as 1855, Bordeaux officially classified the quality levels of some of its châteaus. Hundreds have been officially recognized

Bordeaux (Proprietary)	Regional	Château

for their quality. In the Médoc, for example, the 61 highest-level châteaus are called Grand Cru Classé. There are also more than 400 châteaus in the Médoc that are entitled to be called Cru Bourgeois, a step below Grand Cru Classé. Other areas, such as St-Émilion and Graves, have their own classification systems.

Here are the major classifications:

Médoc (Grands Crus Classés)—1855, 61 châteaus

Médoc (Crus Bourgeois)—1932–1978, 419 châteaus

Graves (Grands Crus Classés)—1959, 16 châteaus

Pomerol—no official classification

St-Émilion—1955, 13 Premiers Grands Crus Classés and 55 Grands Crus Classés

What's a château?

When most people think of a château, they picture a grandiose home filled with Persian rugs and valuable antiques and surrounded by rolling hills of vineyards. Well, I'm sorry to shatter your dreams, but most châteaus are not like that at all. Yes, a château could be a mansion on a large estate, but it could also be a modest home with a two-car garage.

Château wines are usually considered the best quality wines from Bordeaux. They are the most expensive wines, some examples of the best known of the Grand Cru Classé commanding the highest wine prices in the world!

Let's take a closer look at the châteaus. One fact I've learned from my years of teaching wine is that no one wants to memorize the names of thousands of châteaus, so I'll shorten the list by starting with the most important classification in Bordeaux.

According to French law, a château is a house attached to a vineyard having a specific number of acres, as well as having winemaking and storage facilities on the property. A wine may not be called a château wine unless it meets these criteria. The terms "domaine," "clos," and "cru" are also used.

If you see a château on the label, French law dictates that a château really exists. What you see is what you get.

THE GREAT RED WINES OF BORDEAUX

Médoc—Grand Cru Classé, 1855, 61 Châteaus

When and how were the château wines classified?

Some 145 years ago in the Médoc region of Bordeaux, a wine classification was established. Brokers from the wine industry were asked in 1855 to rate the top Médoc wines according to price, which at that time was directly related to quality. (After all, don't we class everything, from cars to restaurants?) The brokers agreed, provided the classification would never become official. *Voilà!* Turn the page for the Official Classification of 1855.

The only château included in the 1855 classification that was not a part of the Médoc was Château Haut-Brion of Graves. This château was so famous at the time that the wine brokers had no choice but to include it. Today the château is owned by an American family, the Dillons.

THE OFFICIAL (1855) CLASSIFICATION OF THE GREAT RED WINES OF BORDEAUX

The Médoc

FIRST GROWTHS—PREMIERS CRUS (5)

VINEYARD	COMMUNE
Château Lafite-Rothschild	Pauillac
Château Latour	Pauillac
Château Margaux	Margaux
Château Haut-Brion	Pessac (Graves)
Château Mouton-Rothschild	Pauillac

SECOND GROWTHS—DEUXIÈMES CRUS (14)

VINEYARD	COMMUNE
Château Rausan-Ségla	Margaux
Château Rausan Gassies	Margaux
Château Léoville-Las-Cases	St-Julien
Château Léoville-Poyferré	St-Julien
Château Léoville-Barton	St-Julien
Château Durfort-Vivens	Margaux
Château Lascombes	Margaux
Château Gruaud-Larose	St-Julien
Château Brane-Cantenac	Cantenac-Margaux
Château Pichon-Longueville (formerly Pichon Longueville-Baron)	Pauillac
Château Pichon-Longueville-Comtesse (formerly Pichon-Longueville-Lalande)	Pauillac
Château Ducru-Beaucaillou	St-Julien
Château Cos d'Estournel	St-Estèphe
Château Montrose	St-Estèphe

THIRD GROWTHS—TROISIÈMES CRUS (14)

VINEYARD	COMMUNE
Château Giscours	Labarde
Château Kirwan	Cantenac-Margaux
Château d'Issan	Cantenac-Margaux
Château Lagrange	St-Julien
Château Langoa-Barton	St-Julien
Château Malescot-St-Exupéry	Margaux
Château Cantenac-Brown	Cantenac-Margaux
Château Palmer	Cantenac-Margaux

Château La Lagune	Ludon
Château Desmirail	Margaux
Château Calon-Ségur	St-Estèphe
Château Ferrière	Margaux
Château d'Alesme (formerly Marquis d'Alesme)	Margaux
Château Boyd-Cantenac	Margaux

FOURTH GROWTHS—QUATRIÈMES CRUS (10)

VINEYARD	COMMUNE
Château St-Pierre	St-Julien
Château Branaire-Ducru	St-Julien
Château Talbot	St-Julien
Château Duhart-Milon-Rothschild	Pauillac
Château Pouget	Cantenac-Margaux
Château La Tour-Carnet	St-Laurent
Château Lafon-Rochet	St-Estèphe
Château Beychevelle	St-Julien
Château Prieuré-Lichine	Cantenac-Margaux
Château Marquis de Terme	Margaux

FIFTH GROWTHS—CINQUIÈMES CRUS (18)

VINEYARD	COMMUNE
Château Pontet-Canet	Pauillac
Château Batailley	Pauillac
Château Grand-Puy-Lacoste	Pauillac
Château Grand-Puy-Ducasse	Pauillac
Château Haut-Batailley	Pauillac
Château Lynch-Bages	Pauillac
Château Lynch-Moussas	Pauillac
Château Dauzac	Labarde
Château d'Armailhac (called Château Mouton-Baron-Philippe from 1956 to 1988)	Pauillac
Château du Tertre	Arsac
Château Haut-Bages-Libéral	Pauillac
Château Pédesclaux	Pauillac
Château Belgrave	St-Laurent
Château Camensac	St-Laurent
Château Cos Labory	St-Estèphe
Château Clerc-Milon-Rothschild	Pauillac
Château Croizet Bages	Pauillac
Château Cantemerle	Macau

Don't be misled by the term "growth." It might make the concept easier to understand if you substitute the word "classification." Instead of saying a wine is "first growth," you could say, "first classification."

"The classified growths are divided in five classes and the price difference from one class to another is about 12%"
—Traité Sur Les Vins du Médoc. William Frank, 1855

For a given vintage there is quite a consistent ratio between the prices of the different classes, which is of considerable help to the trade. So a fifth growth would always sell at about half the price of a second. The thirds and fourths would get prices halfway between the seconds and the fifths. The first growths are getting about 25% over the second growths."
—Bordeaux et Ses Vins, Ch. Cocks, 1868

Is the 1855 classification still in use today?

Every wine person knows about the 1855 classification, but much has changed since then. Some vineyards have doubled or tripled their production by buying up their neighbor's land, which is permitted by law. In some well-known "first growth" vineyards, such as Château Margaux, the quality of the wine degenerated for a while when the family that owned the château wasn't putting enough money and time into the vineyard. In 1977, Château Margaux was sold to a Greek-French family (named Mentzelopoulos) for $16 million, and since then the quality of the wine has gone back even beyond its "first growth" standards.

Château Gloria, in the commune of St-Julien, is an example of a vineyard that didn't exist at the time of the 1855 classification. The late mayor of St-Julien, Henri Martin, bought many parcels of "second growth" vineyards. As a result, he produced top-quality wine that is not included in the 1855 classification. It's also important to consider the techniques used to make wine today. They're a lot different from those used in 1855. Once again, the outcome is better wine. As you can see, some of the châteaus listed in the 1855 classification deserve a lesser ranking, while others deserve a better one.

That said, however, I can also say that, in general, I believe, even though this classification was done 145 years ago, in most cases it is still a very valid classification.

Have there ever been any changes in the 1855 classification?

Yes, but only once, in 1973. Château Mouton-Rothschild was elevated from a "second growth" to a "first growth" vineyard. There's a little story behind that, which is told below.

Exception to the Rule...

In 1920, when the Baron Philippe de Rothschild took over the family vineyard, he couldn't accept the fact that back in 1855 his château had been rated a "second growth." He thought it should have been classed a "first growth" from the beginning—and he fought to get to the top for some fifty years. While the Baron's wine was classified as a "second growth," his motto was:

First, I cannot be.

Second, I do not deign to be.

Mouton, I am.

When his wine was elevated to a "first growth" in 1973, Rothschild replaced the motto with a new one:

First, I am.

Second, I was.

But Mouton does not change.

Is there an easier way to understand the 1855 classification?

I've always found the 1855 classification to be a little cumbersome, so one day I sat down and drew up my own chart. I separated the classification into "growths" (first, second, third, etc.) and then I listed the communes (Pauillac, Margaux, St-Julien, and so on) and set down the number of distinctive vineyards in each one. My chart shows which communes of Bordeaux have the most "first growths"—all the way down to "fifth growths." It also shows which commune corners the market on *all* "growths." Since I was inspired to figure this out during baseball's World Series, I call my chart a "box score" of the 1855 classification.

A quick glance at my box score gives you some instant facts that may guide you when you want to buy a Bordeaux wine from Médoc.

Tallying the score, Pauillac has three of the five "first growths." Margaux practically clean-sweeps the "third growths." In fact, Margaux is the overall winner, because it has the greatest number of classed vineyards in all of Médoc. Margaux is also the only area to have a château rated in each category. St-Julien has no "first" or "fifth growths," but is very strong in the "second" and "fourth."

On the 1945 Mouton-Rothschild bottle there is a big "V" that stands for Victory and the end of World War II. Each year thereafter, Philippe de Rothschild asked a different artist to design his labels, a tradition continued by the Baroness Philippine, his daughter. Some of the most famous artists in the world have agreed to have their work grace the Mouton label, among them:

Jean Cocteau—1947
Salvador Dali—1958
Henry Moore—1964
Joan Miró—1969
Marc Chagall—1970
Pablo Picasso—1973
Robert Motherwell—1974
Andy Warhol—1975
John Huston—1982
Saul Steinberg—1983
Keith Haring—1988
Francis Bacon—1990
Setsuko—1991
Antoni Tàpies—1995
Gu Gan—1996

Kevin Zraly's Box Score of the 1855 Classification

COMMUNE	1ST	2ND	3RD	4TH	5TH	TOTAL
Margaux	1	5	10	3	2	21
Pauillac	3	2	0	1	12	18
St-Julien	0	5	2	4	0	11
St-Estèphe	0	2	1	1	1	5
St-Laurent	0	0	0	1	2	3
Haut-Médoc	0	0	1	0	1	2
Graves	1	0	0	0	0	1
	5	14	14	10	18	61

Total = 61 châteaus

Larose-Trintaudon is the largest vineyard in the Médoc area, making nearly 90,000 cases of wine per year.

The Graves region produces 60% red wine, 40% white wine.

In 1987, a communal appellation was established to create a higher-level appellation in the Graves region. It's called Pessac-Léognan (for both reds and whites).

Cru Bourgeois—1920 (Revised 1932–1978)
329 Châteaus

What does Cru Bourgeois mean?

The Crus Bourgeois of the Médoc are châteaus that were originally classified in 1920, and not in the 1855 classification. In 1932 there were 444 properties listed, but by 1962 there were only 94 members. Today there are over 300, with 150 belonging to the syndicate. The last classification of Crus Bourgeois of the Médoc and Haut-Médoc was in 1978. Because of the high quality of the 1995 and 1996 vintages, some of the best values in wine today are in the Cru Bourgeois classification.

The following is a partial list of Crus Bourgeois to look for:

Château d'Angludet
Château Les Ormes-de-Pez
Château Les Ormes-Sorbet
Château Phélan-Ségur
Château Coufran
Château Chasse-Spleen
Château Meyney
Château Sociando-Mallet
Château Fourcas-Hosten
Château Larose-Trintaudon
Château Greysac
Château Marbuzet
Château Haut-Marbuzet
Château Patache d'Aux
Château La Cardonne
Château Poujeaux
Château Siran

Château Gloria
Château Pibran
Château Monbrison
Château Labégorce-Zédé

Graves (Pessac-Léognan)—1959

The most famous château—we have already seen it in the 1855 classification—is Château Haut-Brion. Other good red Graves classified in 1959 as Grands Crus Classés are:

Château Bouscaut
Château Haut-Bailly

Château Carbonnieux

Domaine de Chevalier

Château de Fieuzal

Château Olivier

Château Malartic-Lagravière

Château La Tour-Martillac

Château Smith-Haut-Lafitte

Château Pape-Clément

Château La Mission-Haut-Brion

Château La Tour-Haut-Brion

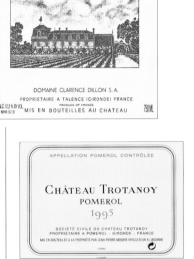

Pomerol—No Official Classification

This is the smallest of the top red-wine districts in Bordeaux. Pomerol produces only fifteen percent as much wine as St-Émilion; as a result, Pomerol wines are relatively scarce. And if you do find them, they'll be expensive. Although no official classification exists, here's a list of some of the finest Pomerols on the market:

Château Pétrus

Château Le Pin

Château La Conseillante

Château Petit-Village

Château Trotanoy

Château l'Évangile

Vieux Château-Certan

Château La Pointe

Château Lafleur

Château La Fleur-Pétrus

Château Gazin

Château Beauregard

Château Nénin

Château Latour-à-Pomerol

The vineyard at Château Pétrus makes the most expensive wine of Bordeaux. It's planted with 95% Merlot.

It takes Château Pétrus one year to make as much wine as Gallo makes in six minutes.

The red wines of Pomerol tend to be softer, fruitier, and ready to be drunk sooner than the Médoc wines.

The major grape used to produce wine in the Pomerol region is Merlot. Very little Cabernet Sauvignon is used in these wines.

St-Émilion—1955 (Revised 1996), 13 Premiers Grands Crus Classés, 55 Châteaus Grands Crus Classés

This area produces about two-thirds as much wine as the entire Médoc, and it's one of the most beautiful villages in France (my own bias). The wines of St-Émilion were finally classified officially in 1955, one century after the Médoc classification. There are thirteen "first growths" comparable to the "cru classé" wines of the Médoc.

THE THIRTEEN FIRST GROWTHS OF ST-ÉMILION
(PREMIERS GRANDS CRUS CLASSÉS)

Château Ausone

Château Cheval Blanc

Château Angélus

Château Beau-Séjour-Bécot

Château Beauséjour-Duffau-
  Lagarosse

Château Belair

Château Canon

Château Figeac

Château La Gaffelière

Château Magdelaine

Château Pavie

Château Trottevieille

Clos Fourtet

Some other appellations to look for in Bordeaux red wines:

Fronsac
Côtes de Blaye
Côtes de Bourg

Important "Grands Crus Classés" and other St-Émilion wines available in the U.S.:

Château Canon-La Gaffelière

Château La Tour-Figeac

Château Trimoulet

Château Dassault

Château Simard

Château Monbousquet

Clos des Jacobins

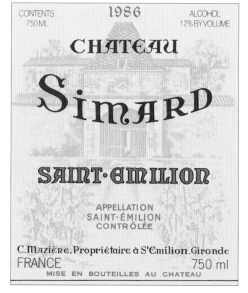

Now that you know all the greatest red wines of Bordeaux, let me take you a step further and show you some of the best vintages.

Bordeaux Vintages

	1960s	1970s	1980s	1990s
Great Wines	1961	1970	1982	1990
	1966	1975	1985	1995
		1978	1986	1996
			1988	
			1989	
Good Wines	1962	1971	1981	1993
	1964	1973	1983	1994
	1967	1976	1984	1997
		1979	1987	1998

How do I buy—and drink—a red Bordeaux?

One of the biggest misconceptions about Bordeaux wines is that they are all very expensive. In reality, there are more than 9,000 châteaus at all different price ranges.

First and foremost, ask yourself if you want to drink the wine now, or if you want to age it. A great château in a great vintage needs a *minimum* of ten years to age. Going down a level, a Cru Bourgeois or Petit Château in a great vintage needs a *minimum* of five years to age. A regional wine can be consumed within two or three years of the vintage year, while a wine labeled simply *Appellation Bordeaux Contrôlée* is ready to drink as soon as it's released.

The next step is to be sure the vintage is correct for what you want. If you're looking for a wine you want to age, in order to be able to age it you must look for a great vintage. If you want a wine that's ready to drink now and you want a greater château, you should choose a lesser vintage. If you want a wine that's ready to drink now and you want a great vintage, you should look for a lesser château.

Another consideration in buying the red wines of Bordeaux is to remember that Bordeaux wines are a blend. Ask yourself if you're looking for a Merlot-style Bordeaux, such as St-Émilion or Pomerol, or if you're looking for a Cabernet style, such as Médoc or Graves, remembering that the Merlot is more accessible and easier to drink when young.

About vintages, the late Alexis Lichine, a noted wine expert, said: "Great vintages take time to mature. Lesser wines mature faster than the greater ones....Patience is needed for great vintages, hence the usefulness and enjoyment of lesser vintages." He summed it up: "Often vintages which have a poorer rating—if young—will give a greater enjoyment than a better-rated vintage—if young."

Drink your 1993, 1994, and 1997 Bordeaux while you wait for your '95 and '96 to mature.

1997 was the earliest harvest since 1893.

What separates a $15 red Bordeaux from a $200 red Bordeaux?

- The place the grapes are grown

- The age of the vines (usually the older the vine, the better the wine)

- The yield of the vine (lower yield means higher quality)

- The winemaking technique (for example, how long the wine is aged in wood)

- The vintage

Is it necessary to pay a tremendous sum of money to get a great-tasting red Bordeaux wine?

Château Lafite-Rothschild $200/bottle

Fifth Growth Pauillac $50/bottle

Cru Bourgeois $25/bottle

Regional Pauillac $15/bottle

It's nice if you have it to spend, but sometimes you don't. The best way to get the most for your money is to use what I call the reverse pyramid method. For example: Let's say you like Château Lafite-Rothschild, which is at the top of our pyramid on the left ($$$$), but you can't afford it. What do you do? Look at the region. It's from Pauillac. You have a choice: You can go back to the 1855 classification and look for a "fifth growth" wine from Pauillac that will give you a flavor for the region at a lesser price ($$$), though not necessarily one-fifth the price of a "first growth." Still too pricey? Drop down one level farther on the inverted pyramid and go for a Crus Bourgeois from Pauillac ($$). Your other option is to buy a regional wine labeled "Pauillac" ($).

Since I didn't memorize the 9,000 châteaus myself, when I go to my neighborhood retailer, I look at the shelf and find a château I've never heard of. If it's from Pauillac, from a good vintage, and it's $15, I buy it. My chances are good. Everything in wine is hedging your bets.

A Bordeaux for Valentine's Day: Château Calon-Ségur

At one time the Marquis de Ségur owned Château Lafite, Château Latour, and Château Calon-Ségur. He said, "I make my wines at Lafite and Latour, but my heart is at Calon." Hence the label.

WINE AND FOOD

Denise Lurton-Moulle (Château La Louvière, Château Bonnet)—With Château La Louvière Rouge, roast leg of lamb or grilled duck breast.

Jean-Michel Cazes (Château Lynch-Bages, Château Haut-Bages-Averous, Château Les Ormes-de-Pez)—"For Bordeaux red, simple and classic is best! Red meat, such as beef and particularly lamb, as we love it in Pauillac. If you can grill the meat on vine cuttings, you are in heaven."

Bruno Prats (Château Cos d'Estournel)—He recommends simple food that is not too rich or served with too much sauce: leg of lamb in its own juice with a touch of garlic, veal with butter sauce, and roast duck with eggplant.

Antony Perrin (Château Carbonnieux)—For red Bordeaux, serve magret de canard (duck breast) with wild mushrooms, or Guinea hen with grapes (pintade aux raisins).

Christian Moueix (Château Pétrus)—With red Bordeaux, especially Pomerol wine, lamb is a must.

For further reading on Bordeaux wines: *Bordeaux* by Robert Parker; *Wines of Bordeaux,* by David Peppercorn, M.W.; and *Grands Vins,* by Clive Coates, M.W.

Since 1882, when the venerable French company Guerlain first produced a lip balm containing Bordeaux wine, nursing mothers have used it as a salve for chapped nipples. "It's a wonderfully soothing emollient, and red wine's tannic acid has healing properties," says Elisabeth Sirot, *attaché de presse* at Guerlain's Paris office. "Frenchwomen have always known this secret." Sirot used it when nursing all four of her children (she learned the tip from her own mother). How sensual—especially considering the American alternative is petroleum jelly.

Had you dined at the Four Seasons restaurant in New York when it first opened in 1959, you could have had a 1918 Château Lafite-Rothschild for $18, or a 1934 Château Latour for $16. Or if those wines were a bit beyond your budget, you could have had a 1945 Château Cos d'Estournel for $9.50.

While Napoleon Bonaparte preferred the Burgundy Chambertin, the late President Richard Nixon's favorite wine was Château Margaux. Nixon always had a bottle of his favorite vintage waiting at his table from the cellar of the famous "21" Club in New York.

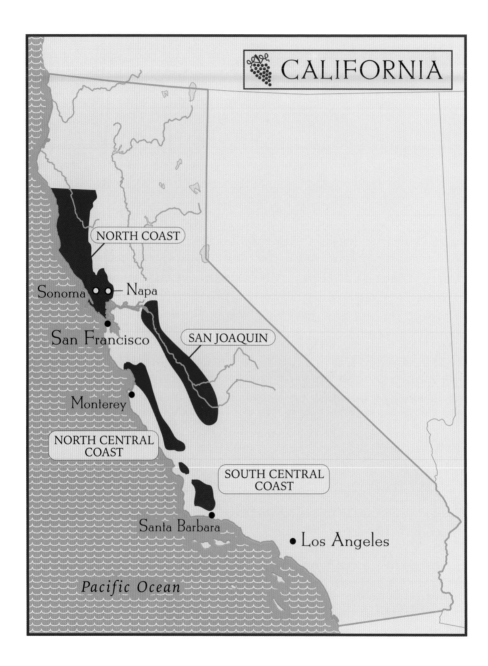

CALIFORNIA

NORTH COAST

Sonoma ○○ Napa

San Francisco

SAN JOAQUIN

Monterey

NORTH CENTRAL
COAST

SOUTH CENTRAL
COAST

Santa Barbara

Los Angeles

Pacific Ocean

The Red Wines of California

Since we've already covered the history and geography of California in "Class 2," it might be a good idea to go back and review the main viticultural areas of California wine country on page 57; before you continue with the red wines of California. Then, consider the following question that inevitably comes up in my class at the Windows on the World Wine School.

Are Americans drinking more white wine or red?

The chart below shows you the trend of wine consumption in the United States over the last thirty years. When I first began studying wines in 1970, people were more interested in red wine than white. From the mid-'70s, when I started teaching, into the mid-'90s, my students showed a definite preference for white wine. Fortunately for me (since I am a red wine drinker), the pendulum is slowly but surely swinging back to more red wine drinkers as we enter the new millennium.

Acreage in California: Currently there are 216,984 acres in red grapes and 190,247 in white grapes planted in California.

Top three red grapes planted in California
1. Zinfandel
2. Cabernet Sauvignon
3. Merlot

Red vs. White——Consumption in the United States

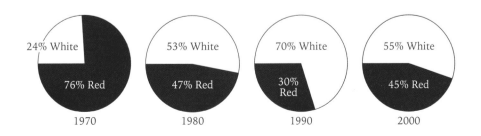

24% White	53% White	70% White	55% White
76% Red	47% Red	30% Red	45% Red
1970	1980	1990	2000

Why this change?

Looking back at the American obsession with health and fitness in the '70s and '80s, many people switched from meat and potatoes to fish and vegetables—a lighter diet that called more for white wine than red. "Chardonnay" became the new buzz word that replaced the call for "a glass of white wine." Bars that never used to stock wine—or at least, nothing decent—began to carry an assortment of fine wines by the glass, with Chardonnay, by far, the best-selling wine. Today, steak is back and the new buzz words are Cabernet Sauvignon and Merlot.

Another major reason for the dramatic upturn in red-wine consumption is the power of the media:

Finally, perhaps the most important reason why red wine has increased in the U.S. is that California is producing a much better quality red wine than ever before. One of the reasons for improved quality is the replanting of vines over the last ten years due to the phylloxera problem. Some analysts thought the replanting would be financially devastating to the California wine industry, but in reality it may have been a blessing in disguise, especially with regard to quality.

The opportunity to replant allowed vineyard owners to increase their red grape production. It enabled California grape growers to utilize the knowledge they have gained over the years with regard to soil, climate, microclimate, trellising, and other viticultural practices.

Bottom line: If you *like* California reds now, you're going to *love* them over the next few years!!

What are the major red grapes in California?

Cabernet Sauvignon—Considered the most successful red grape in California, it yields some of the greatest red wines in the world. Cabernet Sauvignon is the predominant variety used in the finest red Bordeaux

From 1991 to 1997, sales of red wine in the United States has grown over 150%.

Napa Is Red Wine Country
Napa is really red wine country, with over 22,500 acres in red grapes vs. 13,000 acres in whites. Leading the red grapes is Cabernet Sauvignon, while Chardonnay is king of the whites.

114

wines, such as Château Lafite-Rothschild and Château Latour. Almost all California Cabernets are dry, and depending upon the producer and vintage, they range in style from light and ready to drink, to extremely full-bodied and long-lived. California Cabernet has become the benchmark for some of the best California wines.

Most Cabernet Sauvignons are blended with other grapes, primarily Merlot. The winemaker must use at least 75% Cabernet Sauvignon for the wine to be labeled "Cabernet Sauvignon."

My favorite California Cabernet Sauvignons are:

Arrowood
Beaulieu Private Reserve
Beringer Private Reserve
Caymus Special Selection
Chateau Montelena
Chateau St. Jean, Cinq Cepages
Diamond Creek
Duckhorn
Dunn Howell Mountain
Groth Reserve
Heitz
Hess Collection
Jordan
Laurel Glen
Mondavi Reserve
Opus One
Ridge Monte Bello
Spottswoode
Shafer Hillside Select
Silver Oak
Stag's Leap Cask 23

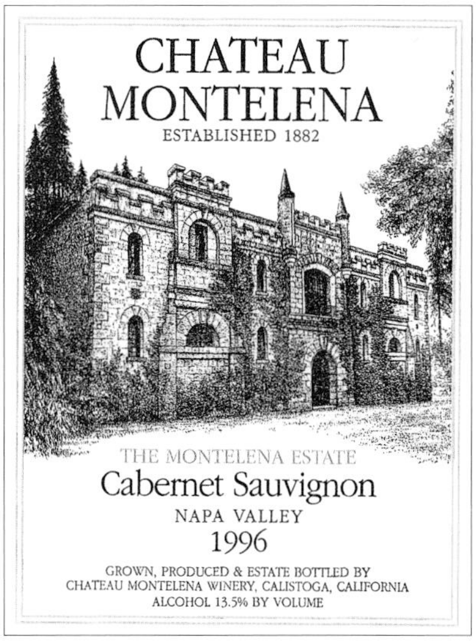

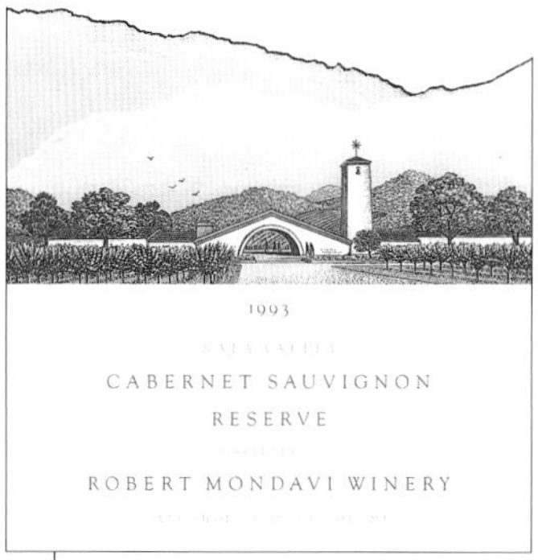

"Reserve" on the label has no legal meaning. In other words, there is no law that defines it. Some wineries, such as Beaulieu Vineyards and Robert Mondavi Winery, still mark some of their wines "Reserve." BV's "Reserve" is from a particular vineyard. Mondavi's "Reserve" is made from a special blend of grapes, presumably his best. Others include "Cask" wines, "Special Selections," or "Proprietor's Reserve." The California Wine Institute has proposed a definition of Reserve, for B.A.T.F. approval, to meet the requirement by some export markets.

Best Bets for Cabernet Sauvignon

1984 1985❖ 1986 1987❖ 1990❖ 1991❖
1992 1993 1994❖ 1995 1996 1997❖ 1999

Note: ❖ signifies exceptional vintage

Pinot Noir—Known as the "headache" grape because of its fragile quality, Pinot Noir is difficult to grow and make into wine. The great grape of the Burgundy region of France—responsible for such famous wines as Pommard, Nuits-St-Georges, and Gevrey-Chambertin—is also one of the principal grapes in French Champagne. In California, many years of experimentation in finding the right location to plant the Pinot Noir and to perfect the fermentation techniques have elevated some of the Pinot

Noirs to the status of great wines. Pinot Noir is usually less tannic than Cabernet and matures more quickly, generally in two to five years. Because of the extra expense involved in growing this grape, the best examples of Pinot Noirs from California may cost more than other varietals.

My favorite California Pinot Noirs are:

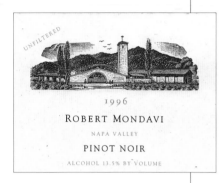

The Carneros district is one of the better places to grow Pinot Noir because of its cooler climate.

Acacia
Au Bon Climat
Calera
Carneros Creek
Dehlinger
Etude
Gary Farrell
Robert Mondavi
Morgan
Saintsbury
Williams Selyem

Best Bets for Pinot Noir
1994   1995   1996   1997

Zinfandel—The surprise grape of California, Zinfandel was used to make "generic" or "jug" wines in the early years of California winemaking. Over the past fifteen years, however, it has developed into one of the best red varietal grapes. It is unique among grapes grown in the United States in that its European origin is unknown. The only problem in choosing a Zinfandel wine is that so many different styles are made. Depending on the producer, the wines can range from a big, rich, intensely flavored style with substantial tannin, to a very light, fruity wine. And let's not forget white Zinfandel!

My favorite Zinfandels are:

One of the hottest wines today in terms of popularity is white Zinfandel, which at twenty million cases sold in 1998 far outsells red Zinfandel, and is also the largest-selling varietal wine in the United States.

Overheard at a wine shop in New York City from a customer buying a white Zinfandel: "You mean they make a red Zinfandel, too?"

Dry Creek Winery
Rafanelli
Ravenswood
Ridge
J. Rochioli

Rosenblum

Signorello

Turley

Best Bets for Zinfandel

1994❖ 1995❖ 1997❖ 1999

Note: ❖ signifies exceptional vintage

Merlot—For many years Merlot was thought of as a grape only to be blended with Cabernet Sauvignon, because Merlot's tannins are softer and its texture more supple. Merlot has now achieved its own identity as a superpremium varietal. Of red grape varietals in California, Merlot has seen the fastest rate of new plantings in the last ten years. It produces a soft, round wine that generally does not need the same aging as a Cabernet Sauvignon. It is a top-seller at restaurants, where its early maturation and compatibility with food make it a frequent choice by consumers.

Ridge Winery may make six different Zinfandels every vintage!

Merlot Madness
There were only two acres of Merlot planted in all of California in 1960. Today there are over 30,000!!

My favorite Merlots are:

Beringer Howell Mountain

Cline

Clos du Bois

Duckhorn

Franciscan

Markham

Martinelli

Matanzas Creek

Newton

Pine Ridge

St. Francis

Shafer

Whitehall Lane

Best Bets for Merlot

1994❖ 1995 1996 1997 1999

Note: ❖ signifies exceptional vintage

Some examples of Meritage® wines of California:

  Cinq Cepages (Chateau St. Jean)
  Dominus (Christian Moueix)
  Insignia (Phelps Vineyards)
  Marlstone (Clos du Bois)
  Rubicon (Niebaum Coppola Estate)
  Opus One (Mondavi/Rothschild)
  Cain Five

Red-Grape Boom

Look at the chart below to see how many acres of the major red grapes were planted in California in 1970, and how those numbers have increased in thirty years. Rapid expansion has been the characteristic of the California wine industry!

Total Acreage of Red-Wine Grapes Planted

GRAPE-BY-GRAPE COMPARISON

GRAPE	1970	1980	1990	2000 (estimated)
Cabernet Sauvignon	11,486	21,800	24,100	40,400
Pinot Noir	4,985	9,200	8,600	9,600
Zinfandel	23,786	27,700	28,000	46,500
Merlot	1,014	2,600	4,962	32,800

What are Meritage® wines?

Meritage® (which rhymes with "heritage") is the name for red and white wines made in America from a blend of the classic Bordeaux wine-grape varieties. This category was created because many winemakers felt stifled by the required minimum amount (75%) of a grape that must go into a bottle for it to be named for that variety. Some winemakers knew they could make a better wine with a blend of, say, sixty percent of the major grape and forty percent of secondary grapes. This new style of wines allows producers of Meritage® wines the same freedom that Bordeaux winemakers have in making their wines.

For red wine, the varieties include Cabernet Sauvignon, Merlot, Cabernet Franc, Petit Verdot, and Malbec. For white wine, the varieties include Sauvignon Blanc and Sémillon.

Opus One

Amidst grand hoopla in the wine world, Robert Mondavi and the late Baron Philippe de Rothschild released Opus One. "It isn't Mouton and it isn't Mondavi," said Robert Mondavi. Opus One is a Bordeaux-style blend made from Cabernet Sauvignon, Merlot, and Cabernet Franc grapes grown in Napa Valley. It was originally produced at the Robert Mondavi Winery in Napa Valley, but is now produced across Highway 29 in its own spectacular winery.

When I buy a Cabernet, Zinfandel, Merlot, Pinot Noir, or Meritage® wine, how do I know which style I'm getting? Is the style of the wine indicated on the label?

Unless you just happen to be familiar with a particular vineyard's wine, you're stuck with trial-and-error tastings. You're one step ahead, though, just by knowing that you'll find drastically different styles from the same grape variety.

With over 900 wineries in California and over half of them producing red wines, it is virtually impossible to keep up with the ever-changing styles that are being produced. One of the recent improvements in labeling is that more wineries are adding important information to the back label indicating when the wine is ready to drink, if it should be aged, and many even offer food suggestions.

To avoid any unpleasant surprises, I can't emphasize enough the importance of an educated wine retailer. One of the strongest recommendations I give—especially to a new wine drinker—is to find the right retailer, one who understands wine and your taste.

Do California red wines age?

Absolutely, especially from the best wineries that produce Cabernet Sauvignon and Zinfandel. I have been fortunate to taste some early examples of Cabernet Sauvignon going back to the '30s, '40s, and '50s, which for the most part were drinking well, proving to me the longevity of certain Cabernets. Cabernet Sauvignons and Zinfandels from the best wineries in great vintages will need a minimum of five years before you drink them, and they will get better over the next ten years. That's at least fifteen years of great enjoyment.

However, one of the things I have noticed in the last ten years, not only tasting as many California wines as I have, but also tasting so many European wines, is that California wines seem to be more accessible when young, as opposed to, say, a Bordeaux. I believe this is one of the reasons California wines sell so well in retail stores and in restaurants.

What have been the trends in the red wines of California over the last fifteen years?

To best answer that question, we should go back even further to see where the trends have been going for the last thirty or so years. The 1960s was a decade of expansion and development. The 1970s was a decade of growth, especially in terms of the number of wineries that were

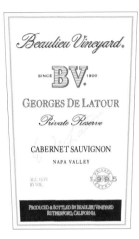

One of the most memorable tastings I have ever attended in my career was for the fiftieth anniversary of Beaulieu's Private Reserve wine. Over a two-day period, we tasted every vintage from 1936 to 1986 with the winemaker, André Tchelistcheff. I think everyone who attended the tasting was amazed and awed by how well many of these vintages aged.

established in California and the corporations and individuals that became involved. The 1980s was the decade of experimentation, in grape growing as well as in winemaking and marketing techniques.

Over the past ten years, I have seen the winemakers finally get a chance to step back and "fine tune" their wine. Today, they are producing wines that have tremendous structure, finesse, and elegance that many lacked in the early years of the California winemaking renaissance. They are also making wines that can give pleasure when young, and also great wines that I will hopefully be around to share with my grandchildren. The benchmark for quality has increased to such a level that the best wineries have gotten better, but more important to the consumer, even the everyday wines (under $10) are better than ever before.

Though California winemakers have settled down, they have not given up experimentation altogether, if you consider the many new grape varieties coming out of California these days. I expect to see more wines made with grapes such as the Viognier, Mourvèdre, Syrah, Grenache, and Sangiovese, continuing the trend toward diversity in California red wines.

Red wines are no longer the sole domain of Napa and Sonoma. Many world-class reds are being produced in the Central Coast regions of California such as Monterey and Santa Barbara.

WINE AND FOOD

Margrit Biever and Robert Mondavi (Robert Mondavi Winery)—With Cabernet Sauvignon: lamb, or wild game such as grouse and caribou. With Pinot Noir: pork loin, milder game such as domestic pheasant, coq au vin.

Tom Jordan (Jordan Vineyard & Winery)—"Roast lamb is wonderful with the flavor and complexity of Cabernet Sauvignon. The wine also pairs nicely with sliced breast of duck, and grilled squab with wild mushrooms. For a cheese course with mature Cabernet, milder cheeses, such as young goat cheeses, St. André and Taleggio, are best so the subtle flavors of the wine can be enjoyed."

Margaret and Dan Duckhorn (Duckhorn Vineyards)—"With a young Merlot, we recommend lamb shanks with crispy polenta, or grilled duck with wild rice in Port sauce. One of our favorites is barbecued leg of lamb with a mild, spicy fruit-based sauce. With older Merlots at the end of the meal, we like to serve cambazzola cheese and warm walnuts."

Janet Trefethen (Trefethen Vineyards)—With Cabernet Sauvignon: prime cut of well-aged grilled beef; also—believe it or not—with chocolate and chocolate-chip cookies. With Pinot Noir: roasted quail stuffed with peeled kiwi fruit in a Madeira sauce. Also with pork tenderloin in a fruity sauce.

Piero Antinori, the famous Italian winemaker, is a joint venture partner at Napa Valley's Atlas Peak Winery. They have planted many acres of Sangiovese, the primary grape used to make Chianti.

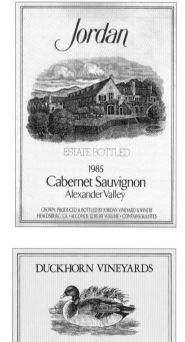

Paul Draper (Ridge Vineyards)—With Zinfandel: a well-made risotto of Petaluma duck. With aged Cabernet Sauvignon: Moroccan lamb with figs.

Warren Winiarski (Stag's Leap Wine Cellars)—With Cabernet Sauvignon: lamb or veal with a light sauce.

Josh Jensen (Calera Wine Co.)—"Pinot Noir is so versatile, but I like it best with fowl of all sorts—chicken, turkey, duck, pheasant, and quail, preferably roasted or mesquite grilled. It's also great with fish such as salmon, tuna, and snapper."

Richard Arrowood (Arrowood Vineyards & Winery)—With Cabernet Sauvignon, Mr. Arrowood suggests Sonoma County spring lamb or lamb chops prepared in a rosemary herb sauce.

David Stare (Dry Creek Vineyard)—"My favorite food combination with Zinfandel is marinated, butterflied leg of lamb. Have the butcher butterfly the leg, then place it in a plastic bag. Pour in half a bottle of Dry Creek Zinfandel, a cup of olive oil, six mashed garlic cloves, salt and pepper to taste. Marinate for several hours or overnight in the refrigerator. Barbecue until medium rare. While the lamb is cooking, take the marinade, reduce it, and whisk in several pats of butter for thickness. Yummy!"

Bo Barrett (Chateau Montelena Winery)—With Cabernet Sauvignon, Bo Barrett enjoys a good rib eye, barbecued with a teriyaki-soy-ginger-sesame marinade. Another favorite dish is venison or even roast beef prepared with olive oil and tapenade with rosemary, or even lamb. But when it comes to a good Cabernet Sauvignon, Bo is happy to enjoy a glass with "nothing at all—just a good book."

Patrick Campbell (Owner/Winemaker, Laurel Glen Vineyard)—"With Cabernet Sauvignon, try a rich risotto topped with wild mushrooms."

Jack Cakebread (Cakebread Cellars)—"I enjoy my 1994 Cakebread Cellars Napa Valley Cabernet Sauvignon with farm-raised salmon with a crispy potato crust or an herb-crusted Napa Valley rack of lamb, with mashed potatoes and a red wine sauce."

Ed Sbragia (Winemaker, Beringer Vineyards)—"I like my Cabernet Sauvignon with rack of lamb, beef, or rare duck."

Tom Mackey (Winemaker, St. Francis Merlot)—With St. Francis Merlot Sonoma County, the winemaker suggests Dungeness crab cakes, rack of lamb, pork roast, or tortellini. With St. Francis Merlot Reserve, Mr. Mackey enjoys hearty minestrone or lentil soup, venison or filet mignon, or even a Caesar salad.

For further reading on California wines I recommend *The Wine Atlas of California,* by Bob Thompson; *Atlas of California,* by James Halliday; and *Making Sense of California Wine,* by Matt Kramer. Cabernet lovers should read James Laube's *California's Great Cabernets.*

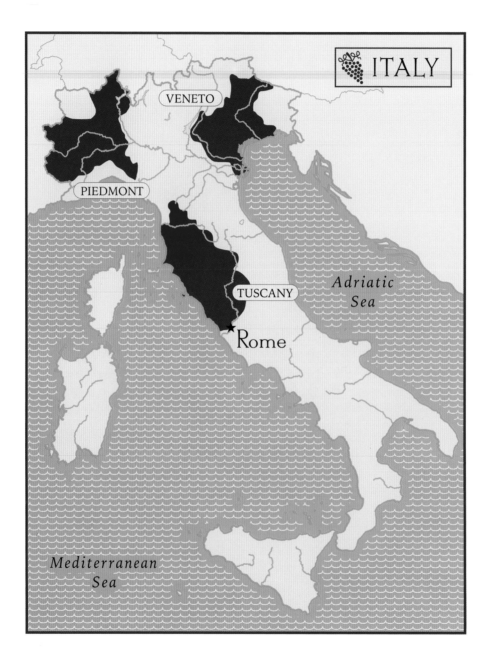

ITALY

VENETO

PIEDMONT

TUSCANY

Adriatic
Sea

★ Rome

Mediterranean
Sea

Wines of the World: Italy, Spain, Australia, Chile & Argentina

The Red Wines of Italy

Italy is the world's largest producer of wine. It has been producing wine for more than 3,000 years, and the vines grow everywhere. As one retailer of fine Italian wine once told me, "There is no country. Italy is one vast vineyard from north to south."

Italian wines are good for any occasion—from quaffing to serious tasting. Some of my favorite wines are Italian. In fact, 25 percent of my personal wine cellar is stocked with them.

There are more than 2,000 different wine labels, if you care to memorize them, 20 regions, and 96 provinces. But don't worry. If you want to know the basics of Italian wines, concentrate on the three regions listed below, and you'll be well on your way to having Italy in the palm of your hand.

Piedmont   Tuscany   Veneto

What are the major red-grape varieties in Italy?

In Tuscany, the major red-grape variety is Sangiovese, and in Piedmont, it is Nebbiolo. There are several others, but these are the best.

How are Italian wines controlled?

As mentioned before, the Denominazione di Origine Controllata (abbreviated D.O.C.), the Italian equivalent of the French A.O.C., controls the production and labeling of the wine. Italy's D.O.C. laws went into effect in 1963.

Two-thirds of all Italian wines are red.

Top three wine regions in production of Italian wines
1. Veneto   17.7%
2. Piedmont   17.1%
3. Tuscany   10.7%

My Italian wine friends sometimes refer to Veneto as Tri-Veneto, which includes Trentino, Alto-Aldige and Friuli. Some of the best white wines of Italy come from these regions.

Many wine producers in Italy are now making wines from Cabernet Sauvignon, Merlot, and Chardonnay.

There are more than 300 D.O.C. wines accounting for 20% of Italy's total wine production.

Of all Italian D.O.C. wines, 60% are red.

The biggest difference between the A.O.C. of France and the D.O.C. of Italy is that the D.O.C. has aging requirements.

D.O.C.G. wines from regions other than Tuscany and Piedmont include Taurasi from Campania, Albana di Romagna from Emilia-Romagna, Torgiano Rosso Riserva and Montefalco Sagrantino from Umbria, Franciacorta and Valtellina Superiore from Lombardy, and Vermentino de Gallura from Sardinia.

At present, there are a total of twenty wines that are entitled to the D.O.C.G. designation.

In Italy, vineyards aren't classified as they are in Bordeaux and Burgundy. There are neither Grands Crus nor Premiers Crus.

How many of you, during your college days, bought a straw-covered bottle of Chianti to use as a candle-holder?

D.O.C. Laws

The D.O.C. governs:
1. The geographical limits of each region
2. The grape varieties that can be used
3. The percentage of each grape used
4. The maximum amount of wine that can be produced per acre
5. The minimum alcohol content of the wine
6. The aging requirements, such as how long a wine should spend in wood or bottle, for certain wines

---

In 1980 the Italian wine board took quality control even one step beyond the regular D.O.C., when they added the higher-ranking D.O.C.G. The "G" stands for *Garantita*, meaning that, through tasting-control boards, they absolutely guarantee the stylistic authenticity of a wine.

As of 2000, the wines from Piedmont and Tuscany that qualified for the D.O.C.G. were:

TUSCANY	PIEDMONT
Vernaccia di San Gimignano	Moscato d'Asti/Asti
Chianti	Gattinara
Chianti Classico	Barbaresco
Vino Nobile di Montepulciano	Barolo
Carmignano Rosso	Brachetto d'Acqui
Brunello di Montalcino	Ghemme
	Gavi

Seven of the Italian D.O.C.G. wines are from Piedmont and six are from Tuscany. That tells you why these are two of the regions you should study.

Tuscany–the Home of Chianti

Why did Chianti have such a bad image until recently?

One reason was the little straw-covered flasks (*fiaschi*) that the wine was bottled in—nice until restaurants hung the bottles from the ceiling next to the bar, along with the sausage and the provolone. So Chianti developed an image as a cheap little red wine to be bought for $5 a jug.

My own feeling is that Chianti Classico Riserva is one of the best values in Italian wine today.

What are the different levels of Chianti?

Chianti—the first level (Cost: $)

Chianti Classico—from the inner historic district of Chianti (Cost: $$)

Chianti Classico Riserva—from a Classico area, and must be aged for a minimum of two years, three months (Cost: $$$$)

How should I buy Chianti?

First of all, find the style of Chianti you like best. There is a considerable variation in Chianti styles. Second, always buy from a shipper or producer whom you know—one with a good, reliable reputation. Some quality Chianti producers are: Antinori, Badia a Coltibuono, Brolio, Frescobaldi, Melini, Monsanto, Nozzole, Ricasoli, Ruffino, Castello Banfi, and Fontodi.

Which grapes are used in Chianti?

According to updated D.O.C.G. requirements, winemakers are required to use at least 75 percent Sangiovese to produce Chianti. The D.O.C.G. is also encouraging the use of "nontraditional" grapes, such as Cabernet Sauvignon, by allowing an unprecedented ten percent "optional grape." These changes, along with better winemaking techniques and better

That's Tradition!
The name "Chianti" was first recorded in 700 A.D. Brolio, a major producer of Chianti, has been in business since 1057. Thirty-two generations of this family have tended to the vineyards and made the wine.

Only one-fifth of all Chianti is Chianti Classico Riserva. Today you'll find that the best Chiantis are sold in Bordeaux-style bottles.

As in California, some Italian winemakers wanted to experiment with grape varieties and blends beyond what was permitted by the D.O.C. regulations, so they decided to produce their own styles of wine. In Tuscany, these wines have become known as the "Super Tuscans." Among the better known of these proprietary Italians wines are Sassicaia, Tignanello, Ornellaia, Cabreo Il Borgo, Solaia, Summus, and Excelsus.

Before the D.O.C. laws were created, some producers of Chianti established their own minimum standards that were quite strict. Their symbol was the black rooster.

Brunello di Montalcino, because of its limited supply, is sometimes very expensive. For one of the best values in Tuscan red wine, look for Rosso di Montalcino.

Brunello Is Changing
Beginning with the 1995 vintage, Brunellos are required to be aged in oak for a minimum of two years instead of the previous three. Result? A fruitier, more accessible style wine.

Some Tuscan winemakers are saying that the 1997 vintage is the best since 1947.

Older great vintages of Tuscany: 1982, 1985, 1988

It is said that when you begin drinking the red wines of Piedmont, you start with the lighter-style Barbera and Dolcetto, move on to the fuller-bodied Barbaresco, until finally you can fully appreciate a Barolo. As the late vintner Renato Ratti said, "Barolo is the wine of arrival."

vineyard development, have all contributed to greatly improving Chianti's image over the last fifteen years. A separate D.O.C.G. has been established for Chianti Classico, and producers of this wine may now use 100 percent Sangiovese.

Which other high-quality wines come from Tuscany?

Three of the greatest Italian red wines are Brunello di Montalcino, Vino Nobile di Montepulciano, and Carmignano. If you purchase the Brunello, keep in mind that it probably needs more aging (five to ten years) before it reaches peak drinkability. The best-known producers of Brunello are: Biondi-Santi (one of the most expensive wines in Italy), Barbi, Altesino, Il Poggione, Col d'Orcia, Castello Banfi, and Caparzo. Those of Vino Nobile are: Avignonesi, Boscarelli, Fassati, and Poggio alla Sala. For Carmignano, look for Villa Capezzana, Poggiolo, and Artimino.

Best Bets for Tuscany

| 1990✣ | 1993 | 1995 | 1997* | 1998 | 1999 |

Note: ✣ signifies exceptional vintage

Piedmont—the Big Reds

Some of the finest red wines are produced in Piedmont. Two of the best D.O.C.G. wines come from this region in northwest Italy are Barolo and Barbaresco.

The grapes of Piedmont:

Dolcetto **Barbera** **Nebbiolo**

Barolo and Barbaresco, the "heavyweight" wines from Piedmont, are made from the Nebbiolo variety. These wines have the fullest style and a high alcoholic content. Be careful when you try to match young vintages of these wines with your dinner; they may overpower the food.

Barolo vs. Barbaresco

BAROLO	BARBARESCO
Nebbiolo grape	Nebbiolo grape
Minimum 12.5% alcohol	Minimum 12.5% alcohol
More complex flavor, more body	Lighter; less body than Barolo, but fine and elegant
Must be aged at least three years (one in wood)	Requires two years of aging (one in wood)
"Riserva" = five years of aging	"Riserva" = four years of aging

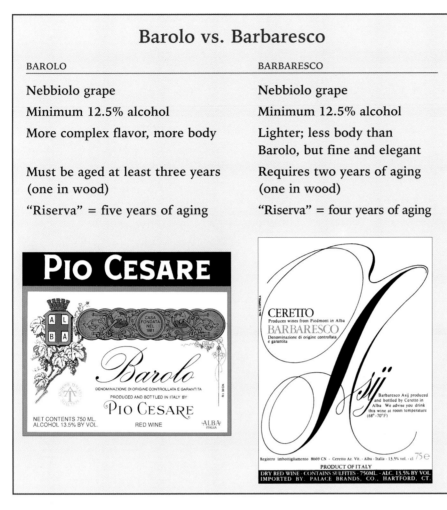

In one of the biggest changes in the D.O.C.G. regulations, the wines of Barolo now only have to be aged in wood for one year, and the minimum alcohol has been changed to 12.5 percent. Before 1999, Barolo had a mandatory two years of wood aging and 13% minimum alcohol.

Piedmont's production:
65% red
18% spumante (sparkling white)
17% white

My favorite producers of Piedmont wines are: Antonio Vallana, Borgogno, Fontanafredda, Gaja, Pio Cesare, Prunotto, Renato Ratti, Ceretto, G. Conterno, A. Conterno, M. Chiarlo, B. Giacosa, Marchesi di Gresy, Marchesi di Barolo, Vietti, and Marcarini.

How Italian Wines Are Named

Winemaking regions have different ways of naming their wines. In California, you look for the grape variety on the label. In Bordeaux, most often you will see the name of a château. But in Italy, there are three different ways that wine is named—by grape variety, village or district, or simply a proprietary name. See the examples below:

GRAPE VARIETY	VILLAGE OR DISTRICT	PROPRIETARY
Barbera	Chianti	Tignanello
Nebbiolo	Barolo	Sassicaia
Sangiovese	Montalcino	Summus

Giuseppe Colla of Prunotto offers his "Best Bets" in the form of advice. His general rule: In a good vintage, set a Barbaresco aside for a minimum of four years before drinking. In the same situation, put away a Barolo for six years. However, in a great vintage year, lay down a Barbaresco for six years and a Barolo for eight years. As they say, "Patience is a virtue"—especially with wine.

127

An interesting trend in Italy: Bottled water and beer consumption are both increasing, while wine consumption is decreasing.

Have Piedmont wines changed over the last 10 years? Many have. The wines of the past were more tannic and difficult to appreciate when young, while many of the present-day wines are easier to drink.

What have been the trends in the red wines of Italy over the last two decades?

Going back a little further, we can see that as recently as 25 years ago Italian wine was made to be consumed in Italy, and not for the export market. As one wine producer commented, "They didn't drink the wine, they ate the wine." To the Italians, wine was an everyday thing like salt and pepper on their table to enhance the taste of the food.

But over the last 25 years, winemaking became more of a business, and the Italian winemakers' philosophy has changed considerably from making casual-drinking wines to much better-made wines that are also much more marketable around the world. They've accomplished this by using modern technology, modern vinification procedures, and updated vineyard management as a basis for experimentation.

Another area of major experimentation is with non-traditional grape varieties such as Cabernet Sauvignon and Merlot. One of the newest trends is single-vineyard labeling. As a result, the biggest news in the whole wine industry is the change in Italian wines over the last fifteen years. When I talk about experimentation, you must remember that this isn't California we're talking about, but Italy, with thousands of years of traditions that are being changed. In Italy, the producers have had to unlearn and relearn in order to make better wines.

The prices of Italian wines have also increased tremendously over the last ten years, which may be good news for the Italian wine producers (in that it enhances the image of their wines), but it isn't such good news for consumers. Some of the wines from Italy have become among the most expensive in the world. That's not to say they're not worth it, but the pricing situation isn't the same as it was ten years ago.

Best Bets for Piedmont
1990* 1995 1996* 1997* 1998* 1999*

Note: * denotes exceptional vintage

Older Great Vintages of Piedmont:
1982, 1985, 1988, 1989

The Piedmont region has had five great vintages in a row: 1995–1999.

Veneto—the Home of Soave

This is one of Italy's largest wine-producing regions. Even if you don't recognize the name immediately, I'm sure you've had Veronese wines at one time or another, like Valpolicella, Bardolino, and Soave. All three are very consistent, easy to drink, and ready to be consumed whenever you buy them. They don't fit into the category of a Brunello di Montalcino or a Barolo, but they're very good table wines and they're within everyone's budget.

Easy-to-find Veneto producers are Bolla, Folonari, and Santa Sofia. Also, look for Allegrini, Anselmi, and Quintarelli.

The top five wines imported to the U.S. from Italy are:
1. Riunite "Classics"
2. Bolla
3. Casarsa
4. Folonari
5. Cella
The above wines equal 43% of all imported table wine in the U.S.

What's Amarone?

Amarone is a type of Valpolicella wine made by a special process in the Veneto region. Only the ripest grapes from the top of each bunch are used. After picking, they're left to "raisinate" (dry and shrivel) on straw mats. Does this sound familiar to you? It should, because this is similar to the process used to make German Trockenbeerenauslese and French Sauternes. One difference is that with Amarone, the winemaker ferments most of the sugar, bringing the alcohol content to fourteen to sixteen percent.

My favorite Amarone producers are Masi, Bertani, and Allegrini.

In the last five or six years, Italians have become more weight- and health-conscious, so they're changing their eating habits. As a result, the leisurely four-hour lunch and siesta is a thing of the past. Yes, all good things must come to an end.

Italian Whites

Pinot Grigio is a white grape variety that is also found in Alsace, France, where it is called Pinot Gris.

Is Pinot Grigio Hot?
In 1970, Italy produced 11,000 cases of Pinot Grigio. And in 1998, they produced over 2.5 million cases!!

"Piedmontese wines show better with food than in a tasting."
—Angelo Gaja

I am often asked why I don't teach a class on Italian white wines. The answer is quite simple. Take a look at the most popular white wines: Soave, Frascati, and Pinot Grigio, among others. Most of them retail for less than $10. The Italians just don't put the same effort into most of their white wines that they put into their reds—in terms of style or complexity—and they are the first to admit it.

Recent plantings of international white varieties such as Chardonnay and Sauvignon Blanc are now coming into fashion, and over the next few years they could change the white wine outlook in Italy.

Wine and Food

In Italy, the wine is made to go with the food. No meal is served without wine. Take it from the experts.

The following food-and-wine suggestions are based on what some of the Italian wine producers enjoy having with their wine. You don't have to take their word for it. Get yourself a bottle of wine, a tasty dish, and *mangia!*

Ambrogio Folonari (Ruffino)—He enjoys Chianti with prosciutto, chicken, pasta, and of course, pizza. When it comes to a Chianti Classico Riserva, Dr. Folonari prefers a hearty prime-rib dinner or a steak.

Ezio Rivella (Castello Banfi)—He says that Chianti is good with all meat dishes, but he saves the Brunello for "stronger" dishes, such as steak, wild boar, pheasant, and other game, as well as Pecorino Toscano cheese.

Angelo Gaja—He has Barbaresco with meat and veal, and also with mature cheeses that are "not too strong," such as Emmenthaler and Fontina. Mr. Gaja advises against Parmesan and goat cheese when you have a Barbaresco. And if you're having a Barolo, Mr. Gaja's favorite is roast lamb.

Giuseppe Colla (Prunotto)—Mr. Colla says light-style Dolcetto goes well with all first courses and all white meat—chicken and veal especially. He prefers not to have Dolcetto with fish. The wine doesn't stand up well to spicy sauce, but it's great with tomato sauce and pasta.

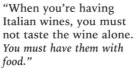

> "When you're having Italian wines, you must not taste the wine alone. *You must have them with food.*"
> —Giuseppe Colla of Prunotto

Renato Ratti—Mr. Ratti once told us that both Barbera and Dolcetto are good with chicken and lighter foods. However, Barolo and Barbaresco need to be served with heavier dishes to match their own body. Mr. Ratti also suggested:

- a roast in its natural sauce or, better yet, try it *Brasato al Barolo*—cooked with Barolo
- meat cooked with wine
- pheasant, duck, wild rabbit
- cheeses
- for a special dish, try risotto al Barolo (rice cooked with Barolo wine)

Mr. Ratti said that Italians even serve wine with dessert—his favorite was strawberries or peaches with Dolcetto wine. The dryness in the wine, contrasted with the natural sweetness of the fruit, makes for a taste sensation!

Lorenza de'Medici (Badia a Coltibuono)—Since Tuscan cooking is very simple, this winery owner recommends an assortment of simple foods. She prefers herbs to heavy sauces. With young Chianti, she suggests roast chicken, squab, or pasta with meat sauce. To complement an older Chianti, she recommends a wide pasta with:

- braised meat in Chianti
- pheasant or other game
- wild boar
- roast beef

Piero Antinori (Antinori)—Mr. Antinori enjoys Chianti with the grilled foods for which Tuscany is famous, especially its bistecca alla Fiorentina (beefsteak). He suggests poultry and even hamburgers as other tasty possibilities.

For Chianti Classico Riserva, Mr. Antinori enjoys having the best of the vintages with wild boar and fine aged Parmesan cheese. He says the wine is a perfect match for roast beef, roast turkey, lamb, or veal.

For further reading on Italian wine: *The Pocket Guide to Italian Wines* and *Wine Atlas of Italy,* both by Burton Anderson; and *Italian Wine* by Victor Hazan.

Spain

The main winemaking regions in Spain are:

La Rioja
Cataluña (Penedés and Priorato)
Ribera del Duero
The Sherry District

Another up-and-coming area in Spain is called Rías Baixas, in the northwestern province of Galicia, producing some excellent white wines made with the Albariño grape.

Also, look for the great rosés of the Navarra region.

Marqués de Cáceres is owned by a Spaniard, who also owns Château Camensac, a fifth-growth Bordeaux.

We'll put aside the region of Sherry for now, since you'll become a Sherry expert in the next chapter. Let's start with Rioja, which is located in northern Spain, very near the French border.

In fact, it's less than a five-hour drive to Bordeaux from Rioja, so it's no coincidence that Rioja wines often have a Bordeaux style. Back in the 1800s, many Bordeaux wine producers brought their expertise to this region.

Why would a Frenchman leave his château in Bordeaux to go to a Spanish bodega in Rioja?

I'm glad you asked. It so happens that Frenchmen did travel from Bordeaux to Rioja at one point in history. Do you remember phylloxera? (See Prelude to Wine, on page 13.) It's a plant louse that at one time killed nearly all the European vines and almost wiped out the Bordeaux wine industry.

Phylloxera started in the north and moved south. It first destroyed all the vines of Bordeaux, and some of the Bordeaux vineyard owners decided to establish vineyards and wineries in the Rioja district. It was a logical place for them to go because of the similar climate and growing

Grenache is the French spelling of Garnacha, a Spanish grape, which was brought to France from Spain during the time of the Popes of Avignon, some of whom were Spanish.

The Viura is the most used grape in white Rioja.

conditions. The influence of the Bordelaise is sometimes apparent even in today's Rioja wines.

Which grapes are used in Rioja wines?

The major grapes used in Rioja wine are:

Tempranillo   Garnacha

These grapes are blended with others to give Rioja wines their distinctive taste. On some labels you will see the word *"cosecha,"* which in Spanish means "harvest" or "vintage."

Spain's Wine Renaissance

Spain is the world's third-largest producer of wine, behind France and Italy. Spain has more land dedicated to vines than any other country: 4.5 million acres!

Spain is also a country with a rich winemaking tradition. Many types of wine are produced: Cava (*Méthode Champenoise* sparkling wines) are produced in the Penedés region not far from Barcelona. Red wines and rosés are produced throughout the entire country. Fortified wines are produced mainly in the south. The best-known region for such wines is Jerez (Sherry).

A 20th-century renaissance extends nationwide to Spain's wine industry, where tremendous investments have been made throughout the country in viticulture and winemaking equipment. In Rioja alone, the number of wineries has increased from 42 to 184 since 1982.

Have Rioja wines changed in style over the last twenty years?

Yes, without a doubt. As has been the case in countries like Chile and Italy, modern technology and new viticultural procedures have made for much better wines, many of which merit long-term aging. In particular, wines that in the past were aged for a long time in wood—both reds and whites—are now being taken out of the wood sooner and placed in the bottle to retain the fruit flavor.

Why are Rioja wines so easy to understand?

All you need to know when buying a Rioja wine is the style (level) and the reputation of the Rioja winemaker/shipper. The grape varieties are not found on the wine labels, and there's no classification to be memorized. The three major levels of Rioja wines are:

1. *Crianza* ($)—released after two years of aging, with a minimum of one year in oak barrels
2. *Reserva* ($$)—released after three years of aging, with a minimum of one year in oak barrels
3. *Gran Reserva* ($$$$)—released after five to seven years of aging, with a minimum of two years in oak barrels

How would I know which Rioja wine to buy in the store?

You mean besides going with your preferred style and the reputation of the winemaker/shipper? You may also be familiar with a Rioja wine by its proprietary name. The following are some bodegas to look for, along with some of their better-known proprietary names:

Bodegas Muga—Muga Reserva, Prado Enea, Torremuga
Remelluri
Contino
Bodegas Riojanas—Monte Real, Viña Albina

Although there are nearly 800 different wineries in Spain, about 80% of its production comes from a handful of companies.

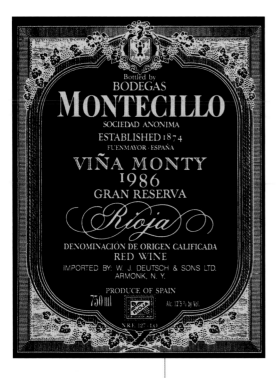

C.U.N.E.—Imperial, Viña Real
Marqués de Cáceres
Marqués de Riscal
Marqués de Murrieta
Bodegas Montecillo—Viña Cumbrero, Viña Monty
La Rioja Alta—Viña Alberdi, Viña Ardanza
Martínez Bujanda—Conde de Valdemar
Bodegas Breton
Palacios Remondo

Best Bets for Rioja
1982 1989 1990 1994 1995 1996 1997

The two other famous winegrowing regions in Spain are Penedés (outside Barcelona) and the Ribera del Duero (between Madrid and Rioja). The most famous wine of the Penedés region is the sparkling wine called "cava," of which the two best-known names in the United States are Codorniu and Freixenet. These are two of the biggest producers of bottle-fermented sparkling wine in the world, and one of the best features of these wines is their reasonable price. The Penedés region is also known for high-quality table wine. The major producer of this region (and synonymous with the quality of the area) is the Torres family. Their famous wine, Gran Coronas Black Label, is made with 100 percent Cabernet Sauvignon, and is rare and expensive, though the Torres family produces a full range of fine Spanish wines in all price categories.

The Ribera del Duero has been around since the 1800s (though it was officially delimited in 1982), but is now becoming quite prominent in the United States. It's considered to be the "new" area of Spain. One of the most expensive Spanish wines, called Vega Sicilia, is produced there. Two others, which are less expensive but more readily available, are called Pesquera and Viña Mayor.

Further reading: *The Wines of Rioja,* by Hubrecht Duijker.

Ribera del Duero wines are made from the Tinto Fino grape, a close cousin of Rioja's Tempranillo. The laws also allow the use of Cabernet Sauvignon, Malbec, Merlot, and small amounts of a white grape called Albillo.

Priorato
This area just south of Barcelona near the Mediterranean produces some of the fullest-bodied wines of Spain, primarily from the Garnacha grape.

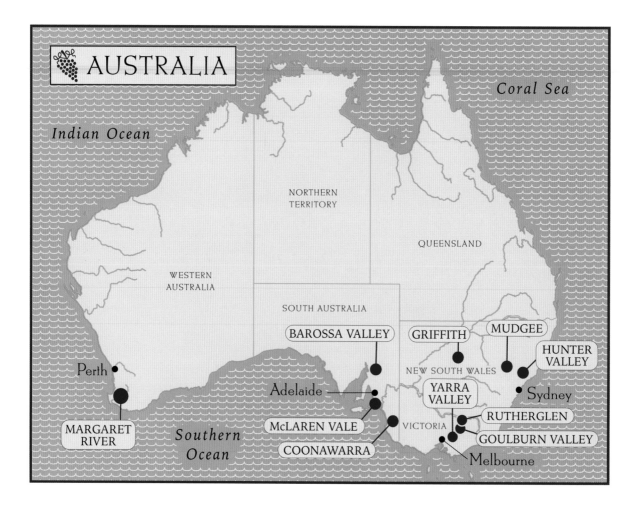

The Wines of Australia

There are about forty distinct winegrowing regions in Australia, with over eighty districts and subdistricts. Do you need to know them all? Probably not, but within Australia's six states you should be familiar with the best districts in four of them:

New South Wales (N.S.W.)
—Griffith, Hunter Valley, Mudgee

South Australia (S.A.)
—Barossa Valley, McLaren Vale, Coonawarra

Victoria (Vic.)
—Yarra Valley, Goulburn Valley, Rutherglen

Western Australia (W.A.)
—Margaret River, Pemberton

The wine industry is by no means new to Australia. In fact, many of Australia's leading wine companies were established more than 175 years ago. Lindemans, Penfolds, Orlando, Henschke, and Seppelt are just a few of the companies that were founded during the 19th century. They are now among Australia's largest, or most prestigious, companies, and they produce excellent wines.

The Top Five Australian Wine Brands Imported into the U.S.
Lindemans
Rosemount Estate
Black Opal
Jacob's Creek
Hardy's

The Australian wine industry began in 1788 with the planting of Australia's first grapevines.

Australian wine exports to the United States
1989   1 million cases
2000   7 million cases

In 1832, James Busby brought back Shiraz cuttings from the Chapoutier vineyards in the Rhône Valley, which he planted in the Hunter Valley.

In the 1830s, Cabernet Sauvignon vine cuttings from Château Haut-Brion in Bordeaux were planted near Melbourne.

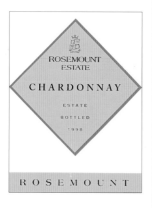

Aussie reds on the Move: Only a few years ago, 65% of Australian wine grapes were white varieties. Today, white wines account for 53% and the reds contribute the remaining 47% to the harvest.

Which grape varieties are grown in Australia?

Major red-grape varieties are:

Shiraz—Called Syrah in the Rhône Valley of France, it can produce spicy, robust, long-lived, and full-bodied wines. It is the most widely planted red grape in Australia.

Cabernet Sauvignon—As in Bordeaux and California, it produces some of the best wines in the country. Always dry, and depending on the producer and the region, Cabernet yields wines that range in style from medium to extremely full-bodied. It is often blended with Shiraz.

Pinot Noir—The great grape of Burgundy. In many cooler districts of Victoria, South Australia, and Western Australia, it is beginning to show signs of reaching quality levels similar to those of its famous brethren.

Merlot—A relative newcomer to Australia, but it is quickly gaining on Pinot Noir in terms of production.

The main white-grape varieties are:

Chardonnay—As in Burgundy and California, Chardonnay makes dry, full-flavored wines, as well as being the base wine for sparkling wines.

Sémillon—In France, this grape is blended with Sauvignon Blanc to make white Bordeaux. In Australia it makes medium-style dry wines, is often blended with Chardonnay, and the best can benefit from aging.

Riesling—A variety also grown in Germany, Alsace, and California, this grape ranges in style from dry to sweet.

Sauvignon Blanc—Over the past few years, this grape has shown the largest increase in Australia's white wine production.

What kinds of wine are produced in Australia?

Australia produces many different kinds of table wine, ranging from light, fruit-driven whites made from blends of grapes from different areas to vineyard-specific, barrel-aged reds from vines over 100 years old. It is not unusual to find Shiraz on original—not grafted—rootstock, because many of Australia's wine regions were not affected by phylloxera or other diseases.

Among the most interesting winemaking practices of Australia are the white blends made from Chardonnay and Sémillon and the red blends made of Cabernet and Shiraz. Many of these represent high quality at reasonable prices, and they are also very enjoyable everyday wines.

How are wines labeled?

Effective with the 1990 vintage, the Australian wine industry's Label Integrity Program (L.I.P.) took effect. Although it does not govern as many aspects as France's A.O.C. laws, the L.I.P. does regulate and oversee vintage, varietal, and geographical indication claims. In order to conform to L.I.P. and other regulations set by the Australian Food Standards Code, Australian wine labels, such as the one below, give a great deal of information.

One of the most important pieces of information is the producer's name. In this case, the producer is Penfolds. If a single grape variety is printed on the label, the wine must be made from at least 85 percent of that variety. In a blend listing the varieties, as above, the percentages of each must be shown. (Note that the first grape listed is always the larger percentage.) If the label specifies a particular wine-growing district (for example, Clare Valley), at least 85 percent of the wine must originate there. If a vintage is given, 95 percent of the wine must be of that vintage.

What about vintages?

Australian winegrowing regions extend across 3,000 miles with many diverse climatic and microclimatic conditions. As in California, there are not the extreme highs and lows that one may find in European vineyards, which is why I sometimes refer to them as "hassle free" vintages. Case in point: Over the past ten years, Australia has had a string of good-to-great vintages. As for value, the Australian dollar in 1999 was worth less than 80% of our own, so Australian wines remain an excellent buy.

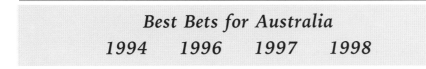

Best Bets for Australia
1994   1996   1997   1998

Up until the 1960s, Australian wine was primarily sweet wine and port-like products. The Australians have graduated (with honors, I might add) to producing excellent dry table wines, but many of the best producers still pride themselves on luscious "stickies," the Australian term for dessert wine. They do tawnies, late-harvest, and *botrytis* (Sémillon and Riesling, mainly) wines that are well-priced and world class. Note those of Peter Lehmann, Cranswick Estate, and Yalumba, for example.

Out of the 120 different Australian wineries distributed in the United States, here is my list of the top wineries: Hardy's, Lindemans, Orlando, Michelton, Yalumba, Rothbury, Penfolds, Petaluma, Rosemount, Wolf Blass, Henschke, Mountadam, D'Arenberg, Peter Lehmann, Leeuwin.

"Cask" or "bag-in-box" are Australian wine terms for bulk or "jug" wines.

The vintage in Australia occurs in the first half of the year. The grapes are harvested from February to May. For any given vintage, Australia will have its wines approximately six months before Europe or America.

The 1998 vintage in Australia was the largest harvest ever, and one of the finest.

CHILE AND ARGENTINA

Pacific Ocean

CHILE

ARGENTINA

Santiago ★

Buenos Aires ★

Atlantic Ocean

ACONCAGUA

CASABLANCA

Santiago ★

MAIPO

RAPEL

MENDOZA

CURICÓ

ARGENTINA

CHILE

The Wines of South America: Chile & Argentina

Chile

Why is Chile the hottest wine-growing region in the world?

First and foremost is the quality of the wines vs. the price. In my opinion, the best value in red wines of the world comes from Chile. These are definitely the best South American wines today.

I did not include the wines of Chile in the first edition of this book, in 1985, but I followed the country's progress from the sidelines while tremendous expansion was taking place with plantings of international grape varieties. Since my most recent visit to wine country there, tasting the fruit of their labor, I am absolutely convinced that the Chileans are producing world-class wines, especially the reds.

Why did it take so long for Chile to produce world-class wines?

Chile has been making wine for almost 450 years, since the first grapes were planted in Chile in 1551 and the first wine was produced in 1555. Things really started getting interesting in the mid-1800s when French varietals such as Cabernet Sauvignon and Merlot were imported into Chile.

But all this progress came to a grinding halt in 1938 when the government of Chile decreed that no new vineyards could be planted. This

The number-one wine imported into the United States is Concha y Toro.

After Italy and France, Chile is the third largest exporter of wine to the United States.

Exports to the U.S.: In 1996, Chile exported 100,000 cases of wine to the U.S. In 1998, Chilean wine exports increased to over three million cases.

The country of Chile runs almost 2,500 miles, north to south.

Chile is the largest importer of stainless-steel fermentor tanks in the world.

In 1995 there were only twelve wineries in Chile. Today there are over seventy.

Wine Regions and Their Specialties

REGION	SPECIALTY
Casablanca	Chardonnay and Sauvignon Blanc
Maipo Valley	Cabernet Sauvignon
Rapel	Merlot

In 1985 there were thirty acres of Chardonnay planted in Chile.

Cabernet Sauvignon accounts for 47% of the total acreage of premium grapes planted in Chile.

Which Grape Is It?
It was recently discovered that 40% of the Merlot planted in Chile is not really Merlot, but another grape called Carmenere.

law lasted until 1974. The renaissance or the modern wine industry of Chile really only began in the early 1980s, when the new technology of stainless-steel fermentors and the old technology of French oak barrels were combined to produce higher-quality wines.

What's happening in Chile today?

It's exciting. Going to Chile today is like going to California 25 years ago. And like California and Australia, there's no tradition of technique. Chile is a work in progress.

The Chilean winemakers have everything going for them: The economy is better than ever, the climate in Chile is between that of California and Bordeaux, and those Andes are spectacular. No matter where you are in the country, those majestic, snowcapped Andes always catch your eye.

What are the major winemaking regions in Chile?

There are twelve different regions for wine production in Chile. The six most important are:

Aconcagua Valley	1,000 acres
Casablanca Valley	5,000 acres
Maipo Valley	16,000 acres
Curicó Valley	29,000 acres
Rapel Valley	31,000 acres
Maule	41,000 acres

What are the major grapes grown in Chile?

The main white varieties are:

Sauvignon Blanc	15,848 acres
Chardonnay	14,353 acres
Muscat	13,400 acres

The main red varieties are:

Cabernet Sauvignon	38,547 acres
País (Mission Grape)	36,872 acres
Merlot	13,040 acres

How do I buy the wines of Chile?

Almost all Chilean wines are dry, and there are no official classifications. Most of the wineries in Chile produce wines of different quality levels and price points, and label their wines by grape variety. The wine laws are very much like those in California. For example, if the grape variety is named on the label, the wine must contain a minimum of 75 percent of that grape. The best Chilean wineries also have their own special names for their highest-quality wines.

The best way to buy Chilean wines is from the top producers. The following is a list of my favorite wineries. In parentheses are names of best wines:

Caliterra (Reserve)
Carmen
Casa Lapostolle (Cuvée Alexandre)
Concha y Toro (Don Melchor)
Cousiño Macul (Finis Terrae)
Domaine Paul Bruno
Errazúriz (Don Maximiano)
Los Vascos (Reserva de Familia)
Montes (Alpha)
Santa Rita (Casa Real)
Seña
Stonelake
Undurraga (Reserve)
Veramonte (Primus)

The Seven Largest Wineries in Chile

WINERY	DATE FOUNDED
Concha y Toro	1883
San Pedro	1865
Santa Rita	1880
Santa Carolina	1875
Errazúriz	1870
Undurraga	1885
Viña Canepa	1930

Chile is a melting pot of Germans, French, Spanish, Italians, and Swiss.

The French Connection

(French Investment in Chile)

FRENCH INVESTOR	CHILEAN WINERY
Grand Marnier	Casa Lapostolle
Domaines Lafite Rothschild	Los Vascos
Bruno Prats & Paul Pontalier	Aquitania/Paul Bruno
William Fèvre	Fèvre
Château Larose-Trintaudon	Casas del Toqui
Baron Philippe de Rothschild	Concha y Toro

Other foreign investors in Chile include:

Robert Mondavi (Mondavi Winery, California)	Seña
Augustin Hunneus (Franciscan Winery, California)	Veramonte
Miguel Torres (Torres Winery, Spain)	Miguel Torres Winery

Best Bets for Chile: Red Vintages
1990   1992   1994   1997

Will Chilean wines age?

On my most recent visit to Chile, I was lucky enough to taste the 1969, 1965, and 1960 vintages of Cousiño Macul Antiguas Cabernet Sauvignon, which were just coming into their prime.

Argentina

What's happening in Argentina?

Great things are happening in Argentina's wine industry! A growing number of wineries have changed their philosophy and now concentrate on producing higher-quality wines rather than manufacturing large quantities.

Until recently, Argentina was more interested in producing inexpensive bulk wine. Now its winemakers are beginning to understand the worldwide demand for quality wine. Still today 90 percent of Argentina's wine is consumed in Argentina, which is the problem.

As it was in Spain and Italy twenty years ago (and Chile ten years ago), wineries were confronted with the dilemma of whether to produce wine for the domestic market—wine that was sometimes bland and oxidized—or trying to make better wine for the export market. Today a new, higher style of Argentinian wine is emerging.

You are very lucky if you are just starting out with Chilean wine. The 1997, which is available now, was one of the best vintages ever produced in Chile.

The 1999 Chilean harvest is one of the smallest in years, due to severe drought conditions.

Argentina has been producing wine for over 400 years. The first grapes in Argentina were planted in 1554.

Argentina is the largest producer of wines in South America. It's the fifth-largest wine producer in the world. Argentina is also the fourth-largest consumer per capita of wines in the world.

When it comes to quality, 5% of the wines of Argentina were considered quality in 1973. Today, 25% are considered quality wines.

Why has it taken so long for Argentina to become a player in the wine world?

Any wine region must have capital to produce great wine. In the last five years, more investment has been poured into Argentina's wine industry than over the past fifty years.

Who's investing in Argentina?

From California, Jess Jackson (Kendall-Jackson); from Bordeaux, Jean Michel Arcaute (Château Clinet); the owners of Château Cheval Blanc; and also from Bordeaux, the Lurton family.

Even wineries from Chile, such as Concha y Toro and Santa Rita, are investing their money and expertise in Argentina.

Why is Argentina easier to understand than Chile?

Think red. Think Mendoza. Think Malbec. The best wines of Argentina are red. The major region is Mendoza, which produces 75 percent of all wines coming from Argentina. Malbec is the best quality grape planted in Mendoza. Other red grapes produced are Cabernet Sauvignon and Merlot. In the future, look for Syrah.

How do I buy wine from Argentina?

As with Chile, buy from the best producers. There are eighty wineries in Argentina, but at this time, you only need to know a dozen:

1. Bianchi	7. Lopez
2. Catena	8. Luis Bosca
3. Esmeralda	9. Navarro Correas
4. Etchart	10. Norton
5. Finca Flichman	11. Trapiche
6. Mariposa	12. Weinert

Best Bets for Argentina
1996   1997

Argentina's European Ancestry

"They like to dress like the English, talk like the French, and they think they're Italian."

All varietal wines are 100% the grape named.

With 300 days of sunshine and only eight inches of rain annually, the Argentinians have set up an elaborate network of canals and dams to irrigate their vineyards.

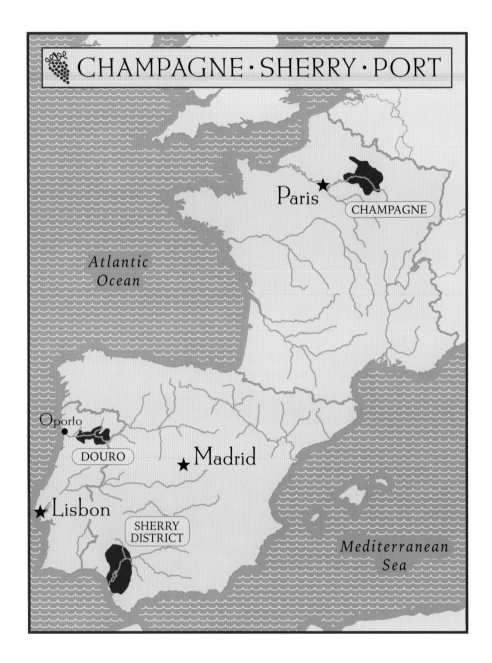

Champagne, Sherry, and Port

Now we're beginning our last class—the last chapter on the wine itself. This is where the course ends—on a happy note, I might add. What better way to celebrate than with Champagne?

Why do I group Champagne, Sherry, and Port together? Because as diverse as these wines are, the way the consumer will buy them is through the reputation and reliability of the shipper. Since these are all blended wines, the shipper is responsible for all phases of the production—you concern yourself with the house style. In Champagne, for example, Moët & Chandon is a well-known house; in Port, the house of Sandeman; and in Sherry, the house of Pedro Domecq.

> The Champagne region covers about 85,000 acres, or 2.5% of French vineyards. Production is about 280 million bottles a year, which represents about 10% of world production of sparkling wines.

Champagne

What's Champagne?

We all know that Champagne is a sparkling bubbly that everyone drinks on New Year's Eve. It's more than that. Champagne is a region in France—the country's northernmost winemaking region, to be exact—and it's an hour and a half northeast of Paris.

Why do I stress its northern location? Because this affects the taste of the wines. In the Champagne region, the grapes are picked with higher acidity than in most other regions, which is one of the reasons for Champagne's distinct taste. The Champagne region is divided into four main areas:

> Acidity in Champagne not only gives freshness to the wines, but is also important to their longevity.
>
> The balance of the fruit and acidity, together with the bubbles (CO_2), are what make good Champagne.

Valley of the Marne   **Côte des Blancs**

Mountain of Reims   **Côte des Bar**

Three grapes can be used to produce Champagne:

Pinot Noir—accounts for 37 percent of all grapes planted.

Pinot Meunier—accounts for 37 percent of all grapes planted.

Chardonnay—accounts for 26 percent of all grapes planted.

In France, only sparkling wines that come from the region of Champagne may be called "Champagne." Some American producers have borrowed the name "Champagne" to put on the label of their sparkling wines. These cannot and should not be compared with Champagne from France.

What are the three major types of Champagne?

- **non-vintage/multiple vintage**—a blend of different years
- **vintage**—from a single vintage
- **"prestige" cuvée**—from a single vintage with longer aging requirements

Why is there such a tremendous price difference between non-vintage and "prestige" cuvée Champagnes?

"Prestige" Champagnes usually meet the following requirements to be designated as such:

- Made from the best grapes of the highest-rated villages
- Made from the first pressing of the grapes
- Spent more time aging in the bottle than non-vintage Champagnes
- Made only in vintage years
- Made in small quantity, and the demand is high. Price is dictated largely by supply and demand.

Non-vintage Champagne is more typical of the house style than vintage Champagne.

Vintage Champagne must contain 100% of that vintage year's harvest.

Over 80% of the Champagnes produced are not vintage dated. This means they are blends of several years' wines.

Dom Pérignon Champagne is aged six to eight years before it is put on the market.

Is every year a vintage year?

No, but 1985, 1986, 1988, 1989, 1990, 1995, 1996, and 1997 were. *Note:* These were vintage years for most Champagne houses. "Vintage" in Champagne is different from other wine regions, because each house makes its own determination on whether or not to declare a vintage year.

How's Champagne made?

Champagne is made by a process called *Méthode Champenoise,* which begins with Champenois soil and climate. When a similar method is used outside La Champagne, it is called *Méthode Traditionnelle* or Classic Method or *Método Tradicional,* etc. The use of the expression *Méthode Champenoise* is not allowed in the European Union outside of Champagne.

Méthode Champenoise

Harvest—The normal harvest usually takes place in late September or early October.

Pressing the Grapes—Only two pressings of the grapes are permitted. Prestige cuvée Champagnes are usually made exclusively from the first pressing. The second pressing, called the *taille,* is generally blended with the cuvée to make vintage and non-vintage Champagnes.

Fermentation—All Champagnes undergo a first fermentation when the grape juice is converted into wine. Remember the formula: Sugar + Yeast = Alcohol + CO_2. The carbon dioxide dissipates. The first fermentation takes two to three weeks and produces still wines.

Blending—The most important step in Champagne production is the blending of the still wines. Each of these still wines is made from a single grape variety from a single village of origin. The winemaker has to make many decisions here. Three of the most important ones are: 1) Which grapes to blend—how much Chardonnay, Pinot Noir, and Pinot Meunier? 2) From which vineyards should the grapes come? 3) Which years or vintages should be blended? Should the blend be made only from the wines of the harvest, or should several vintages be blended together?

Liqueur de Tirage—After the blending process, the winemaker adds *Liqueur de Tirage*—a blend of sugar and yeast—which will begin the wine's second fermentation. At this point, the wine is placed in its permanent bottle with a temporary bottle cap.

Second Fermentation—During this fermentation, the carbon dioxide stays in the bottle. This is where the bubbles come from. The second fermentation also leaves natural sediments in the bottle. Now the problems begin. How do you get rid of the sediments without losing the carbon dioxide? Go on to the next steps.

Shippers don't always agree on the quality of the wines produced in any given vintage, so the years for vintage Champagnes vary from shipper to shipper. Each house usually declares a vintage three years out of each decade.

Two methods of making rosé Champagne: 1) add red wine to the blend; 2) leave the red grape skins in contact with the must for a short period of time.

Wine presses are placed throughout the vineyards so the winemaker can press the grapes immediately without extracting any of their color.

Most Champagnes are fermented in stainless steel.

151

Classic Champagnes (non-vintage) must be aged for a minimum of fifteen months in the bottle after bottling. Vintage Champagnes must be aged for a minimum of three years after bottling.

Aging—The amount of time the wine spends aging on its sediments is one of the most important factors in determining the quality of the wine.

Riddling—The wine bottles are now placed in A-frame racks, necks down. The *remueur*, or riddler, goes through the racks of Champagne bottles and gives each bottle a slight turn while gradually tipping the bottle farther downward. After six to eight weeks, the bottle stands almost completely upside down, with the sediments resting in the neck of the bottle.

Dégorgement—The top of the bottle is dipped into a brine solution to freeze it, and then the temporary bottle cap is removed and out fly the frozen sediments, propelled by the carbon dioxide.

Dosage—A combination of wine and cane sugar is added to the bottle after *dégorgement*. At this point, the winemaker can determine whether he wants a sweeter or a drier Champagne.

Recorking—The wine is recorked with real cork instead of a bottle cap.

Until around 1850, all Champagne was sweet.

Occasionally a Champagne will be labeled "extra brut," which is drier still than brut.

Dosage

The dosage determines whether the wine will be the driest style, brut, a sweet demi-sec or any style in between. The following shows you the guidelines the winemaker uses when he adds the dosage.

**Brut—driest   Extra dry—less dry   Sec—more sweet
Demi-sec—sweetest**

Brut and extra-dry are the wines to serve as apéritifs, or throughout the meal. Sec and Demi-sec are the wines to serve with desserts and wedding cake!

Blanc de Blancs is white wine made from 100% white grapes—Chardonnay.

What accounts for the different styles of Champagne?

Going back to the three grapes we talked about that are used to make Champagne, the general rule is:

The more white grapes in the blend, the lighter the style of the Champagne.

The more red grapes in the blend, the fuller the style of the Champagne.

Also, some producers ferment their wines in wood. Bollinger ferments some, and Krug ferments all their wines this way. This gives the Champagne fuller body and bouquet than those fermented in stainless steel.

How do I buy a good Champagne?

First, determine the style you prefer, whether full-bodied or light-bodied, a dry brut or a sweet demi-sec. Then make sure you buy your Champagne from a reliable shipper/producer. Each producer takes pride in its distinctive house style, and strives for a consistent blend, year after year.

The following are some brands in national distribution to look for. While it is difficult to be precise, the designations generally conform to the style of the houses.

Light, Delicate
A. Charbaut et Fils
Jacquesson
Lanson

Light to Medium
Billecart-Salmon
Deutz
Nicolas Feuillatte
Laurent-Perrier
G.H. Mumm
Perrier-Jouët
Pommery
Ruinart Père & Fils
Taittinger

Medium
Charles Heidsieck
Moët & Chandon
Piper-Heidsieck
Pol Roger

Medium to Full
Henriot
Louis Roederer

Full, Rich
Bollinger
A. Gratien
Krug
Veuve Clicquot

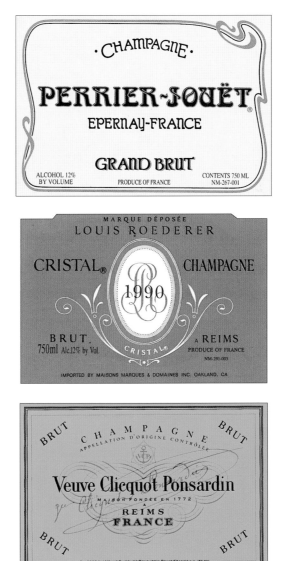

The top five Champagne houses in shipments to the United States in 1999:
Moët & Chandon
Veuve Clicquot
Perrier-Jouët
Mumm
Taittinger

There are more than 100 Champagne houses in France and about 40 Champagnes available in the United States.

Champagne houses market about two-thirds of Champagne's wines, but they own less than ten percent of the vineyards.

When is Champagne ready to drink?

As soon as you buy it. Champagne is something you can drink right away. Non-vintage Champagnes are meant to be drunk within two to three years, and vintage and prestige cuvée Champagnes can be kept longer, about ten to fifteen years. So if you're still saving that Dom Pérignon that you received for your 10th wedding anniversary fifteen years ago, don't wait any longer. Open it!!

"It's not a Burgundy; it's not a Bordeaux; it's a white wine; it's a sparkling wine that should be kept no longer than two to three years. It should be consumed young."

—*Claude Taittinger*

The pressure in a bottle of Champagne is close to 90 pounds per square inch (or "six atmospheres," or roughly three times the pressure in your automobile tire).

Champagne is put into heavy bottles to hold the pressurized wine. This is another reason why Champagne is more expensive than ordinary wine.

Women and Champagne
Women, particularly ones attached to royal courts, deserve much of the credit for Champagne's international fame. Madame de Pompadour said that Champagne was the only drink that left a woman still beautiful after drinking it. Madame de Parabère once said that Champagne was the only wine to give brilliance to the eyes without flushing the face.

It is rumored that Marilyn Monroe once took a bath in 350 bottles of Champagne. Her biographer George Barris said that she drank and breathed Champagne "as if it were oxygen."

When a London reporter asked Madame Lilly Bollinger when she drank Champagne, Madame Bollinger replied: "I drink it when I'm happy and when I'm sad. Sometimes I drink it when I'm alone. When I have company I consider it obligatory. I trifle with it if I'm not hungry and drink it when I am. Otherwise I never touch it—unless I'm thirsty."

As beautiful as Helen was, the resulting glass was admittedly wide and shallow.

What's the correct way to open a bottle of Champagne?

Before we sip Champagne in class, I always take a few moments to show everyone how to open a bottle of Champagne properly. I do this for a good reason. Opening a bottle of Champagne can be dangerous, and I'm not kidding. I've always stressed this to all the servers and captains at Windows on the World. If you know the pounds per square inch that are under pressure in the bottle, you know what I'm talking about.

Opening Champagne Correctly

1. It is especially important that the bottle be chilled before you open it.

2. Cut the foil around the top of the bottle.

3. Place your hand on top of the cork, never removing your hand until the cork is pulled out completely. (I know this may seem a bit awkward, but it's very important.)

4. Undo the wire. At this point, it is probably safer to leave the wire on.

5. Carefully put a cloth napkin over the top of the cork; in case the cork pops, it will go safely into the napkin.

6. Remove the cork gently, slowly turning the bottle in one direction and the cork in another. The idea behind opening a bottle is to ease the cork out gently rather than cracking the bottle open with a loud pop and letting it foam. That may be a lot of fun, but it does nothing for the Champagne. When you pop off the cork, you allow the carbon dioxide to escape. That carbon dioxide is what gives Champagne its sparkle. If you open a bottle of Champagne in the way I've just described, then it can be opened hours before your guests arrive with no loss of carbon dioxide.

Which glasses should Champagne be served in?

No matter which Champagne you decide to serve, you should serve it in the proper glass. There's a little story behind the Champagne glass, dating back to Greek mythology. The first "coupe" was said to be molded from the breast of Helen of Troy. The Greeks believed that wine-drinking was a sensual experience, and it was only fitting that the most beautiful woman take part in shaping the chalice.

Centuries later, Marie Antoinette, Queen of France, decided it was time to create a new Champagne glass. She had coupes molded to her own breasts, which changed the shape of the glass entirely, since Marie Antoinette was—shall we say—a bit more endowed than Helen of Troy.

The glasses shown to the right are the ones commonly used today—the flute and the tulip-shaped glass. Champagne does not lose its bubbles as quickly in these glasses as it did in the old-fashioned model, and these shapes also enhance the smell and aromas of the wine in the glass.

How many bubbles are in a bottle of Champagne? According to scientist Bill Lembeck, 49 million bubbles per bottle!

WINE AND FOOD

Champagne is one of the most versatile wines that you can drink with a number of foods, from apéritif to dessert. Here are some Champagne-and-food combinations that a few experts suggest:

Christian Bizot (Bollinger)—Mr. Bizot's favorite accompaniments to Champagne are a cheese soufflé made with a mild cheese like Gruyère, or grilled fish with a light cream sauce, but not too spicy. He explains, "The heavier the food, the heavier the style of Champagne."

Another favorite of Mr. Bizot is Bollinger R.D. with game meats.

Some dishes that Mr. Bizot finds do *not* do justice to the wine: melon, because the sugary taste offsets the taste of the Champagne; vinegar, as in a salad dressing, or vinaigrette; any dessert with Brut Champagne.

Claude Taittinger (Taittinger)—Mr. Taittinger's general rule is: "Never with sweets." Instead, he offers, "May I suggest a Comtes de Champagne Blanc de Blancs drunk with seafood, caviar, or pâté of pheasant." Another note from Mr. Taittinger: He doesn't serve Champagne with cheese because, he says, "The bubbles do not go well." He prefers red wine with cheese.

Christian Pol Roger—With Brut non-vintage: light hors d'oeuvres, mousse of pike. With vintage: pheasant, lobster, other seafood. With rosé: a strawberry dessert.

What's the difference between Champagne and sparkling wine?

As I've already mentioned, Champagne is the wine that comes from the Champagne region of France. In my opinion, it is the best sparkling wine in the world, because the region has the ideal combination of elements conducive to excellent sparkling-wine making. The soil is fine chalk, the grapes are the best grown anywhere for sparkling wine, and the location is perfect. This combination of soil, climate, and grapes is reflected in the wine.

To evaluate Champagne, look at the bubbles. The better wines have smaller bubbles and more of them. Also, with a good Champagne, the bubbles last longer. Bubbles are an integral part of the wines of Champagne. They create texture and mouthfeel.

Domaine Chandon is owned by the Moët-Hennessy Group, which is responsible for the production of Dom Pérignon in France. In fact, the same winemaker is flown into California to make the blend for the Domaine Chandon.

Piper-Heidsieck has sold the Piper-Sonoma and its vineyards to Jordan Winery. Jordan will now produce the wines for Piper-Sonoma.

Champagne Bottle Sizes
Magnum—2 bottles
Jeroboam—4 bottles
Rehoboam—6 bottles
Methuselah—8 bottles
Salmanazar—12 bottles
Balthazar—16 bottles
Nebuchadnezzar—
   20 bottles

About 20% of the sparkling wines made in the United States are made by the *Méthode Champenoise*.

Sparkling wine, on the other hand, is produced in many areas, and the quality varies from wine to wine. The Spanish produce the popular Codorniu and Freixenet—both excellent values and good sparkling wines, known as *cavas*. The German version is called *Sekt*. Italy has *spumante,* which means "sparkling." The most popular Italian sparkling wine in the United States is Asti Spumante.

New York State and California are the two main producers of sparkling wine in this country. New York is known for Great Western, Taylor, and Gold Seal. California produces many fine sparkling wines, such as Chandon, Korbel, Piper-Sonoma, Schramsberg, Mumm Cuvée Napa, Roederer Estate, Domaine Carneros, Iron Horse, and "J", by Jordan Winery. Many of the larger California wineries also market their own sparkling wines.

Is there a difference between the way Champagne and sparkling wines are made?

Sometimes. All authentic Champagnes and many fine sparkling wines are produced by *Méthode Champenoise,* described earlier in this chapter, and which, as you can see, is laborious, intensive, and very expensive. If you see a bottle of sparkling wine for $3.99, you can bet that the wine was not made by this process. The inexpensive sparkling wines are made by other methods. For example, in one method the secondary fermentation takes place in large tanks. Sometimes these tanks are big enough to produce 100,000 bottles of sparkling wine.

Sherry

The two greatest fortified wines in the world are Port and Sherry. These wines have much in common, although the end result is two very different styles.

What exactly is fortified wine?

Fortified wine is made when a neutral grape brandy is added to wine to raise the wine's alcohol content. What sets Port apart from Sherry is *when* the winemaker adds the neutral brandy. It's added to Port *during* fermentation. The extra alcohol kills that yeast and stops the fermentation, which is why Port is relatively sweet. For Sherry, on the other hand, the brandy is added after fermentation.

Where is Sherry made?

Sherry is produced in sunny southwestern Spain, in Andalusia. An area within three towns makes up the Sherry triangle. They are:

> **Jerez de la Frontera**
> **Puerto de Santa María**
> **Sanlúcar de Barrameda**

Which grapes are used to make Sherry?

There are two main varieties:

> **Palomino** (this shouldn't be too difficult for horse lovers to remember)
> **Pedro Ximénez** (named after Peter Siemons, who brought the grape from Germany to Sherry)

What are the different types of Sherry:

> **Manzanilla**—dry
> **Fino**—dry
> **Amontillado**—dry to medium-dry
> **Oloroso**—dry to medium-dry
> **Cream**—sweet

Another fortified wine is Madeira. Although it is not as popular as it once was, Madeira wine was probably the first wine imported into America. It was favored by the colonists, including George Washington, and was served to toast the Declaration of Independence.

The neutral grape brandy, when added to the wine, raises the alcohol content to 15%–20%.

Two other famous fortified wines are Marsala (from Italy) and Vermouth (from Italy and France).

For you historians, Puerto de Santa María is where Christopher Columbus's ships were built and where all the arrangements were made with Queen Isabella for his journey of discovery.

The Palomino grape accounts for 90% of the planted vineyards in Sherry.

Here's another abbreviation for you—PX. Do you remember B.A.T.F., T.B.A., QbA, A.O.C., and D.O.C.? If you want to know Sherry, you may have to say "PX," which is the abbreviation for the Pedro Ximénez grape.

PX is used to make Cream Sherry, like Harvey's Bristol Cream, among others. Cream Sherry is a blend of PX and Oloroso.

What are the unique processes that characterize Sherry production?

Controlled oxidation and fractional blending. Normally a winemaker guards against letting any air into the wine during the winemaking process. But that's exactly what *makes* Sherry—the air that oxidizes the wine. The winemaker places the wine in barrels and stores it in a bodega.

What's a bodega?

No, I'm not talking about a Latino grocery store at 125th Street and Lexington Avenue in New York City. In Spain, a *bodega* is an above-ground structure used to store wine. Why do you think winemakers would want to store the wine above ground? For the air. Sherry is an oxidized wine. They fill the barrels approximately two-thirds full, instead of all the way, and they leave the bung (cork) loosely in the barrel to let the air in.

> ### The Angel's Share
>
> When Sherry is made, not only do winemakers let air into the barrels, but some wine evaporates as well. Each year they lose a minimum of 3% of their Sherry to the angels, which translates into 7,000 bottles *per day* lost through evaporation!
>
> Why do you think the people of Sherry are so happy all the time? Besides the excellent sunshine they have, the people breathe in oxygen *and* Sherry.
>
> So much for controlled oxidation. Now for fractional blending. Fractional blending is carried out through the *Solera System*.

What's the Solera System?

The Solera System is an aging and maturing process that takes place through the dynamic and continuous blending of several vintages of Sherry that are stored in rows of barrels. At bottling time, wine is drawn out of these barrels—never more than one-third the content of the barrel—to make room for the new vintage. The purpose of this type of blending is to maintain the "house" style of the Sherry by using the "mother" wine as a base and refreshing it with a portion of the younger wines.

How do I buy Sherry?

Your best guide is the producer. It's the producer, after all, who buys the grapes and does the blending. Ten producers account for sixty percent of the export market:

Sherry accounts for less than 3% of Spanish wine production.

In today's Sherry, only American oak is used to age the wine.

Some Soleras can be a blend of 10–20 different harvests.

I'm sure you're familiar with these four top-selling Sherries: Harvey's Bristol Cream, Dry Sack, Tio Pepe, and La Ina.

The Top Sherry Producers

1. González Byass
2. Croft
3. Pedro Domecq
4. Harvey's
5. Sandeman

6. Williams & Humbert
7. Savory and James
8. Osborne
9. Emilio Lustau
10. Hidalgo

How long does a bottle of Sherry last once it's been opened?

Sherry will last longer than a regular table wine, because of its higher alcoholic content, which acts as a preservative. But once Sherry is opened, it *will* lose its freshness. To drink Sherry at its best, you should consume the bottle within two weeks of opening it and keep the opened bottle refrigerated. Manzanilla and Fino Sherry should be treated as white wines and consumed within a day or two.

Wine and Food

Mauricio González—He believes that Fino should always be served well chilled. He enjoys having Fino as an apéritif with Spanish tapas (hors d'oeuvres), but he also likes to complement practically any fish meal with the wine. Some of his suggestions: clams, shellfish, lobster, prawns, langoustines, fish soup, or a light fish, such as salmon.

José Ignacio Domecq—He suggests that very old and rare Sherry should be served with cheese. Fino and Manzanilla can be served as an apéritif or with light grilled or fried fish, or even smoked salmon. "You get the taste of the smoke better than if you have it with a white wine," says Mr. Domecq.

Amontillado is not to be consumed like a Fino. It should be served with light cheese, *chorizo* (sausage), ham, or shish kebab. It is a perfect complement to turtle soup or a consommé.

According to Mr. Domecq, dry Oloroso is known as a sporty drink in Spain—something to drink before hunting, riding, or sailing on a chilly morning.

With Cream Sherry, Mr. Domecq recommends cookies, pastries, and cakes. Pedro Ximénez, however, is better as a topping for vanilla ice cream or a dessert wine before coffee and brandy.

For further reading: *Sherry,* by Julian Jeffs.

To clarify the Sherry and rid it of all sediment, beaten egg whites are added to the wine. The question always comes up: "What do they do with the yolks?" Did you ever hear of flan? That's the puddinglike dessert made from all the yolks. In Sherry country, this dessert is called *tocino de cielo,* which translated means "the fat of the angels."

Of the Sherry consumed in Spain, 90% is Fino and Manzanilla. As one wine-maker said, "We ship the sweet and drink the dry."

Port

Port comes from the Douro region in northern Portugal. In fact, in recent years, to avoid the misuse of the name "Port" in other countries, the true Port from Portugal has been renamed "Porto" (for the name of the port city from which it's shipped).

Just a reminder: Neutral grape brandy is added to Port *during* fermentation, which stops the fermentation and leaves behind up to nine to eleven percent residual sugar. This is why Port is on the sweet side.

What are the two types of Port?

Wood Port—This type includes **Ruby Port,** which is dark and fruity, blended from young non-vintage wines (Cost: $); and **Tawny Port,** which is lighter and more delicate, blended from many vintages, aged in casks—sometimes up to forty years and longer (Cost: $$/$$$).

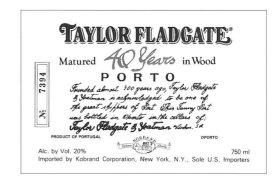

Vintage Port—This wine is aged two years in wood and will mature in the bottle over time (Cost: $$$$).

Is every year a vintage year for Port?

No, it varies from shipper to shipper. And in some years, no vintage Port is made at all. For example, in 1991 and 1994, two of the better vintages for Port, most producers declared a vintage. On the other hand, in 1990 and 1993, Port, in general, was not considered vintage quality.

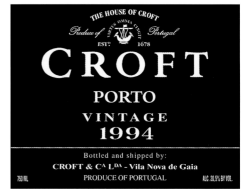

Port wine has been shipped to England since the 1670s. During the 1800s, to help preserve the Port for the long trip, shippers fortified it with brandy, resulting in Port as we know it today.

Port is usually 20% alcohol. Sherry, by comparison, is usually around 18%.

As with Sherry, evaporation is a problem—some 15,000 bottles evaporate into the air every year.

Another less expensive method of making Tawny Port is to add white Port to a young Tawny Port. A *true* Tawny Port is always expensive. You get what you pay for.

In France, the major importer of Port, the wine is used mainly as an apéritif.

In a typical year, 60% of the Port is Tawny and Ruby; 30% is vintage character; 7% is old Tawny; and 3% is vintage.

On average, only three years in ten are declared vintage years.

Wood Port vs. Vintage Port

The biggest difference between wood Port (Ruby and Tawny) and vintage Port is this: The wood Port is ready to drink as soon as it is bottled and it will not improve with age. Vintage Port, on the other hand, gets better as it matures in the bottle. A great vintage Port will be ready to drink fifteen to thirty years after the vintage date, depending upon the quality of the vintage.

How do I buy Port?

Once again, as with Sherry, the grape variety should not dictate your choice. Find the style and the blend you prefer, but even more important, look for the most reliable producers. Of the Port available in the United States, the most important producers are:

Cockburn
Croft
Dow
A. A. Ferreira
Fonseca
W. & J. Graham
Robertson's
Sandeman
Taylor Fladgate
Warre & Co.
Niepoort & Co., Ltd.
Quinta do Noval
Harvey's of Bristol
C. da Silva
Ramos Pinto

Best Bets for Vintages of Port

1963*	1966	1970*	1977*	1983	1985
1991	1992	1994*	1995	1997*	

*Note: *signifies exceptional vintage*

Vintage Port only began in 1870.

Other Port Styles

LBV ("Late Bottled Vintage")—a wood Port made from a single vintage, bottled four to six years after the harvest. Similar in style to vintage Port, but lighter, ready to drink on release, no decanting needed.

"Colheita"—also from a single vintage, but wood-aged a minimum of 7 years.

Vintage Character—similar style to LBV, but a blend of vintages from the better years.

Quinta means individual vineyard.

Of the Port made in Portugal, 85–90% is for export.

The British are known to be Port lovers. Traditionally, upon the birth of a child, parents buy bottles of Port to put away for the baby until its 21st birthday, not only the age of maturity of a child, but also that of a fine Port.

"The 1994 vintage is the greatest for Port since the legendary 1945."
—James Suckling, author, *Vintage Port*

There are more than
forty different grape
varieties planted in the
Douro region.

Should vintage Port be decanted?

Yes, because you are likely to find sediment in the bottle. By making it a
practice to decant vintage Port, you'll never be bothered by sediment.

How long will Port last once it's been opened?

Port has a tendency to last longer than ordinary table wine because of its
higher alcohol content. But if you want to drink Port at its prime, drink
the contents of the open bottle within one week.

Recommended reading: *Vintage Port: The Wine Spectator's Ultimate Guide,* by
James Suckling and *The Port Companion,* by Godfrey Spence.

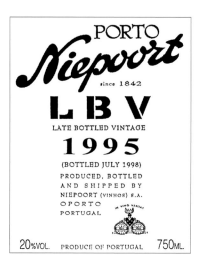

Matching Wine and Food

By Kevin Zraly and Andrea M. Immer

You've just tasted your way through eight chapters of this book and discovered at least a shopping-cart's worth of wines to really enjoy. And for what purpose? Food! The final stop on the wine odyssey—and the whole point of the trip—is the dinner table. Quite simply, wine and food were meant for each other. Just look at the dining habits of the world's best eaters (the French, the Italians, the Spanish); wine is the seasoning that livens up even everyday dishes. Salt and pepper shakers are a fixture of the American table, but in Europe it's the wine bottle.

Are you a menu maven or a wine-list junkie? Personally, I look at the wine list first, choose my wine, and then make my meal selection.

Wine-and-Food Matching Basics

First, forget everything you've ever heard about wine-and-food pairing. There's only one rule when it comes to matching wine and food: The best wine to pair with your meal is whatever wine you like. No matter what!

Here's where I get to turn the tables on one of New York's most famous gossip columnists, whose wine order at Windows on the World was always, no matter the dish, Pouilly-Fuissé—on the rocks! If you know what you want, by all means have it. Worried that your preference of a Chardonnay with a sirloin steak might not seem "right"? Remember, it's your own palate that you have to please.

Chardonnay is a red wine masquerading as a white wine, which, in my opinion, makes it a perfect match for steak.

What's wine-and-food synergy?

Sounds like a computer game for gourmets, right? If up until now you haven't been the wine-with-dinner type, you're in for a great adventure. Remember, the European tradition of wine with meals was not the result of a shortage of milk or iced tea. Rather, it results from what I call wine-and-food synergy—when the two are paired, both taste better.

How does it work? In the same way that combining certain foods improves their overall taste. For example, you squeeze fresh lemon onto your oysters, or grate parmesan cheese over spaghetti marinara, because it's the combination of flavors that makes the dish.

Now apply that idea to food-and-wine pairing; foods and wines have different flavors, textures, and aromas. Matching them can give you a new, more interesting flavor than you would get if you were washing down your dinner with, say, milk (unless you were dining on chocolate-chip cookies).

Do I have to be a wine expert to choose enjoyable wine-and-food matches?

Why not just use what you already know? Most of us have been tasting and testing the flavors, aromas, and textures of foods since before we got our first teeth, so we're all food experts! As I'll show you, just some basic information about wine and food styles is all you'll need to pick wines that can enhance your meals.

What about acidity?

Acid acts as a turbocharger for flavor. It enhances and lengthens the flavor of the dish. Watch television's Food Network. They're always using lemons and limes—acidic ingredients. Even dishes that aren't "sour" have a touch of an acid ingredient to pump up the flavor. As chef Emeril Lagasse says, "Kick it up a notch!"

What role does texture play?

There's an obvious difference in texture or firmness between different foods. Wine also has texture, and there are nuances of flavor in a wine that can make it an adequate, outstanding, or an unforgettable, selection with the meal. Very full-style wines have a mouth-filling texture and bold, rich flavors that make your palate sit up and take notice. But when it comes to food, these wines tend to overwhelm most delicate dishes (and clash with boldly flavored ones). Remember, we're looking for harmony. A general rule is, the sturdier or fuller in flavor the food, the more full-bodied the wine should be.

Once you get to know the wines, matching them with food is no mystery. Here is a list with some suggestions based on the texture of the wine and the foods they can match.

Probably one of the reasons that classic French cuisine is noted for its subtlety is because the French want to let their wines "show off." This is an especially good idea if the wine is a special or "splurge" bottle.

164

White Wines

Light-Bodied Whites	Medium-Bodied Whites	Full-Bodied Whites
Alsace Pinot Blanc	Pouilly-Fumé	Chardonnay*
Alsace Riesling	Sancerre	Chablis Grand Cru
Chablis	White Graves	Meursault
Muscadet	Chablis Premier Cru	Chassagne-Montrachet
German Kabinett and Spätlese	Mâcon-Villages	Puligny-Montrachet
Sauvignon Blanc*	Pouilly-Fuissé	Viognier
Orvieto	St-Véran	
Soave	Montagny	
Verdicchio	Sauvignon Blanc*/Fumé Blanc	
Frascati	Chardonnay*	
Pinot Grigio	Gavi	
	Gewürztraminer	

Matching Foods

sole	snapper	salmon
flounder	bass	tuna
clams	shrimp	swordfish
oysters	scallops	lobster
	veal paillard	duck
		roast chicken

A "fail-safe" food: When in doubt, order roast chicken, which acts like a blank canvas for almost any wine style—light, medium, or full-bodied.

When selecting a white wine to go with your meal, don't forget Champagne. After all, Champagne, before it actually becomes Champagne with its full bubbly splendor, is the ultimate white wine that is very versatile with food. (See page 153 for textures and styles of Champagne.)

*Note that starred wines are listed more than once. That's because they can be vinified in a range of styles from light to full, depending on the producer. When buying these, if you don't know the style of a particular winery, it's a good idea to ask the server or wine merchant for help.

Red Wines

Light-Bodied Reds	Medium-Bodied Reds	Full-Bodied Reds
Bardolino	Cru Beaujolais	Barbaresco
Valpolicella	Côtes du Rhône	Barolo
Chianti	Crozes-Hermitage	Bordeaux (great châteaux)*
Rioja-Crianza	Burgundy Premiers and Grands Crus	Châteauneuf-du-Pape
Beaujolais	Bordeaux (Crus Bourgeois)	Hermitage
Beaujolais-Villages	Cabernet Sauvignon*	Cabernet Sauvignon*
Burgundy (Village)	Merlot*	Merlot*
Barbera	Zinfandel*	Zinfandel*
Bordeaux (proprietary)	Chianti Classico Riserva	Syrah/Shiraz*
Pinot Noir*	Dolcetto	
	Rioja Reserva and Gran Reserva	
	Syrah/Shiraz*	
	Pinot Noir*	

Pinot Noir is a white wine masquerading as a red wine, which makes it a perfect wine for fish and fowl.

Matching Foods

salmon	game birds	lamb chops
tuna	veal chops	leg of lamb
swordfish	pork chops	beefsteak (sirloin)
duck		game meats
roast chicken		

*Note that starred wines are listed more than once. That's because they can be vinified in a range of styles from light to full, depending on the producer. When buying these, if you don't know the style of a particular winery, it's a good idea to ask the server or wine merchant for help.

Do sauces play a major role when you're matching wine and food?

Yes, because the sauce can change or define the entire taste and texture of a dish. Is the sauce acidic? Heavy? Spicy? Subtly flavored foods let the wine play the starring role. Dishes with bold, spicy ingredients can overpower the flavor nuances and complexity that distinguish a great wine.

Let's consider the effect sauces can have on a simple boneless breast of chicken. A very simply prepared chicken paillard might match well with a light-bodied white wine. If you add a rich cream sauce or a cheese sauce, then you might prefer a medium-bodied or even a full-bodied white wine. A red tomato-based sauce, such as a marinara, might call for a light-bodied red wine.

No-Fault Wine Insurance

Drinking wine with your meals should add enjoyment, not stress; but it happens all too often. You briefly eye the wine list or scan the wine-shop shelf, thinking well, maybe...a beer. In the face of so many choices, you end up going with the familiar. But it can be easy to choose a wine to enjoy with your meal.

From endless experimentation at home and in the restaurant, I've come up with a list of "user-friendly" wines that will go nicely with virtually any dish. What these wines have in common is that they are light- to medium-bodied, and they have ample fruit and acidity. The idea here is that you will get a harmonious balance of flavors from both the wine and the food, with neither overwhelming the other. Also, if you want the dish to play center stage, your best bets are wines from this list.

User-Friendly Wines

Rosé wines

Virtually any rosé or
  blush wine fills the bill

White wines

Pinot Grigio

Sauvignon Blanc/Fumé Blanc

German Riesling Kabinett
  and Spätlese

Pouilly-Fumé and Sancerre

Mâcon-Villages

Champagne and sparkling wines

Red Wines

Chianti Classico

Rioja Crianza

Beaujolais-Villages

Côtes du Rhône

Pinot Noir

Merlot

These wines work well for what I call "restaurant roulette"—where one diner orders fish, another orders meat, and so on. They can also match well with distinctively spiced ethnic foods that might otherwise clash with a full-flavored wine. And, of course, all these wines are enjoyable to drink on their own.

Wine and Cheese—Friends or Foes?

As in all matters of taste, the topic of wine and food comes with its share of controversy and debate. Where it's especially heated is on the subject of matching wine and cheese.

But wait! Isn't it common wisdom that wine and cheese are "naturals" for each other? It's absolutely true that a good cheese is sometimes the best food choice to make the most of a wine's flavors and complexity. That's why our wine-and-food dinners at Windows on the World always pair a cheese course with the last, best wine of the night (before dessert), usually a mature and full-bodied red, because we believe this is the best way to showcase a great wine.

The key to this match is in carefully selecting the cheese; therein lies the controversy. Some chefs and wine-and-food experts caution that some of the most popular cheeses for eating are the least appropriate for wine because they overpower it—a ripe cheese like Brie is a classic example.

The "keep-it-simple" approach applies again here. At Windows on the World, we find that the best cheeses for wines are the following: Parmigiano Reggiano, fresh Mozzarella, Pecorino, Talleggio, and Fontina from Italy; Chèvre, Montrachet, Tomme, and Gruyère from France; Dutch Gouda; English or domestic cheddar; domestic aged or fresh goat cheese and Monterey Jack; and Manchego from Spain.

My favorite wine-and-cheese matches:

Chèvre/fresh goat cheese—Sancerre, Sauvignon Blanc

Montrachet, aged (dry) Monterey Jack—Cabernet Sauvignon, Bordeaux

Pecorino—Chianti Classico Riserva, Brunello

Parmigiano Reggiano—Amarone, Cabernet Sauvignon, Bordeaux, Barolo

Manchego—Rioja, Brunello di Montalcino

What to drink with Brie? Try Champagne or sparkling wine. And blue cheeses, because of their strong flavor, overpower most wines except—get ready for this—dessert wines! The classic (and truly delicious) matches are Roquefort cheese with French Sauternes, and Stilton cheese with Port.

Sweet Satisfaction: Wine with Dessert, Wine as Dessert

I remember my first taste of a dessert wine—a Sauternes from France's Bordeaux region. It was magical! Then there are also Port, Cream Sherry, Beerenauslese, to name a few—all very different wines with one thing in common: sweetness. Hence the name "dessert" wines—their sweetness closes your palate and makes you feel satisfied after a good meal. But with wines like these, dessert is just one part of the wine-and-food story.

"Wine with dessert?" you're thinking. At least in this country, coffee is more common, a glass of brandy or liqueur if you're splurging. But as more and more restaurants add dessert wines to their by-the-glass offerings, perhaps the popularity will grow for these kinds of wine. (Because they're so rich, a full bottle of dessert wine isn't practical unless several people are sharing it. For serving at home, dessert wines in half-bottles are a good alternative.)

At Windows on the World, we serve the dessert wine a few minutes before the dessert itself, to prepare you for what is to come. But you certainly can serve a sweet dessert wine with the course.

Here are some of our favorite wine-and-dessert combinations.

Port—dark chocolate desserts, walnuts, poached pears, Stilton cheese

Madeira—milk chocolate, nut tarts, crème caramel, coffee- or mocha-flavored desserts

Pedro Ximénez Sherry—vanilla ice cream (with the wine poured over it), raisin-nut cakes, desserts containing figs or dried fruits

Beerenauslese and Late Harvest Riesling—fruit tarts, crème brûlée, almond cookies

Sauternes—fruit tarts, poached fruits, crème brûlée, caramel and hazelnut desserts, Roquefort cheese

Muscat Beaumes-de-Venise—crème brûlée, fresh fruit, fruit sorbets, lemon tart

Asti Spumante—fresh fruits, biscotti

Vouvray—fruit tarts, fresh fruits

Vin Santo—biscotti (for dipping in the wine)

Often, I prefer to serve the dessert wine as dessert. That way I can concentrate on savoring the complex and delicious flavors with a clear palate. It's especially convenient at home—all you have to do to serve your guests an exotic dessert is pull a cork! And if you're counting calories, a glass of dessert wine can give you the satisfying sweetness of dessert with a lot less bulk (and zero fat!).

Wine-Buying Strategies for Your Wine Cellar

Buying and selecting wines for your cellar is the most fun and interesting part of wine appreciation—besides drinking it, of course! You've done all your studying and reading on the wines you like, and now you go out to your favorite wine store to banter with the owner or wine manager. You already have an idea what you can spend and how many bottles you can safely store until they're paired with your favorite foods and friends.

Wine-buying has changed dramatically over the last twenty years. Many liquor stores have become wine-specialty stores, and the consumer and retailer both are much more knowledgeable. Even fifteen years ago, the wines of California, Australia, and Chile were not the wines the consumer cared to buy. Back then, the major players were the wines of France and Italy. Today there's so much more diversity in wine styles and wine prices, it's almost impossible to keep up with every new wine and new vintage that comes on the market. You can subscribe, among many publications, to *Wine Spectator*, *The Wine Enthusiast*, *Wine & Spirits*, or *Wine Advocate*, Robert Parker's newsletter, to help you with your choices, but ultimately you'll find the style of wine to suit your own personal taste.

In this book I don't recommend specific wines from specific years because I don't believe that everyone will enjoy the same wines, or that everyone has the same taste buds as I do. I think it's very important that every year the consumer have a general overview of what's hot and what's not. Here are some of my thoughts and strategies for buying wine this year.

There is, and will continue to be, an abundance of fine wine over the next few years. The vintage years of 1995 and 1996 in Bordeaux and 1997, 1998, and 1999 in Germany, Piedmont, and Tuscany, as well as the 1999 Burgundy reds, will give us great wines to drink over the next few years. The 1992 through 1997 vintages for California Cabernet Sauvignon and Chardonnay are generally excellent. The 1994, 1995, and 1997 vintage Ports are now available. Although many of these wines are high-priced, there still remain hundreds of wines under $15 that you can drink now or cellar for the future.

Anyone can buy expensive wines! The real challenge is finding the best values—the $10 bottle that tastes like a $20 bottle. The following is a list of my buying strategies for my own wine cellar.

Everyday Wines

($10 and under)

California

R.H. Phillips Cabernet Sauvignon Barrel Cuvée
Robert Mondavi Woodbridge Selections
Beaulieu Coastal
Monterey Vineyards Classic
Buena Vista Sauvignon Blanc
Round Hill Chardonnay
Beringer Merlot Founders Estate

France

Côtes du Rhône Parallele "45" Jaboulet
J. Vidal-Fleury Côtes du Rhône
La Vieille Ferme Côtes du Ventoux
Hugel Gentil
Mâcon-Villages
Louis Latour Ardèche Chardonnay
Château Bonnet Blanc
Beaujolais-Villages Louis Jadot or Georges Duboeuf
Michel Lynch
Maître d'Estournel
Fortant de France
Réserve St.-Martin

Spain

Conde de Valdemar Crianza
Bodegas Montecillo Cumbrero

Chile

Concha y Toro Casillero del Diablo

Walnut Crest Merlot

Caliterra Cabernet Sauvignon

Santa Rita Cabernet Sauvignon 120

Australia

Rosemount Chardonnay or Shiraz/Cabernet (Diamond Label)

Lindemans Chardonnay Bin 65

Italy

Montepulciano Red, Casal Thaulero

Chiarlo Barbera d'Asti

Antinori Sangiovese Santa Cristina

Taurino Salice Salentino

Corvo

Sparkling Wines

Codorniu Brut Classico

Freixenet Brut

Once-a-Week Wines

($10 to $15)

France

Château Greysac

Château Larose Trintaudon

Château La Cardonne

Crozes-Hermitage Les Jalets, Jaboulet

Alsace Riesling—Trimbach, Hugel, or Zind-Humbrecht

Château de Sancerre, Lapostolle

Pouilly Fuisse, Georges Deboeuf

California

Silverado Sauvignon Blanc

Simi Sauvignon Blanc

Ferrari-Carano Fumé Blanc

Fetzer Sundial Chardonnay

Chateau St. Jean Chardonnay

Gallo of Sonoma Chardonnay, Cabernet Sauvignon, Pinot Noir, and Merlot

Ravenswood Vintners Blend
Rosenblum Zinfandel Vintners Cuvée
Ridge Zinfandel (Sonoma)
Forest Glen Merlot
Benziger Chardonnay or Merlot
Hawk Crest Chardonnay, Cabernet Sauvignon or Merlot
Raymond Amberhill Cabernet Sauvignon
Estancia Chardonnay or Cabernet Sauvignon
Kendall-Jackson Chardonnay Vintners Reserve or Cabernet Sauvignon
Fetzer Barrel Select Cabernet Sauvignon
Louis Martini Cabernet Sauvignon
Liberty School Cabernet Sauvignon
Meridian Chardonnay or Cabernet Sauvignon
Beaulieu Rutherford Cabernet Sauvignon
Napa Ridge Chardonnay, Cabernet Sauvignon, and Pinot Noir

Washington State

Columbia Crest Merlot and Cabernet Sauvignon
Hogue Cabernet and Merlot
Covey Run Chardonnay

Italy

Rosso di Montalcino Col d'Orcia
Antinori Badia a Passignano Chianti Classico
Badia a Coltibuono Chianti Classico Riserva
Lungarotti Rubesco
Pighin Pinot Grigio
Anselmi Soave

Spain

C.U.N.E. Contino Reserva
Bodegas Muga Reserva

Chile

Santa Rita Cabernet Sauvignon Casa Real
Montes Merlot
Cousiño Macul Antiguas-Reserva Cabernet Sauvignon
Los Vascos Reserve Cabernet Sauvignon

Argentina

Navarro Correas Cabernet Sauvignon "Collection Privada"

Germany

Kabinett/Spätlese—Wehlener Sonnenuhr by J.J. Prüm or
Niersteiner Olberg by Strub

Australia

Lindemans Shiraz Bin 50

Sparkling Wines

Bouvet Brut
Korbel

Once-a-Month Wines

($15 to $30)

California

Chardonnay

Mondavi

Chalone

Ferrari-Carano

Sonoma-Cutrer

Cuvaison

Beringer

Cabernet Sauvignon

Beringer

Mondavi

Joseph Phelps

Clos du Val

Pinot Noir

Mondavi

Saintsbury (Carneros)

Etude

Calera

Au Bon Climat

Zinfandel

Ridge Geyserville

Merlot

Markham

Clos du Bois

Shafer

St. Francis

France

Non-vintage Champagne
Ladoucette Pouilly-Fumé
Château Carbonnieux Blanc
Château Olivier Blanc
Mercurey, Faiveley

Château Fourcas-Hosten
Château Meyney
Château Gloria
Château Phélan-Ségur
Château Les Ormes de Pez
Château Pontesac
Château de Sales
Domaine Leroy Bourgogne Rouge

Australia

Rosemount Show Reserve Chardonnay
Penfolds Bin 389

Italy

Mastroberardino Taurasi
Antinori Chianti Classico Tenute Marchese Riserva
Ruffino Chianti Classico Riserva

Spain

Pesquera
La Rioja Alta Viña Ardanza

Chile

Casa Lapostolle Cabernet Sauvignon or Merlot Cuvée Alexandre
Concha y Toro Cabernet Sauvignon Don Melchor
Errazúriz Don Maximiano Founders Reserve

Argentina

Catena Cabernet Sauvignon Alta
Bodegas Weinert Carrascal

Ports

Sandeman Founders Reserve
Fonseca Bin #27

Once-a-Year Wines
($$$$+)

It's easy to buy these kinds of wine when money is no object! Any wine retailer would be more than happy to help you spend your money!!

Creating an Exemplary
Restaurant Wine List

Preface

When I first conceived the ideas for this book in the early '80s, I had two purposes in mind. One was that my wine students were telling me that they needed an easier-to-understand text than the one I was using, and two, that there was a tremendous need in the hotel and culinary schools in the United States for a beginning guide to wine.

If you are a consumer, you may find the next two chapters to be interesting reading since they were written for the young student who is about to embark on a career in the restaurant or hotel business.

Today the *Windows on the World Complete Wine Course* is used at fine educational institutions such as the Culinary Institute of America, Cornell University, Michigan State University, University of Nevada (Las Vegas), Florida International University, and over 100 other schools specializing in the hospitality industry.

Anyone who is even marginally aware of market trends knows that the popularity of wine has increased dramatically. Wine lists are no longer the province of an elite group of high-ticket, white-tablecloth culinary temples. There are ever-increasing ranks of customers who actively seek to enjoy wine in restaurants of all price levels.

To attract these potential customers, many a restaurateur has toyed with the idea of revamping and expanding his wine list. Yet, when confronted with the stark reality of such a task, many panic and accept the judgment of others, who have their own profit motives in mind. Once the restaurateur has acknowledged that it's time to start carrying more than house red, white, and rosé wines, he must lay the groundwork for building a list.

To illustrate: The hypothetical restaurant to which you've just taken the deed is a picturesque 100-seat establishment located in a moderate-size city. Your restaurant is open for both lunch and dinner, and doesn't possess any definite ethnic identity, falling under that umbrella label of "Continental/American."

The following is a step-by-step procedure in question-and-answer format for building a wine list for your restaurant. Remember, the most important aspects of your wine list are that it should complement your menu offerings, be attractively priced, offer an appealing selection, and be easy for the customer to select from and understand.

What's your competition?

Before you consider which wineries to choose, or fret about whether to have forty or 400 wines, take the time to investigate your market. Visit both the restaurants that attract the clientele you're aiming for (your target market) and the ones above and below your scale. Study how they merchandise wine, how well their staff serves it, and obtain a copy of their wine list—provided it's not chained to the sommelier's neck. Go during a busy dinner hour and observe how many bottles of wine are nestled in ice buckets or present on tables. Get a feeling for your competition's commitment to wine.

Can wine distributors offer help?

Contact the various suppliers in your area and explain to them what your objectives are. Ask them to suggest a hypothetical wine list—you're under no obligation to use it. Many wine distributors have specially trained people to work along with restaurateurs on their wine lists. They can also suggest ways of merchandising and promotion. Use them as a resource.

What's your storage capacity?

Wine requires specific storage conditions: an ideal temperature range of 55°F to 60°F, away from direct sunlight and excessive vibration. Your wine storage does not belong next to the dishwashing machine or the loading dock. How large a space do you have? Does it allow room for shelving? You'll want to store the bottles on their sides. How accessible is the wine to service personnel?

What are your consumers' preferences?

Preliminary research reveals that in the United States, eighty percent of the wine consumed is domestic and twenty percent is imported. The consumer preferences for our hypothetical restaurant's audience are predominantly American and French wines.

How long should your list be?

This is, in part, determined by storage space and capital investment. For our hypothetical restaurant, we decided to feature sixty wines on the list. Initially, this might seem like a lot for a 100-seat restaurant, but consider that those wines will be divided among sparkling, red, white, and rosé, and encompass the regions of France, the United States, Italy, Spain, Germany, Chile, and Australia. Sixty is almost the minimum number that will allow you the flexibility to offer a range of types and tastes and wine for special occasions, as well as for casual quaffing. We want our customers to know that wine matters in our restaurant.

What proportion of red to white?

In the Wine School at Windows on the World, I always ask my students about their wine preferences. Ten years ago, the majority of my students preferred white wine, but today I find that my students have a decided preference for red wines. Though red wines have become more important to restaurant wine lists in general, our hypothetical restaurant has only three red-meat entrées out of ten. So based on wine and food combinations, the decision to feature more whites than reds is a sound one.

How should prices be set?

Don't plan on paying your mortgage with profits from your wine list! Pricing is dictated according to your selections. Aim for sixty percent of these wines to be moderately priced. Why? Because this is the price category in which the highest volume of sales will take place. For our purposes, mid-priced wines sell for between $25 and $35. Therefore, we want 36 of our wines priced in this range. Of the remaining wines, twenty percent (twelve wines) would be priced less than $25, and twenty percent for more than $35.

The percentage of profit realized on wine is less than that realized on cocktails. However, the dollar-value profit is greater since the total sale is much more. Too many restaurateurs have intimidated much of the potential wine market by stocking only very rare, expensive wines and pricing them into the stratosphere. You want a wine list that will enable all your customers to enjoy a bottle (or two) of wine with their meal without having to float a bank loan. The bulk of your customers are looking for a good wine at a fair price—not a rare vintage wine at $400 a bottle.

What's your capital investment?

Determine with your accountant the amount of money you'll initially invest. Decide whether you want an inventory that will turn over in thirty to sixty days, or if you wish to make a long-term investment in cellaring wines. The majority of restaurants make short-term wine investments.

What will it actually cost?

Once we've decided on the number of wines on the list, and the general pricing structure, it's easy to determine what it will cost for one case of each wine. With some wines—the ones we anticipate will be very popular—our initial order will be for two cases, and for the more expensive wines, we'll start off with a half-case. Our sixty-selection wine list will require an initial investment of approximately $8,500. Here's how we arrived at that "ballpark" figure:

Low-priced wines:
12 cases @ $75 per case average $900.00

Medium-priced wines:
36 cases @ $130 per case average $4,680.00

High-priced wines:
12 cases @ $240 per case average $2,880.00

Total: $8,460.00

What goes on the wine list?

There are many different styles of wine list. Some opt for long descriptions of the wine's characteristics and feature facts and maps of viticultural regions.

For our restaurant, we're going to adopt a very straightforward approach.

- The list is divided into categories by type, and each type is divided into regions.
- The progression is: sparkling wine, white, red, and blush.

Each entry on the wine list should have the following information:

- Bin Number—This simplifies inventory and reordering, and assists both customer and staff with difficult pronunciation.
- Name of wine—Be precise.
- Vintage—This is often omitted on wine lists by restaurateurs who want to be able to substitute whatever is available. This practice is resented by anyone with a passing interest in wine, and with today's laser-printed wine lists, it is, in my opinion, unacceptable.
- Shipper—This information is very important for French wines, particularly those from Burgundy.
- The type, style, and color of the paper you choose for your wine list are personal decisions. However, double-check all spelling and prices before the list is sent to the printer. It is very embarrassing when your customers point out spelling errors.

Which categories of wine should be used?

Our wine list includes six sparkling wines (three French, two American, and one Spanish). There are 29 white wines, 24 red wines, and one blush, for a grand total of 60. Here is one example of how the categories might be broken down. Of course, each restaurant should choose the wines according to availability and price.

Building a Basic Restaurant Wine List

White and Sparkling Wines (35)

FRENCH (10)

1 Mâcon Blanc
1 Chablis (Premier Cru)
1 Meursault
1 Puligny-Montrachet
1 Pouilly-Fuissé
1 Pouilly-Fumé or Sancerre
2 Alsace (1 Riesling, 1 Gewürztraminer)
2 Bordeaux (1 Graves, 1 Sauternes)

AMERICAN (14)

1 Riesling
3 Sauvignon Blanc/Fumé Blanc
10 Chardonnay

ITALIAN (2)

1 Soave
1 Pinot Grigio

AUSTRALIAN (1)

1 Chardonnay

GERMAN (2)

1 Rhein (Kabinett or Spätlese)
1 Mosel (Kabinett)

SPARKLING (6)

3 French Champagne (2 Non-Vintage,
   1 Prestige Cuveé)
2 American Sparkling (2 different price
   categories)
1 Spanish Sparkling

Red and Blush Wines (25)

FRENCH (7)

1 Beaujolais
2 Burgundy (such as Nuits-St-Georges,
   Pommard, Volnay)
3 Bordeaux (different price categories)
1 Rhône Valley (Côtes du Rhône,
   Châteauneuf-du-Pape, or Hermitage)

AMERICAN (11)

2 Merlot
2 Pinot Noir
1 Zinfandel
6 Cabernet Sauvignon

ITALIAN (3)

1 Chianti Classico Riserva
1 Bardolino or Valpolicella
1 Barolo or Barbaresco

AUSTRALIAN (1)

1 Shiraz or Cabernet Sauvignon

SPANISH (1)

1 Rioja Reserva

CHILEAN (1)

1 Cabernet Sauvignon

BLUSH (1)

1 White Zinfandel

Should I buy wine without tasting it?

Tasting the wines for the list is of utmost importance. If you've decided to feature a Chardonnay, contact your distributors and ask to taste all the Chardonnays that conform to your criteria of availability and price. Tasting the wines blind will help you make selections on the basis of quality rather than label. These tastings represent quite an investment of time. To choose a wine list of sixty wines, you could easily taste three times that many.

Once you've narrowed the field, try pairing the wines with your menu offerings. If possible, include your staff in these tastings. The more familiar they are with the wines on the list and the foods they complement, the better they'll be able to sell your selections.

Recheck the availability of your selected wines. Place your orders. Remember, you don't have to buy 25 cases of each wine.

Your restaurant's open—what's next?

This is a guideline to establishing an initial list. At Windows on the World, with its high volume, we continually update and revise the list to meet the requirements of our customers and the ever-changing wine market.

Once your list has been implemented, it's imperative that you track wine sales to determine how successful the list has been. Analyze your wine list with respect to the following factors:

- The number of bottles sold per customer (divide the number of bottles sold by the number of covers).
- How much white wine to red (by percentage)—you might find that you need more or fewer whites, or more or fewer reds.
- The average price of a bottle of wine sold in the first three months.
- The ten most popular wines on the list.
- Instruct your staff to report any diner's request for a wine that's not on your list.

The steps involved in compiling our hypothetical list of sixty wines are the same steps that are used in compiling larger, more ambitious lists. Obviously, this list only highlights the major areas—sixty wines barely scratch the surface of what's available. True, with this size restriction we're unable to give great depth of selection, but it's still a list where the average customer, including myself, would find something appealing.

The Progressive Wine List

When Windows on the World reopened in 1996, our "short" list of 100 wines was presented in a different format from the one just discussed for our hypothetical restaurant.

We decided that Americans are more comfortable ordering wines by the specific grape varieties than by country and region. We now feature the three major grape varieties for white wines—Riesling, Sauvignon Blanc/Fumé Blanc, and Chardonnay, and the three major grape varieties for reds—Cabernet Sauvignon,

Pinot Noir, and Merlot. Then, we took all the wines and listed them by the major grape from which they are produced. For other wines made from other grape varietals, we created a separate heading on our wine list called "Worldly Wines."

We took it a step further and placed the wines on the list in order, from the lightest style to the heaviest style wines. This type of list is known as a "Progressive Wine List." There is a distinct advantage to this kind of wine list. By placing your lighter-bodied wines first and your heavier-bodied wines next, it helps your waitstaff to better recommend wines for the food the customer has chosen. To create a Progressive Wine List for your restaurant, you would lead off with the Rieslings, from the lightest to the heaviest style wines, then the Sauvignon Blancs/Fumé Blancs, and then the Chardonnays. For the red wines, you would begin with the Pinot Noirs, the Merlots, and then the Cabernet Sauvignons.

What about wine by the glass?

In my opinion, the most significant change in the past fifteen years since this book was first written has been the selling of wines by the glass. This is a home run for everyone—the consumer now has the opportunity to try different wines at different price points without buying a bottle. The waitstaff gets to learn more about different styles of wines by the glass than they do about wines listed on the wine list, plus they don't have to deal with the opening of a bottle since most of these wines are coming from the bar.

For the restaurant owner, you have a happier customer, a happier staff, faster service, and the potential to make more revenue and profits with an effective wine-by-the-glass program.

A note on pricing wines by the glass: The bottle of wine holds approximately 25 ounces; therefore you should get five 5-ounce pours from each bottle. My rule of thumb is to sell a glass for what the bottle costs me.

How many wines by the glass should I offer?

No matter how many wines you serve by the glass, whether it's only one or twenty, you must cork and store your wines (red and white) in the refrigerator overnight.

When we first began our wine-by-the-glass program at Windows on the World twenty years ago, we had one white and one red wine, which we changed daily. Today we have six wines by the glass—three whites and three reds, available in a low, medium, and high price point for each category. We sometimes offer some very special rare wines by the glass, just as a chef will have specials from his or her menus.

If you plan to have more than ten wines by the glass, invest in a wine preservation system. With under ten, if you are selling an opened bottle of wine within 48 hours and you follow the overnight refrigeration procedure, you can probably do without a preservation system and still maintain the quality of the wine.

If you're a consumer, you now have an idea what's involved in creating a balanced wine list. For restaurateurs, the logistic of creating a wine list may seem Olympian. This chapter was offered to take some of the mystery out of this task.

Wine Service in Restaurants and at Home

Wine Service in Restaurants and at Home

Congratulations! You finished all eight classes. Now you know how to combine wine with food, how to find the best values, and, if need be, you could even create a restaurant wine list!

The last thing you want to do is make a mistake in wine service, whether you are at a restaurant or at home.

Wine in Restaurants

In a restaurant, I strongly recommend that you order all your wines at the beginning of the meal and have them opened so you're not sitting there without wine when your main course arrives. Even better, call the restaurant ahead of time and pre-order your wines.

My Pet Peeves of Restaurant Wine Service

- not enough wine lists
- incorrect information, *i.e.,* wrong vintage and producer
- high markups
- untrained staff
- lack of corkscrews
- out-of-stock wines
- improper glassware
- overchilled whites and warm reds

Wine Service Ritual

In most restaurants, the wine service ritual is as intimidating to the service staff as it is to the new wine consumer.

Picture this scenario: You've ordered your bottle of wine. The server now presents you with the bottle.

What do you do?

First, make sure that the wine presented to you at the table is the same wine you ordered from the wine list and is the correct vintage. Now the fun begins. The server opens the wine and presents you with the cork.

What are you supposed to do with the cork?

Nothing! After thirty years of being in the wine and restaurant industry, I have no idea why we give the customer the cork. In the movies, the bon vivant used to sniff the cork and wave it around ceremoniously. That may look good on film, but why would anyone want to smell a wet winey cork?!

The truth, if you really want to find out whether a wine is good or not, all you have to do is pour it in your glass, swirl it, and smell it. It's all in the smell!

The Magical Mystery Taste Test

Now you have to taste the wine. So many steps, so little time. While everyone at the dinner table is looking at you, the server pours the first taste of wine. Will Mikey like it?

At this point I urge my students to remember that the first taste of wine is always a shock to your taste buds. The truth is, if you really want to determine whether a wine is good or not, all you really need to do is pick up the glass, swirl the wine, and smell it. If you really want to impress your guests, simply smell the wine and nod your approval. If you are unsure, take a small taste or even two to confirm your first impression.

When should you send a wine back in a restaurant?

Whenever you feel there is something wrong with the wine. At Windows on the World we don't have a problem with people sending a bottle of wine back. In actuality, we sell 10,000 bottles of wine per month and

Some wineries, especially in California, are now using synthetic corks to seal their wine.

Did you know?
The wine-tasting ritual goes back to the days of kings, when royal tasters had to sample wine before it was served to the king and his table. Unfortunately there was a high turnover rate of royal tasters.

Today's royal tasters are called *sommeliers*, which is the French word for wine steward. At the real ritzy restaurants, they are clad in tuxedos (a little bit more intimidation) and are usually seen wearing a chain with a little cup at the end of it. The cup is called a *tastevin* and is used by true sommeliers to taste the wine for you.

fewer than ten are sent back. Even then, most of them are in good shape. For those of you who have heard about the server who recommends a wine to a table and adds, "If you don't like it, I'll drink it myself," we do, especially the good stuff!

What are the two major reasons for sending a wine back?

The first reason is that the wine is spoiled or oxidized. It has lost its fruit smell and taste, usually because of poor storage of the wine or the wine has passed its prime and should have been consumed earlier.

The second reason is that the wine is corked. It is estimated that three to five percent of all the world's wines are corked, meaning that the cork that was used to seal the bottle was defective. You'll know immediately if a wine is corked because the smell of the wine is not of fruit, but is more like a dank, wet cellar or moldy newspaper.

An oxidized wine smells like Sherry or Madeira.

Is it necessary to spend a lot of money for wine in restaurants?

I've been in the restaurant business most of my life and also a customer in restaurants at least three times per week. So you might find it interesting that I never order a bottle of wine over $50 (unless someone else is paying!). I do not believe that a restaurant is a great place for experimentation with wine because of the higher markup charged at most restaurants. We all know of great restaurants in our area that charge too much for wine and those that offer a fair markup. I go to the restaurants with the best wine prices.

Wine by the Glass

At Wild Blue, one of our restaurants in the World Trade Center, we offer over fifty wines by the glass from $8 to $30.

In my opinion, the best thing that has happened to wine appreciation for both the consumer and the restaurateur is wine by the glass. If I'm going to do any experimentation in a restaurant, it will definitely be in a restaurant that has a good selection of wines by the glass. This also solves the age-old challenge of what wine to order when one person orders fish and another orders meat. You're no longer stuck with one bottle to accommodate everyone's different menu choices.

Another good thing about wine by the glass is that you get a hassle-free wine experience. That means:

1. You don't have to decipher the wine list. You don't even have to ask for it.
2. You don't have to approve the label.
3. You don't have to smell the cork.
4. You don't have to go through the tasting ritual.

Temperature

One of the biggest complaints in restaurant wine service is that the white wines are served too cold, but for me, being a red wine drinker, my biggest complaint is that the red wines are served too warm.

White wines served too cold will hide the true character and flavor of the wine. Red wines served too warm change the balance of the components and hinder the true taste of the wine, increasing the sensation of alcohol and tannin over the fruit, especially in California wines.

In my own dining-out experience at least fifty percent of the time the wine is served at an improper temperature. It's easier to solve the problem for a white wine by leaving it in the glass and letting it warm up, but to chill down a red wine I have to order a bucket filled with ice and water and leave my wine in it for five to ten minutes to bring it to the correct temperature. I strongly recommend that you follow the same method, even though it may be a hassle. I can assure you that you'll enjoy your wines more.

Quick Tips on Temperatures for Serving Wine

1. Great Chardonnays, for example, are best served at warmer temperatures (55°F to 60°F) than whites made from Sauvignon Blanc or Riesling (45°F to 55°F).

2. Champagnes and sparkling wines taste better served well chilled (45°F).

3. Lighter reds, such as Gamay, Pinot Noir, Tempranillo, and Sangiovese bring out a better balance of fruit to acid when served at a cooler temperature (55°F to 60°F) than wines such as Cabernet Sauvignon and Merlot (60°F to 65°F).

The average temperature of a refrigerator is 38°F to 45°F.

Wine at Home

Storage

National statistics show that most wine purchased at retail stores will be consumed within three days of purchase, but for those of you who are collecting wine, whether you have a dozen bottles or 2,000, you must protect your investment.

If you're lucky enough to have a constant 55°F storage condition all year round, you're way ahead of the game. But since most of us don't have that luxury, keep in mind a few important facts:

1. Warmer temperatures prematurely age wine.

2. Fluctuation of temperature is not healthy for wine. If your storage fluctuates from 55°F to 75°F, you're doing more harm than good to the wine.

3. Higher humidity is better than lower humidity.

4. When all else fails, especially for those living in a cozy apartment, put your wines in the refrigerator—both whites and reds—rather than risk storing them in warm conditions.

Where do you store your wines? If you live in a château, I'm sure you have a beautiful wine cellar, but if you live in an apartment with an average temperature of 70°F and your wines are stored with your shoes, this is not good news for the health of your wine.

If you leave a bottle of wine in a 70°F room, as opposed to in a 55°F room, you are actually prematurely aging the wine twice as quickly.

The Corkscrew

How many of you have seen other people break a cork or even push the cork in the bottle when opening a wine?

Many times this happens because people either use the wrong corkscrew or they open the wine incorrectly.

Of the many different kinds of corkscrew and cork-puller available, the most efficient and easiest tool to use is the pocket model of the "Screwpull," a patented device that includes a knife and a very long screw. Simply by turning in one continuous direction, the cork is extracted effortlessly. This is the best type of corkscrew for home use, and because it is gentle, it is best for removing long, fragile corks from older wines.

The corkscrew most commonly used in restaurants is the "waiter's corkscrew." Small and flat, it contains a knife, screw, and lever, all of which fold neatly into the handle.

How do I open a bottle of wine?

When opening a bottle of wine, the first step is to remove the capsule. You can accomplish this best by cutting around the neck on the underside of the bottle's lip. Once you remove the capsule, wipe the top of the cork clean—often dust or mold adheres to the cork while the wine is still at the winery, and before the capsule is put on the bottle. Next, insert the screw and turn it so that it goes as deeply as possible into the cork. Don't be afraid to go through the cork. I'd rather get a little cork in my wine than not get the cork out of the bottle.

The most important technique in opening a bottle of wine is once you have lifted the cork one-quarter of the way out, stop and turn the screw farther into the cork. Now pull the cork three-quarters of the way out. This is the point where most people feel they're in control and start pulling and bending the cork. And of course, they end up leaving a little bit of the cork still in the bottle. The best method at this point is to use your hand to wiggle out the cork.

Just to make you feel better: I still break at least a dozen corks a year.

To Decant, Perchance to Breathe

Does a wine need to breathe?

One of the most controversial subjects in winedom is breathing, or exposing the wine to air. I always find it interesting when I go to a restaurant and the waiter informs me that the wine must breathe for a minimum of fifteen minutes before I can drink it!

My opinion is that opening a bottle of wine and leaving it "to breathe" on the table at your home or restaurant does nothing to enhance the taste of the wine.

But still, there are many people who maintain that the wine does get better with aeration. If that's your pleasure, let it breathe.

There is another school of thought that agrees that the breathing theory does not work by just opening a bottle of wine, but that by pouring it into a decanter and exposing it to more air surface, the wine will achieve greater taste. So what's my advice after opening thousands and thousands of bottles of wine?

Open it up, pour it in a glass, and enjoy the wine!

When in France, do as the French. My experience in visiting the French wine regions is that in Burgundy they very rarely decant, but in Bordeaux, they almost always decant.

Which wines do I decant?

The three major wine collectibles are the ones that most likely will need to be decanted, especially as they get older and throw more sediment. The three major wine collectibles are:

1. Great châteaus of Bordeaux (ten years and older)
2. California Cabernets (eight years and older)
3. Vintage Port (ten years and older)

My primary reason for decanting a bottle of wine is to separate the wine from the sediment.

How do I decant a bottle of wine?

1. Completely remove the capsule from the neck of the bottle. This will enable you to see the wine clearly as it passes through the neck.

2. Light a candle. Most red wines are bottled in very dark green glass, making it difficult to see the wine pass through the neck of the bottle. A candle will give you the extra illumination you need. A flashlight would do, but candles keep things simple.

3. Hold the decanter (a carafe or glass pitcher can also be used for this purpose) firmly in your hand.

4. Hold the wine bottle in your other hand, and gently pour the wine into the decanter while holding both over the candle at such an angle that you can see the wine pass through the neck of the bottle.

5. Continue pouring in one uninterrupted motion until you begin to see the first signs of sediment.

6. Stop decanting once you begin to see sediment. At this point, if there is still sediment left, leave the wine standing until it settles. Then continue decanting.

Glassware

Whether you're dining out or you're at home, the enjoyment of food and wine is enhanced by fine silver, china, linen, and, of course, glassware. The color of wine is as much a part of its pleasure and appeal as its bouquet and flavor. Glasses that alter or obscure the color of wine detract from the wine itself. The most suitable wine glasses are those of clear glass with a bowl large enough to allow for swirling.

The perfect size glass for a white or red wine is 10 to 12 ounces. To allow for swirling and the development of the wine's bouquet, a wine-glass should not be filled more than halfway.

A variety of shapes are available, and personal preferences should guide you when selecting glasses for home use. Some shapes, however, are better suited to certain wines than to others. For example, a smaller glass that closes in a bit at the top helps concentrate the bouquet of a white wine and also helps it keep its chill. Larger, balloon-shaped glasses are more appropriate for red wines.

The most suitable Champagne glasses and the ones more and more restaurants are using are the tulip or the Champagne flute. These narrow glasses hold between four and eight ounces, and they allow the bubbles to rise from a single point. The tulip shape also helps to concentrate the bouquet.

Award-Winning Wine Lists

I strongly believe that a restaurant with a great wine list will also have excellent food and service. Try one of these restaurants and see what I mean.

The restaurants listed below were chosen by *Wine Spectator*, the largest-selling wine newspaper in the United States, for having the best lists in the world.

Alain Ducasse (since 1998)
Paris, France

Altwienerhof (since 1990)
Vienna, Austria

The American Hotel (since 1981)
Sag Harbor, New York

The Angus Barn (since 1989)
Raleigh, North Carolina

Anthony's in the Catalinas (since 1993)
Tucson, Arizona

Au Crocodile (since 1993)
Strasbourg, France

Beverly's (since 1993)
Coeur d'Alene, Idaho

Billy Crews Dining Room (since 1986)
Santa Teresa, New Mexico

Bistro à Champlain (since 1988)
Ste.-Marguerite du Lac Masson, Quebec,
Canada

Brennan's Restaurant (since 1983)
New Orleans, Louisiana

Canlis (since 1997)
Seattle, Washington

Carlos' Restaurant (since 1990)
Highland Park, Illinois

The Carnelian Room (since 1982)
San Francisco, California

Casanova Restaurant (since 1990)
Carmel, California

The Cellar (since 1992)
Fullerton, California

The Chanticleer Inn (since 1987)
Siasconset, Massachusetts

Charlie Trotter's (since 1993)
Chicago, Illinois

Crabtree's Kittle House Inn (since 1994)
Chappaqua, New York

**The Dining Room at the Ritz-Carlton
  (since 1982)**
Chicago, Illinois

El Paseo Restaurant (since 1987)
Mill Valley, California

Emeril's (since 1999)
New Orleans, Louisiana

Enoteca Pinchiorri (since 1984)
Florence, Italy

Enoteca Pinchiorri-Tokyo (since 1994)
Tokyo, Japan

Felidia Ristorante (since 1988)
New York, New York

Flagstaff House Restaurant (since 1983)
Boulder, Colorado

Florentine Dining Room (since 1981)
Palm Beach, Florida

The French Room (since 1984)
San Francisco, California

Friends Lake Inn (since 1997)
Chestertown, New York

Galileo da Roberto Donna (since 1997)
Washington, D.C.

Georges Blanc (since 1987)
Vonnas, France

Gidleigh Park (since 1984)
Devon, England

Graycliff (since 1988)
Nassau, Bahamas

Guido Ristorante (since 1996)
Costigliole d'Asti, Italy

The Hermitage Inn (since 1984)
Wilmington, Vermont

Il Poeta Contadino (since 1997)
Alberobello, Italy

The Inn at Little Washington (since 1995)
Washington, Virginia

The Inn at Sawmill Farm (since 1992)
West Dover, Vermont

Italian Village Restaurant (since 1984)
Chicago, Illinois

JJ's (since 1996)
Kansas City, Missouri

Kingston 1686 House (since 1992)
Kingston, New Hampshire

La Rive Gauche (since 1983)
Palos Verdes, California

La Tour d'Argent (since 1986)
Paris, France

Landgasthof & Vinothek Farnsburg (since 1992)
Ormalingen, Switzerland

Le Cirque 2000 (since 1986)
New York, New York

Le Louis XV (since 1995)
Monte Carlo, Monaco

Les Amis (since 1996)
Singapore

Lucas Carton (since 1989)
Paris, France

Maison & Jardin Restaurant (since 1995)
Altamonte Springs, Florida

Malliouhana (since 1999)
West Indies

The Manor (since 1988)
West Orange, New Jersey

The Mansion on Turtle Creek (since 1995)
Dallas, Texas

Michel Rostang (since 1993)
Paris, France

Mr. Stox (since 1983)
Anaheim, California

Montrachet (since 1994)
New York, New York

Pacific's Edge Restaurant (since 1991)
Carmel, California

Park and Orchard Restaurant (since 1991)
East Rutherford, New Jersey

Patina Restaurant (since 1994)
Los Angeles, California

Peppone (since 1988)
West Los Angeles, California

The Plumed Horse (since 1987)
Saratoga, California

The Ranch House Restaurant (since 1985)
Ojai, California

The Refectory (since 1990)
Columbus, Ohio

**The Restaurant at the Little Nell
(since 1997)**
Aspen, Colorado

Restaurant Jog Muller (since 1993)
Germany

Restaurant Riesbächli (since 1990)
Zurich, Switzerland

**Restaurant 301 at the Hotel Carter
(since 1998)**
Eureka, California

Rotisserie for Beef and Bird (since 1988)
Houston, Texas

Rubicon (since 1998)
San Francisco, California

The Sardine Factory (since 1982)
Monterey, California

Seasons (since 1987)
Washington, D.C.

Sierra Mar (since 1993)
Big Sur, California

Silks at Stonehedge Inn (since 1996)
Tyngsboro, Massachusetts

Sparks Steak House (since 1981)
New York, New York

Starker's Restaurant (since 1992)
Kansas City, Missouri

Taillevent (since 1984)
Paris, France

Tan Dinh (since 1985)
Paris, France

Top O' The Cove (since 1982)
La Jolla, California

Topper's at the Wauwinet (since 1996)
Nantucket, Massachusetts

Troisgros (since 1996)
Roanne, France

Valentino (since 1981)
Santa Monica, California

Hotel Waldhaus am See (since 1998)
St. Moritz, Switzerland

The Wild Boar Restaurant (since 1993)
Nashville, Tennessee

Windows on the World (since 1981)
New York, New York

Wine Cask (since 1994)
Santa Barbara, California

The WineSellar & Brasserie (since 1989)
San Diego, California

Glossary and Pronunciation Key

Acid: One of the four tastes of wine. It is sometimes described as sour, acidic, or tart and can be found on the sides of the tongue and mouth.

Aloxe Corton (Ah-LOHSS Cor-TAWN): A village in the Côte de Beaune in Burgundy, France.

Amarone (Ah-ma-ROH-nay): A type of Veronese wine made by a special process in which grapes are harvested late and allowed to "raisinate," thus producing a higher alcohol percentage in the wine and sometimes a sweet taste on the palate.

Amontillado (Ah-mone-tee-YAH-doe): A type of Sherry.

A.O.C.: An abbreviation for Appellation d'Origine Contrôlée; the French government agency that controls wine production there.

A.P. number: The official testing number displayed on a German wine label that shows the wine was tasted and passed government quality-control standards.

Aroma: The smell of the grapes in a wine.

Auslese (OUSE-lay-zeh): A sweet white German wine made from selected bunches of late-picked grapes.

A.V.A.: An abbreviation for American Viticultural Area.

Barbaresco (Bar-bar-ESS-coh): A full-bodied, D.O.C.G. red wine from Piedmont, Italy; made from the Nebbiolo grape.

Barbera (Bar-BEAR-ah): A red grape grown primarily in Piedmont, Italy.

Barolo (Bar-OH-lo): A full-bodied D.O.C.G. red wine from Piedmont, Italy; made from the Nebbiolo grape.

B.A.T.F.: An abbreviation for Bureau of Alcohol, Tobacco, and Firearms; the government agency that controls wine production in the United States.

Beaujolais (Bo-zho-LAY): A light, fruity red Burgundy wine from the region of Beaujolais; in terms of quality, the basic Beaujolais.

Beaujolais Nouveau (Bo-zho-LAY New-VOH): The "new" Beaujolais that's produced and delivered to retailers in a matter of weeks after the harvest.

Beaujolais-Villages (Bo-zho-LAY vih-lahzh): A Beaujolais wine that comes from a blend of grapes from designated villages in the region; it's a step up in quality from regular Beaujolais.

Beaune (Bone): French city located in the center of the Côte d'Or in Burgundy.

Beerenauslese (Bear-en-OUSE-lay-zeh): A full-bodied, sweet white German wine made from the rich, ripe grapes affected by "botrytis."

Blanc de Blancs (Blahnk duh BLAHNK): A white wine made from white grapes.

Blanc de Noir (Blahnk duh nwahr): A white wine made from red grapes.

Botrytis cinerea (Bow-TRIED-iss Sin-eh-RAY-ah): A mold that forms on the grapes, known also as "noble rot," which is necessary to make Sauternes and the rich German wines Beerenauslese and Trockenbeerenauslese.

Bouquet: The smell of the wine.

Brix (Bricks): A scale that measures the sugar level of the unfermented grape juice (must).

Brunello di Montalcino (Brew-NELL-oh dee Mon-tahl-CHEE-no): A high-quality D.O.C.G. red Italian wine from the Tuscany region.

Brut (Brute): The driest style of Champagne.

Cabernet Franc (Cah-burr-NAY Frahnk): A red grape of the Bordeaux region and the Loire Valley of France.

Cabernet Sauvignon (Cah-burr-NAY Sow-vee-NYOH): The most important red grape grown in the world, yielding many of the great wines of Bordeaux and California.

Chablis (Shah-BLEE): The northernmost region in Burgundy; a wine that comes from Chardonnay grapes grown anywhere in the Chablis district.

Chambolle-Musigny (Shahm-BOWL Moos-een-YEE): A village in the Côte de Nuits in Burgundy, France.

Champagne: The region in France that produces the only sparkling wine that can be authentically called Champagne.

Chaptalization: The addition of sugar to the must (fresh grape juice) before fermentation.

Chardonnay (Shahr-dun-NAY): The most important and expensive white grape, now grown all over the world; nearly all French white Burgundy wines are made from 100 percent Chardonnay.

Chassagne-Montrachet (Shahs-SAHN-ya mown-rah-shay): A village in the Côte de Beaune in Burgundy, France.

Château (Shah-TOH): The French "legal" definition is a house attached to a vineyard having a specific number of acres with winemaking and storage facilities on the property.

Château wine: Usually the best-quality Bordeaux wine.

Châteauneuf-du-Pape (Shah-toh-nuff-dew-POP): A red wine from the southern Rhône Valley region of France; the name means "new castle of the Pope."

Chenin Blanc: A white grape grown in the Loire Valley region of France and in California.

Chianti (Key-AHN-tee): A D.O.C.G. red wine from the Tuscany region of Italy.

Chianti Classico (Key-AHN-tee Class-ee-ko): One step above Chianti in terms of quality, this wine is from an inner district of Chianti.

Chianti Classico Riserva (Key-AHN-tee Class-ee-ko Re-ser-va): The best-quality level of Italian Chianti, which requires more aging than Chianti and Chianti Classico.

Cinsault (San-SO): A red grape from France's Rhône Valley.

Classified châteaux: The châteaux in the Bordeaux region of France that are known to produce the best wine.

Concord: A red grape used to make some New York State wines.

Colheita (Coal-AY-ta): The term meaning "vintage" in Portuguese.

Cosecha (Coh-SAY-cha): The term meaning "harvest" in Spanish.

Côte de Beaune (Coat duh BONE): The southern portion of the Côte d'Or in Burgundy; known especially for fine white wines.

Côte de Nuits (Coat duh NWEE): The northern portion of the Côte d'Or in Burgundy; known especially for fine red wines.

Côte d'Or (Coat DOOR): The district in Burgundy that is known for some of the finest wines in the world.

Côte Rôtie (Coat Row-TEE): A red wine from the northern Rhône Valley region of France.

Côtes-du-Rhône (Coat dew ROAN): The Rhône Valley region of France; also the regional wine from this district.

Cream Sherry: A type of Sherry made from a mixture of Pedro Ximénez and Oloroso.

Crianza (Cree-AHN-za): A wine aged a year in oak and a year in the bottle. It is the most basic and least expensive quality level of Rioja wine.

Crozes-Hermitage (Crows Air-mee-TAHZH): A red wine from the northern Rhône Valley region of France.

Cru Beaujolais: (Crew-Bo-zho-LAY) The top grade of Beaujolais wine, coming from any one of ten designated villages in that region of France.

Cru Bourgeois: (Crew Bour-ZHWAH) A list of more than 300 châteaus in Bordeaux that have been recognized for their quality.

Decanting: The process of pouring wine from its bottle into a carafe to separate the sediment from the wine.

Dégorgement (Day-gorzh-MOWN): One step of the Champagne method used to expel the sediment from the bottle.

Demi-sec (Deh-mee SECK): A champagne containing a high level of residual sugar.

D.O.C.: An abbreviation for Denominazione di Origine Controllata, the Italian government agency that controls wine production.

D.O.C.G.: An abbreviation for Denominazione di Origine Controllata e Garantita; the Italian government allows this marking to appear only on the finest wines. The "G" stands for "Guaranteed."

Dolcetto (Dohl-CHET-toh): A red wine from Piedmont, Italy, that is lighter in style than a Barolo or Barbaresco.

Dosage (Doh-SAHZH): A combination of wine and cane sugar that is used in making Champagne.

Edelfäule (EH-del-foy-luh): A German name for the mold that forms on the grapevines when the conditions permit it. (See also Botrytis cinerea and "Noble Rot.")

Erzeugerabfüllung (AIR-tzoy-ger-ahb-fue-lung): A German word for an estate-bottled wine.

Estate-bottled: Wine that's made, produced, and bottled by the vineyard's owner.

Extra dry: Less dry than brut Champagne.

Fermentation: The process by which grape juice is made into wine.

Fino (FEE-noh): A type of Sherry.

First growth: The highest-quality Bordeaux châteaux wine from the Médoc Classification of 1855.

Flor: A type of yeast that develops in some Sherry production.

Fortified wine: A wine such as Port and Sherry that has additional grape brandy that raises the alcohol content.

Gamay (Gah-MAY): A red grape used to make Beaujolais wine.

Garnacha (Gar-NAH-cha): A red grape grown in Spain. It is the same grape as the one grown in the Rhône Valley region of France and there called Grenache.

Gevrey Chambertin (Zhehv-RAY Sham-burr-TAN): A village in the Côte de Nuits in Burgundy, France.

Gewürztraminer (Ge-VERTZ-tra-MEE-ner): The "spicy" white grape grown in Alsace, California, and Germany.

Gran Reserva: A Spanish wine that's had extra aging.

Grand Cru (Grawn Crew): The highest classification for wines in Burgundy.

Grand Cru Classé (Grawn Crew Clas-SAY): The highest level of the Bordeaux classification.

Graves (Grahv): Dry wine, red or white, from the Bordeaux region of France.

Grenache (Greh-NAHSH): A red grape of the Rhône Valley region of France.

Hectare: A metric measure that equals 2.471 acres.

Hectoliter: A metric measure that equals 26.42 U.S. gallons.

Halbtrocken: The German term meaning "semi-dry."

Hermitage (Air-mee-TAHZH): A red wine from the northern Rhône Valley region of France.

Jerez de la Frontera (hair-eth day la fron-TAIR-ah): One of the towns in Andalusia, Spain, where Sherry is produced.

Jug wine: A simple drinking wine from California that is sold in "jug" bottles.

Kabinett (Kah-bee-NETT): A light, semi-dry German wine.

Liebfraumilch (LEEB-frow-milch): An easy-to-drink white German wine; it means "milk of the Blessed Mother."

Liqueur de Tirage (Lee-KERR deh Teer-AHZH): A blend of sugar and yeast added to Champagne to begin the wine's second fermentation.

Long-vatted: A term for a wine fermented with the grape skins for a long period of time to acquire a rich red color.

Mâcon Blanc (Mac-CAW blahnk): The most basic white wine from the Mâconnais region of Burgundy, France.

Mâcon-Villages (Mac-CAW vee-LAHZH): A white wine from designated villages in the Mâconnais region of France; a step above the Mâcon Blanc quality.

Manzanilla (Mahn-than-NEE-ya): A type of Sherry.

Margaux (Mar-GO): A village and district in the Bordeaux region in France.

Mechanical harvester: A machine used on flat vineyards. It shakes the vines to harvest the grapes.

Médoc (May-DOCK): A district in the Bordeaux region in France.

Merlot (Mehr-LOW): The red grape grown primarily in the Bordeaux region of France, California, and Chile.

Méthode Champenoise (May-TUD Shahm-pen-WAHZ): The method by which Champagne is made.

Meursault (Mehr-SOH): A village in the Côte de Beaune in Burgundy, France.

Microclimate: A term that refers to an area that has a climate within a climate. While one area may be generally warm, it may have a cooler "microclimate" or region.

Morey-St-Denis (Mor-RAY san duh-NEE): A village in the Côte de Nuits in Burgundy, France.

Mosel-Saar-Ruwer (MO-z'l sahr roo-ver): A region in Germany that produces a light-style white wine.

Müller-Thurgau (MEW-lurr TURR-gow): A cross between the Riesling and the Silvaner grapes of Germany.

Muscadet (Moos-cah-DAY): A light, dry wine from the Loire Valley of France.

Muscat Beaumes-de-Venise (Mus-CAT bome deh ven-EASE): A sweet fortified wine from the Rhône Valley region of France.

Must: Grape juice before fermentation.

Nebbiolo (Nehb-bee-OH-loh): A red grape grown in Piedmont, Italy, which produces some of the finest Italian wine, such as Barolo and Barbaresco.

"Noble Rot": See Botrytis cinerea.

Non-vintage Champagne: Champagne made from a blend of vintages (more than one year's crop); it is more typical of the house style than vintage Champagne.

Nose: The term used to describe the bouquet and aroma of wine.

Nuits-St-Georges (Nwee san ZHORZH): A village in the Côte de Nuits in Burgundy, France.

Official Classification of 1855: A classification drawn up by wine brokers of the best Médoc châteaux of that time.

Pauillac (PAW-yak): A village and district in the Bordeaux region of France.

Petite Sirah: A red grape grown primarily in California.

Petits Châteaus: Lesser-known châteaus in the Bordeaux region that produce good-quality wines for reasonable prices.

Pfalz (Faults): A wine region in Germany.

Phylloxera (Fill-LOCK-seh-rah): A root louse that kills grape vines.

Piedmont (Peed-MON-tay): One of the most important wine districts in Italy.

Pinot Blanc: A white grape grown primarily in the Alsace region of France.

Pinot Grigio (PEE-noh GREE-jee-o): The most popular white wine from Italy made from the grape variety called Pinot Grigio, a.k.a. Pinot Gris in France.

Pinot Meunier (PEE-noh muhn-YAY): A red grape grown primarily in the Champagne region of France.

Pinot Noir (PEE-noh nwahr): A fragile red grape that is difficult to grow; nearly all red French Burgundy wines are made from 100 percent Pinot Noir.

Pomerol (Palm-muh-roll): A district in the Bordeaux region of France.

Pommard (Poh-MAR): A village in the Côte de Beaune in Burgundy, France.

Pouilly-Fuissé (Pooh-yee fwee-SAY): The highest-quality white Mâconnais wine.

Pouilly-Fumé (Pooh-yee fooh-MAY): A dry white wine from the Loire Valley region of France.

Premier Cru: A wine which has special characteristics that comes from a specific designated vineyard in Burgundy, France, or is blended from several such vineyards.

Proprietary wine: A wine that's given a brand name like any other product and is marketed as such, *e.g.,* Riunite, Mouton-Cadet.

Puligny-Montrachet (Pooh-lean-yee mown-rah-SHAY): A village in the Côte de Beaune in Burgundy, France.

Qualitätswein (Kval-ee-TATES-vine): A German term meaning "quality wine."

Qualitätswein mit Prädikat (Kval-ee-TATES-vine mitt pray-dee-KAHT): The highest level of quality German wine.

Reserva/Riserva: A term that means a wine has extra aging; it is often found on Spanish, Portuguese, and Italian wine labels.

Reserve: A term sometimes found on American wine labels. Although it has no legal significance, it usually indicates a better-quality wine.

Residual sugar: An indication of how dry or sweet a wine is.

Rheingau (RHINE-gow): A region in Germany.

Rheinhessen (RHINE-hess-en): A region in Germany.

Rheinpfalz (RHINE-faults): A region in Germany. The official name has now been changed to Pfalz.

Ribera del Duero (Ree-BAY-rah dell Dway-roh): A winegrowing region in Spain.

Riddling: One step of the Champagne-making process in which the bottles are turned gradually each day until they are upside down, with the sediment resting in the neck of the bottle.

Riesling: A white grape grown primarily in Alsace, Germany, and California.

Rioja (Ree-OH-ha): A wine region in Spain.

Ruby Port: A dark and sweet fortified wine blended from non-vintage wines.

Sancerre (Sahn-SEHR): A dry white wine from the Loire Valley region of France.

Sangiovese (San-jo-VAY-zay): A red grape grown primarily in Tuscany, Italy.

Sauternes (Soh-TURN): A sweet white wine from the Bordeaux region of France.

Sauvignon Blanc (SOH-veen-yown blahnk): A white grape grown primarily in the Loire Valley, Graves, and Sauternes regions of France, and in Washington State and California (where the wine is sometimes called Fumé Blanc).

Sémillon (Say-mee-YAW): A white grape found primarily in the Graves and Sauternes regions of Bordeaux, France.

Shiraz (SHEAR-oz): A red grape grown primarily in Australia, aka Syrah.

Short-vatted: A term for a wine fermented with the grape skins for only a short time.

Solera system (So-LEHR-ah): A process used to systematically blend various vintages of Sherry.

Sommelier (So-mel-YAY): The French term for cellarmaster, or wine steward.

Spätlese (SHPATE-lay-zuh): A white German wine made from grapes picked later than the normal harvest.

Stainless-steel tank: A container that (because of its capability for temperature control) is used to ferment and age some wines.

St-Émilion (Sahnt Ay-meel-YOHN): A district in the Bordeaux region of France.

St-Estèphe (Sahnt Ay-STEFF): A village and district in the Bordeaux region of France.

St-Julien (Sahnt Zhoo-lee-EHN): A village and district in the Bordeaux region of France.

St-Véran (Sahn Vay-RAHN): A white Mâconnais wine one step above Mâcon-Villages in quality.

Sulfur dioxide: A substance used in winemaking and grape growing as a preservative, an antioxidant, and also as a sterilizing agent.

Süss-Reserve: The unfermented grape juice added to German wine after fermentation to give the wine more sweetness.

Syrah (See-RAH): A red grape grown primarily in the Rhône Valley region of France, aka Shiraz.

Tafelwein (taf'l VINE): A German table wine.

Tannin: A natural compound and preservative that comes from the skins, stems, and pips of the grapes and also from the wood in which wine is aged.

Tawny Port: A Port that is lighter, softer, and aged longer than Ruby Port.

T.B.A.: An abbreviation for the German wine Trockenbeerenauslese.

Tempranillo (Temp-rah-NEE-yoh): A red grape grown primarily in Spain.

Thompson seedless: A white grape grown in California and used to make jug wines.

Trebbiano (Treb-bee-AH-no): A white grape grown in Italy.

Trockenbeerenauslese (Troh-ken-bear-en-OUSE-lay-zuh): The richest and sweetest wine made in Germany from the most mature grapes.

Tuscany (TUSS-cah-nee): A region in Italy.

Varietal wine: A wine that is labeled with the predominant grape used to produce the wine, *i.e.,* a wine made from Chardonnay grapes would be labeled "Chardonnay."

Veronese wines: The wines from Veneto, Italy: Valpolicella, Bardolino, Soave, and Amarone.

Village wine: A wine that comes from a particular village in Burgundy.

Vino Nobile di Montepulciano (VEE-noh NOH-bee-leh dee Mon-teh-pull-CHAH-noh): A D.O.C.G. red wine from the Tuscany region of Italy.

Vintage: The year the grapes are harvested.

Viognier (Vee-own-YAY): A white grape from the Rhône Valley region of France and California.

Vitis labrusca: A native grape species in America.

Vitis vinifera (VEE-tiss Vih-NIFF-er-ah): The European grape species used to make European and California wine.

Volnay (Vohl-NAY): A village in the Côte de Beaune region of Burgundy, France.

Vosne Romanée (Vohn Roh-mah-NAY): A village in the Côte de Nuits region of Burgundy, France.

Vougeot (Voo-ZHOH): A village in the Côte de Nuits region of Burgundy, France.

Vouvray (Voo-VRAY): A white wine from the Loire Valley region of France; it can be dry, semi-sweet, or sweet.

Wood Port: Ruby and Tawny Port; they're ready to drink as soon as you buy them.

Zinfandel (Zin-fan-DELL): A red grape grown in California.

Index

205

In my thirty years of teaching wine, I've probably been asked over 10,000 questions about wine by my 10,000 students. At the Windows on the World Wine School, every student is given a question card at each class meeting. I've kept these cards for years. In the pages that follow, I've tried to answer some of my students' most frequently asked questions. I hope you find this helpful in your wine journey.

What do I do when I can't finish the whole bottle of wine?

I don't know, this has never happened to me! I belong to the clean-bottle club!

This is actually one of the most frequently asked questions in wine school.

If you still have a portion of the wine left over, whether it be red or white, the bottle should be corked and immediately put into the refrigerator. Don't leave it out on your kitchen counter. Remember, bacteria grow in warm temperatures, and a 70+ degree kitchen will spoil wine very quickly. By refrigerating the wine, most wines will not lose their flavor over a 48-hour period. Some people swear that the wine even tastes better. However, one of my favorite old songs goes like this: "Does your chewing gum lose its flavor on the bedpost overnight?...."

It's the same thing with wine. After 48 hours it will begin to oxidize and possibly even smell like vinegar. This is true of all table wines with an 8–14% alcohol content. Other wines, such as ports and sherries, with a higher alcohol content of 17–21%, will last longer, but I wouldn't consume them after a two-week period.

Another way of preserving wine for an even longer period of time is to buy a small decanter that has a corked top and fill the decanter to the top with the wine.

Or go to a hobby or craft store that also carries home wine making equipment and buy some half bottles and corks.

Remember, the most harmful thing to wine is oxygen, and the less contact with oxygen, the longer the wine will last. That's why some wine collectors also use something called the Vacu-Vin, which pumps air out of the bottle. Other wine collectors spray the bottle with an inert gas such as nitrogen, which is odorless and tasteless, and which preserves the wine from oxygen.

Remember, if all else fails, you'll still have a great cooking wine!

Why do I get a headache when I drink wine?

The simple answer is overconsumption! Seriously though, over ten percent of my students are medical doctors, and none of them has been able to give me the definitive answer to this question.

Some people get headaches from white wine, others from red, but when it comes to alcohol consumption, dehydration definitely plays a major role in how you feel the next day. That's why for every glass of wine I consume, I will have two glasses of water to keep my body hydrated.

There are many factors that influence the way alcohol is metabolized in your system. The top four are:

1. health
2. DNA
3. age
4. gender

Research is increasingly leaning toward genetics as a reason for chronic headaches.

Many doctors have told me that food additives contribute to headaches. There is a chemical in red wine called tyramine, which is said to dilate blood vessels.

Regarding gender, due to certain stomach enzymes, women absorb more alcohol into their bloodstream than men do. A doctor who advises women that one glass of wine a day is a safe limit is likely to tell men that they can drink two glasses.

One final note: For those of you who have allergies, different levels of histamines are present in red wines; these obviously can cause discomfort and headaches. I myself am allergic to red wine and I "suffer" every day.

Why does the label say that my wine contains sulfites?

All wines contain some sulfites, which are a byproduct of fermentation. Some winemakers also add sulfur to a wine, and it is also used in the vineyards. Sulfur dioxide is a preservative that prevents oxidation and off flavors in wine. It also inhibits bacterial growth and is used as a disinfectant.

Many people use sulfur dioxide as a disinfectant. The sensation and smell of sulfur is the same as that of a lit match.

Excessive sulfur in a wine is a negative. Its smell will overpower the fruit, sometimes causing a burning and itching sensation in the nose. It is often used as a preservative in low-alcohol white wines, especially those from Germany, and many sweet wines.

Each person has a different threshold for sulfur dioxide and although most people do not have an adverse reaction, it can be a problem for asthmatics.

Is it necessary to let a wine "breathe"?

This is one of the most controversial subjects among my wine friends, and everyone seems to have a different answer or angle regarding the question.

I think most of my peer group would agree that simply opening a bottle of wine an hour or two before service will not really help the wine. It also will not hurt the wine. It is probably a good idea if you are having a dinner party at home to open your wines before your guests arrive.

What is bothersome to me is when a waiter in a restaurant asks me whether I would like my wine to breathe before he or she serves it. A waiter once told me that the wine I had ordered needed at least thirty minutes' "breathing" before I could drink it. Any waiter at Windows on the World who would say this to a customer would most likely be looking for employment elsewhere. Not only do I disagree, but as a restaurant director, I certainly hope that the customer is ordering a second bottle thirty minutes later.

The major question still remains though. Does a wine improve when it is taken out of the bottle and put into your decanter or glass? There are many schools of thought. I've had students swear to me that certain wines tasted much better after three hours in the decanter than when first served from the bottle. On the other hand, many studies with professional wine people have shown no discernable difference between most wines opened, poured, and consumed immediately and those that have been in a decanter over an extended period of time.

One thing for sure is that very old wine (25+ years) should be opened and consumed immediately. One of the most interesting wine experiences I ever had was in the late '70s, and involved a bottle of a 1945 Burgundy. When I opened the wine, the room filled with the smell of great wine. The first taste of the wine was magnificent. Unfortunately, 15 minutes after opening the bottle, everything about the wine changed, especially the taste. The wine starting losing its fruit, and the acidity overpowered the fruit.

What happened? Oxygen is the culprit here. Just as buried treasure is taken from the sea and kept in salt water in order not to expose it to oxygen, wine is destroyed by exposure to oxygen. If I had decanted that wine first and left it to "breathe," I would never have had that first fifteen minutes of pleasure. This probably will not happen every time you open an old bottle of wine, but it is very important to be aware of how fragile older wines can be.

Is it necessary to "swish" the wine around my mouth before I swallow it?

It must sound strange to people outside my wine class to hear over 150 people making slurping sounds when tasting their wine. Wine tasting certainly loses its romantic appeal when you swish or chew it in your mouth.

There are only four possible tastes to wine—sweet, sour, bitter, and salt. Since there's no salt in wine, that narrows it down to three possible tastes. But the most important aspect of "tasting" wine is smelling it. And the average person can perceive over 2,000 smells in wine.

This "swishing" or bringing air into the mouth actually creates a chimneylike effect, sending vapors to your smell receptors. Another reason to "swish" wine is to get it to all your taste buds. Remember, the average person has 5,000 taste buds! I tell my students, after they've looked at the color of the wine and smelled the wine, to put the wine in their mouth and leave it there for a minimum of three seconds. Some experts believe it is necessary to keep wine in your mouth for 15–20 seconds.

In this period of time that the wine is in your mouth, besides the taste receptors, you will also experience the tactile sensations of temperature, viscosity, tannin, and alcohol. Obviously everyone has a different threshold and sensitivity to these sensations, but through this tasting process, you can make a decision whether you like the wine or not.

Why does wine come in so many different bottle shapes and sizes?

Bottle shape, weight, color, and size usually signify a certain historical area where the wine originates. Here are some examples:

Riesling—elongated bottle

In Germany, Mosels are in green bottles; Rheins, in brown bottles.

Sauvignon Blanc—Bordeaux-tyle bottle

Chardonnay—Burgundy bottles

Pinot Noir—Burgundy bottles

Cabernet Sauvignon and Merlot—Bordeaux-style bottle

Champagne—Heavier and stronger bottles are needed because of the pounds per square inch of pressure in the bottle.

Most rosés are sold in clear glass to entice you to buy them. But most wine bottles are either dark brown, yellow, or green glass to filter out sunlight. All age-worthy wines are bottled with indented bottoms called the "punt." Especially with older red wines, this is where the sediment will end up.

BOTTLE SIZES

12.7 oz=	½ bottle
25.4 oz=	1 standard bottle
**Magnum=	2 bottles
Double Magnum (Jeroboam*)=	4 bottles
Jeroboam (Rehoboam*)=	6 bottles
Imperiale (Methuselah*)=	8 bottles
Salmanazar*=	12 bottles
Balthazar*=	16 bottles
Nebuchadnezzar*=	20 bottles

*Champagne bottle size

**Most wine collectors agree that the best bottle size for long-term aging is a Magnum.

Do all wines need to be corked?

It is a time-honored tradition over two centuries old to use corks to preserve wine. Most corks come from cork oak trees grown in Portugal and Spain.

It is sort of blasphemy for me to tell you that I believe that most wine (over 90%) could be sold without using cork as a stopper. Since 90% of all wine is meant to be consumed within one year, a screwcap (*incroyable!*) or even the soda crown cap would work just as well, if not better, than a cork.

Just think what this would mean to you—no need for a corkscrew, no broken corks, and you don't even have to smell the cork!

Before you try and convict me for wine heresy, I do believe that certain wines—those with potential to age over five years—are much better off using cork. But also keep in mind, for those real wine collectors, that a cork's life span is approximately 25 years, after which you'd better drink the wine or find somebody to recork it.

What is a "corked" wine?

This is a very serious problem for wine lovers! There are some estimates that three to five percent of all wines have been contaminated and spoiled by a faulty cork.

When it happens at the Wine School, we make sure that every student gets a chance to smell a "corked" wine. It's a smell they won't soon forget!!

Some of my students describe it as a dank, wet, moldy, cellar smell, and some describe it as a wet cardboard smell. It overpowers the fruit smell in the wine, making the wine undrinkable. It could happen in a $10 bottle of wine or a $100 bottle of wine.

Some wineries now use a synthetic cork made from high-grade thermoplastic that is FDA-approved and also recyclable.

These corks form a near-perfect seal, so leakage, evaporation, and off-flavors are virtually eliminated. They open with traditional corkscrews and allow wine to be stored upright.

Two well-known wineries in California, St. Francis and Bonny Doon, are now using these synthetic corks for their wine.

Which corkscrews are the best to use?

One of the scariest aspects of enjoying wine is the possibility—with friends looking on—of breaking a cork or even pushing it into the bottle! I have vivid memories of being a 19-year-old waiter and not knowing how to open a bottle of wine properly.

Finding the right corkscrew should be a priority. There are books written just on the subject of corkscrews. At last count, there were over 1,000 different sizes and shapes of corkscrew.

The following are my three recommendations:

1. *Waiter's corkscrew:* This is the one I've been using for the last 30 years. It's the one with the small knife to cut off the foil, and both the screw and knife pull out and fold back easily to fit back into your pocket.

2. *The winged corkscrew, a.k.a. the Jumping Jack corkscrew:* This is the one everyone has. For me, it's cumbersome, but it does work.

3. *The modern-day corkscrew for the modern-day wine lover:* Invented by an American, it is called the Screwpull. It is made of a strong plastic and has a Teflon screw. It is especially advantageous to use the Screwpull with older bottles of wine, whose corks tend to be longer and also become more fragile as the wine ages.

One last secret: I average at least a dozen broken corks a year.

What's that funny-looking stuff attached to the bottom of my cork?

Tartaric acid, or tartrates, are sometimes found on the bottom of a bottle of wine or the cork. Tartaric acid is a harmless crystalline deposit that looks like glass or rock candy. In red wines, the crystals take on a rusty, reddish-brown color from the tannin.

Most tartrates are removed at the winery by lowering the temperature of the wine before it is bottled. Obviously this does not work with all wines, and if you keep your wine at a very cold temperature for a long period of time, you can end up with this deposit on your cork.

Cool-climate regions like Germany have a greater chance of producing the crystallization effect.

What makes a bad wine a bad wine?

Everyone thinks I have such a great life, tasting wine all day long. But remember, you have to go through the bad to get to the good! When judged, sometimes up to 40% of the wines are discounted based on smell and color alone. Some factors that contribute to the making of a bad wine are:

faulty corks

poor selection of grapes

bad weather

bad wine making

high alcohol and tannin (bitterness)

herbaceousness

bacteria and yeast problems

unwanted fermentation in the bottle

hydrogen sulfide (rotten-egg smell)

excess sulfur dioxide

poor winery hygiene

bad barrels

poor storage

Does the age of the vine affect the quality of the wine?

You will sometimes see on French wine labels the term "Vielles Vignes." By law, the term requires the wine be made from grapes on vines that are twenty years or older. In California, I've tasted many Zinfandels that were made from vines that were over 75 years old. Many wine tasters, including myself, believe that these old vines create a different complexity and taste than do younger vines.

In many countries, grapes from vines three-years old or younger cannot be made into a winery's top wine. Château Lafite Rothschild produces a second wine, called Carruades de Lafite Rothschild, which is made from the vineyard's youngest vines.

As a vine gets older, especially over thirty years, it starts losing its fruit-production value. In commercial vineyards, vines will slow down their production at about twenty years of age, and most vines are replanted by their fiftieth birthday.

How should I wash my wine glasses?

For your everyday drinking of wine, wash your glasses in the dishwasher. But I've had many a great wine spoiled because of the detergent used. Therefore, my special wine glasses are not put into the dishwasher. They are washed by hand without any soap or detergent. Glasses are susceptible to scents, so mine are carefully dried hanging from a rack, not upside down on a counter or cloth.

What are wine classifications?

Classifications of wine, a sort of rating system of the best wines, have been a major part of the French wine trade for over 150 years.

The most famous classification in wine is the 1855 classification of the Medoc and Sauternes regions of Bordeaux (see pages 33 and 102–103). St. Emilion and the Graves region of Bordeaux also have their own classification (see pages 106–107).

In Burgundy and Alsace there are also classifications, ranking wines according to their quality. But outside France—most notably in Germany, Italy, and California—there isn't any official classification of best vineyards.

Will storage of wine affect the quality?

You've finished reading all the books there are on wine, you've taken all the wine courses in your area, and you now feel ready to stand toe-to-toe with your local retailer and begin what will be a lifelong hobby of wine collecting.

I'm sure not everything you bought for your new wine cellar is going to be there five years from now, but some wines do improve with age, and you must protect your investment. The fun of wine collecting is trying wines at different stages in their growth.

How important is it to have proper storage for your new wine collectibles? Well, let me put it another way. Without proper storage, you will never know how good the wine could have been!

In wine collecting it seems as if it's always the cart before the horse. First I'll buy the wines, then I'll think about where I'm going to put them. Which of course is the wrong way to begin wine collecting. I've often asked my students how many of them live in châteaux and how many of them live in apartementos? The apartemento people usually store their fine wines in the first door as you enter their *apartemento* next to their muddy shoes. If you are an apartment dweller and you have fine wine, you should look into wine storage in your area or buy a château!

Studies have shown that the best temperature for long-term wine storage is approximately 55 degrees. The same studies have also shown that storing wine at 75 degrees ages wine twice as fast. So my first consideration in wine storage will absolutely be the temperature at which it is stored.

Obviously the optimum temperature is 55 degrees, but I would rather the wine be a consistent 65 degrees all year long than swing in temperature from 50 to 70 degrees. This is the worst scenario and can be very harmful to the wine. And just as warm temperatures will prematurely age the wine, temperatures too cold can freeze the wine, pushing out the cork and immediately ending the aging process.

The second consideration in long-term wine storage (five years or more) is humidity. If the humidity is too low, your corks will dry out. If that happens, wine will seep out of the bottle. Again, if wine can get out, air can get in. Too much humidity, and you are likely to lose your labels. Personally, I'd rather lose my labels than lose my corks. My own wine cellar ranges from 55–60 degrees and stays at a fairly constant 75% humidity. Humidity and temperature are the most important things when it comes to wine storage, but I would also be careful regarding off smells and excessive vibration.

P.S.: The oldest bottle of wine still aging in Bordeaux is a 1797 Lafite Rothschild.

Should my wines be stored horizontally or vertically?

Wine bottles should be stored horizontally, with up to a 10-degree angle, especially for long-term aging. The reason very simply is that when the bottle of wine is stored on its side, the wine will be in contact with the cork. This prevents any oxygen, the major enemy of wine, from getting into the bottle. If the wine is kept in a vertical position, the chances are great that the cork will dry out, the wine will evaporate, and the oxygen getting in will quickly spoil your wine.

P.S.: Whoever wrote that it is important to turn the bottle of wine once a month was probably a beer drinker.

How long should I age my wine?

The *Wall Street Journal* recently came out with an article stating that most people have one or two wines that they've been saving for years for a special occasion. This is probably not a good idea!

Over 90% of all wine—red, white, and rosé—should be consumed within a year. With that in mind, the following is a guideline to aging wine from the *best* producers in the *best* years:

California Chardonnay	3–8+	years
French White Burgundy	2–10+	years
German Riesling *(Auslese, Beerenauslese, and Trockenbeerenauslese)*	3–30+	years
French Sauternes	3–30+	years

RED

Bordeaux Châteaux	5–30+	years
California Cabernet Sauvignon	3–15+	years
Barolo and Barbaresco	5–25+	years
Brunello di Montacino	3–15+	years
Chianti Classico Reservas	3–10+	years
Spanish Riojas *(Gran Reservas)*	5–20+	years
Hermitage/Shiraz	5–25+	years
California Zinfandel	5–15+	years
California Merlot	2–10+	years
California/Oregon Pinot Noirs	2–5+	years
French Red Burgundy	3–8+	years
Vintage Ports	10–40+	years

There are always exceptions to the rules when it comes to generalizing about the aging of wine (especially considering vintages), hence the plus signs. I have had Bordeaux wines over 100 years old that were still going strong. It is also not unlikely to find a great Sauternes or Port that still needs time to age after its fiftieth birthday. But the above age spans represent over 95% of the wines in their categories.

What do I think of wine ratings?

Americans rate everything from cars to restaurants to people. I suppose it was inevitable that rating systems would be devised about wine. When I began my study of wine, there was a rating system that was used primarily at professional wine judgings, called the 20-point system. It went like this:

color and appearance	3
smell *(aroma and bouquet)*	5
taste *(flavor)*	9
length and quality	3
	20 POINTS

Today it seems that all wine publications use the 100-point system developed by Robert M. Parker Jr., which rates all wines at a minimum 50 points all the way to the maximum 100 points. Opinions are divided on whether this is the best way to look at wine. I myself have no use for rating wines by number, and I also have no use for the sometimes poetic descriptions of wines that leave me wondering whether they are talking about a wine or a fruit cocktail! In my classes, the only vote taken is whether you like the wine or you don't.

For the consumer, a high rating gives an immediate credibility to a wine's quality. On the other hand, an 80-point rated wine, for example, might not be purchased by a consumer even though the wine is of sound quality. The debate about the numerical rating system is here to stay, so my advice to the consumer, retailer, and restauranteur is to choose a critic consistent with your style of wine, as you would a movie or theatre critic.

What are futures in wine?

This type of wine-buying actually began in Bordeaux, France, and was primarily used by the trade to buy wine at a lower price before it was even bottled. With the great Bordeaux vintages of the 1980s, buying wine as futures became a major investment strategy for importers, retailers, and consumers of wine, primarily in the U.K. and U.S. markets. Over the last 10 years, many of the best California Cabernet Sauvignons have also been sold in the futures market.

As a consumer, you are paying a retailer in advance to buy the wine at a lower price, hoping the wine itself will be of great quality for drinking or selling later on at a profit.

Is wine a good investment?

It wasn't that long ago that California wines couldn't find any buyers except among wine collectors, who, after tasting the fabulous 1974 vintage Cabernet Sauvignons, realized the potential for these wines in the overall market for fine wines. As the 1997 vintage of Cabernet Sauvignon is now coming to the marketplace, most of it has already been sold to "new" wine collectors, who buy the wines either to enjoy at a later date or to sell at auction five years in the future at a profit.

Investment in wine for profit is a relatively new phenomenon. Even the great Bordeaux châteaux didn't start to make any money until twenty years ago.

Until recently, it was actually illegal in many states to sell wine if you didn't have a liquor license.

Christie's started a wine auction division in 1966, and so did Sotheby's in 1970. Now, you can even go online and see wine as a high-ticket item.

In the early 1990's, with my wine school catering to the Wall Street crowd, I looked into starting a mutual fund for wine lovers. If I had done so, it would have beaten stock market earnings. Even if it had failed, I would have been able to drink my "losses"!

Speculation in wine began in earnest in the U.S. with the 1982 Bordeaux vintage, which the illustrious wine critic Robert M. Parker called one of the best vintages ever from Bordeaux. If you had purchased any of the great châteaux as "futures," you would have easily been able to sell those wines 10 years later at a substantial gain. The same goes for the great vintages of California Cabernet Sauvignon, most recently the 1990 and 1994 vintages.

Today, market conditions are not the same as they were five years ago. Even though the economy is booming in the U.S., there have been only two great vintages in Bordeaux of investment-grade wine and three great vintages of California wine in the last ten years.

With that said, I still am personally investing my money in certain wines I feel will always continue to increase in value. Here is my list:

BLUE CHIPS
1. Great Châteaux of Bordeaux 1995 or 1996

2. The best producers of California Cabernet Sauvignon 1997

3. Rhône Valley, France—especially the great producers of Hermitage 1991 or 1995 Châteauneuf du Pape 1995 or 1998

OTHER GOOD CHOICES
4. Top Italian Super Tuscan 1997

5. Best Estates of Burgundy 1996 or 1999

6. Barolos and Barbarescos 1996, 1997, 1998, or 1999

Is it a good idea to buy wines at auction?

In the last ten years, because of the unbelievable interest in wine and the booming U. S. economy, it has become more and more difficult for consumers to buy great wine through the retail stores and for restaurants to buy from distributors. When Windows on the World opened in 1976, I had no trouble buying wines that were 20, 30, and 40 years old from my distributors. Today, I am lucky to find anything with over five years of age from my distributors. The "Windows" beverage director spends a lot of time at wine auctions, and ten percent of our wine purchases are from auction houses.

I posed this question to Peter D. Meltzer, auction correspondent for *Wine Spectator* magazine: Are wine auctions good for consumers? He believes wine auctions present a good opportunity to acquire fine and rare bottlings in a variety of formats that are not readily available through traditional distribution channels. Mature wines sold at auction often go for less than recent releases offered at retail. Usually prices at auction fall below retail, and occasionally wholesale and mixed lots enable you to sample a wide cross-section of wines without having to purchase by the case, creating a great educational "tasting kit."

What homework should you do before you attend a wine auction?

According to Peter D. Meltzer, these are the most important strategies for buying wine at auction:

♦ Familiarize yourself with retail catalogs and recently realized price lists from the major auction houses. There's no point paying more than the store next door is charging.

♦ Study the condition reports and provenance provided in the auction catalog before considering a bid. Wines with poor levels may have oxidized, ruining the drinking experience and greatly reducing any potential resale value. Avoid lots that have not been stored in temperature- and humidity-controlled storage facilities. Remember that with few exceptions you are buying *as is*.

♦ Try to attend an advertised pre-sale tasting to sample as many of your "candidates" for purchase as possible.

- Remember to factor the buyer's fee (usually 15%) into your bidding strategy, plus applicable sales tax.
- Don't engage in a bidding war. You may win the bottle but lose the price war.
- Stay awake. There's always a point in a large auction where people seem to nod off, and bargains present themselves to the wary. Late afternoon is often the best time for best buys.
- Small lots (three to four bottles) of premium wines often sell for less than complete twelve-bottle cases. Large offerings (two to three dozen bottles) sometimes sell at a relative discount.
- Wines in their original wooden case tend to be more expensive than ones repacked in cardboard. Unless you plan to resell your wine, take advantage of the anomaly.

What are going to be the new, hot areas in wine?

It seems as if most countries are catching the wine craze. Here are some areas where I have seen major growth and improvement in quality, especially with certain grape varieties:

New Zealand—Sauvignon Blanc and Chardonnay

Chile—Cabernet Sauvignon

Argentina—Malbec

Hungary—Tokaj; one of the greatest dessert wines in the world

Austria—Gruner Veltliner

Portugal—not just Port anymore! Try Bacca Velha and you'll see what I mean.

South Africa—Cabernet Sauvignon, Merlot, and Chardonnay

And what will I be writing about in the year 2025?

China! There has been rapid expansion of wine growing and the government has promoted the consumption of wine rather than distilled spirits. Two major companies that have invested in China to plant vineyards are Rémy Martin and Allied Domecq.

Besides the wine recommended in your book, can you recommend other wines from other countries?

Every year when I finish writing a new edition, people invariably ask me, "What did you add to the book this year to make it better?" My philosophy is, what did I learn this year that the beginning and intermediate wine person do not need to know; thus, every year my book gets more concise.

Of course, this is very unfair to great winemakers around the world whose countries or regions are not covered in my book. Here are some of the other great winemakers of the world:

SOUTH AFRICA
Hamilton Russell
Kanonkop
Thelema
Glen Carlou

NEW ZEALAND
Cloudy Bay
Goldwater
Brancott
Morton Estate

ITALY
Lungarotti
Mastroberardino
Jermann

AUSTRIA
Franz Prager
Kracher

HUNGARY
Royal Tokaji
Disznoko

ISREAL
Yarden

FRANCE
Mas de Daumas Gassac

LEBANON
Chateau Musar

CANADA
Inniskilin

SPAIN
Palacios
Alejandro Fernandez

When I am at a restaurant with a group of friends and they all order something different, what's the most versatile wine that will complement everyone's dinner selection?

One of the biggest dilemmas my students confront is what to do when they go out to a restaurant with a large group of people and have to choose a wine that will go with a wide assortment of meat, fish, or vegetarian selections.

Normally, I do not "experiment" with wine in restaurants, because of the prices charged for wines. I will never spend more than $50 a bottle in a restaurant.

With that in mind, I usually order what I would call "safe" wines. My two favorite choices for a white wine are a Chardonnay without oak, such as a Macon from France, or a slightly oak-aged Chardonnay from California or Australia.

As for the reds, my first choice is definitely a Pinot Noir, most likely from California or Oregon, but if I can find a red Burgundy under $50, that would also be one of my choices. Other red choices would be Brunello di Montalcino and Chianti from Italy and Reservas and Gran Reservas from Rioja, Spain.

All of these selections would work well with meat, fish, and vegetarian choices.

What is the tipping policy for sommeliers in restaurants?

When I was a sommelier (wine steward), I always appreciated receiving a gratuity for my knowledge and service. Although it should not be automatic, remember that "TIPS" (To Insure Proper Service) definitely benefit your return trip to the restaurant.

A sommelier can make your dining experience better by:

- making your reservation and getting you a good table
- not trying to sell you the most expensive wine on the list (unless you ask, of course)
- matching your food selection properly
- decanting the wine
- giving special wine suggestions that are not on the list
- being attentive to your table
- taking the label off the bottle

Depending on service, I will tip anywhere from $5 to $20 above the regular waiter gratuity for the sommelier.

What are the most important books for your wine library?

Thank you for buying my wine book, which I hope you have found useful for a general understanding of wine. As with any hobby, there is always a thirst for more knowledge.

I hope that you noticed that at the end of each chapter, I recommended specific wine books for the different wine regions.

The following is a list of books I consider required reading if you want to delve further into this fascinating subject:

Oxford Companion to Wine, Jancis Robinson 1999

The New Sotheby's Wine Encyclopedia, Tom Stevenson 1997

Oz Clarke's New Encyclopedia of Wine, 1999

Hugh Johnson's Modern Encyclopedia of Wine, 1997

World Atlas of Wine, Hugh Johnson 1994

Oz Clarke's Wine Atlas, 1995

Wine for Dummies, Ed McCarthy and Mary Ewing Mulligan 1998

The Essential Wine Book, Oz Clarke 1997

Since the above volumes are sometimes encyclopedic in nature, I always carry with me two pocket guides to wine:

Hugh Johnson's Pocket Encyclopedia of Wine, 2000

Oz Clarke's Pocket Wine Guide, 2000

Where can I get the best wine service in the U.S.?

The James Beard Awards recognizes the following restaurants with the Outstanding Wine Service Award.

The past winners are:

1992 *Bern's Steak House*, Tampa

1993 *Charlie Trotter's*, Chicago

1994 *Valentino*, Santa Monica

1995 *Montrachet*, New York

1996 *Chanterelle*, New York

1997 *The Four Seasons*, New York

1998 *The Inn at Little Washington*, Washington (Virginia)

1999 *Union Square Café*, New York

2000 *Rubicon*, San Francisco

The past winners for Wine & Spirits Professional of the Year Award are:

1991 Robert Mondavi, Mondavi Winery, Oakville

1992 Andre Tchelistcheff

1993 Kevin Zraly, Windows on the World, New York

1994 Randall Grahm, Bonny Doon Vineyard, Santa Cruz

1995 Marvin Shanken, *Wine Spectator*

1996 Jack and Jaimie Davies, Schramsberg Vineyards, Calistoga

1997 Zelma Long, Simi Winery, Healdsburg

1998 Robert Parker, *The Wine Advocate*

1999 Frank Prial, *The New York Times*

2000 Kermit Lynch, Berkeley

I want to continue my wine education and also have a good vacation. Which wine regions would be fun to visit?

A great vacation for me is great wine, fabulous restaurants, perfect climate, proximity to the ocean, beautiful scenery (am I asking too much yet?), and nice people!

My three favorite areas that fulfill these "needs" are:

Napa Valley, California

Tuscany, Italy

Bordeaux, France

What's the difference between California and French wines, and who makes the better wines?

You really think I'm going to answer that? California and France both make great wines, but the French make the best French wines....

From production strategy to weather, each region's profile is distinct. California wines and French wines share many similarities. They also have many differences. The greatest similarity is that both France and California grow most of the same grape varieties. The biggest differences are soil, climate, and tradition.

The French regard their soil with reverence and believe that the best wines only come from the greatest soil. When grapes were originally planted in California, the soil was not one of the major factors in determining which grapes were planted where. Over the last twenty years, this has become a much more important aspect for the vineyard owners in California, and it's not unheard of for a winemaker to say that his/her best Cabernet Sauvignon comes from a specific area.

As far as weather goes, the temperatures in Napa and Sonoma are different from those of Burgundy and Bordeaux. The fact is, that while European vintners get gray hair over pesky problems like cold snaps and rainstorms in the growing season, Californians can virtually count on abundant sunshine and warm temperatures.

Tradition is the biggest difference between the two, and I'm not just talking about winemaking. For example, vineyard and winery practices in Europe have remained virtually unchanged for generations; and these age-old techniques—some of which were written into law—define each region's own style. But in California, where few traditions exist, vintners are free to experiment with modern technology and create new products based on consumer demand. If you've ever had a wine called white Zinfandel, you know what I mean.

It is sometimes very difficult for me to sit in a tasting and compare a California Chardonnay and a French white Burgundy, since they have been making wines in Burgundy for the last 1,600 years and the renaissance of California wines is not yet 40 years old.

I buy both French and California wines for my personal cellar, and sometimes my choice has to do totally with how I feel that day. Do I want to end up in Bordeaux or the Napa Valley?